STEP-BY-STEP
PORTRAITS
FROM SIMPLE SHAPES

A beginner's guide to drawing
faces in proportion

SinArty

DAVID & CHARLES

www.davidandcharles.com

CONTENTS

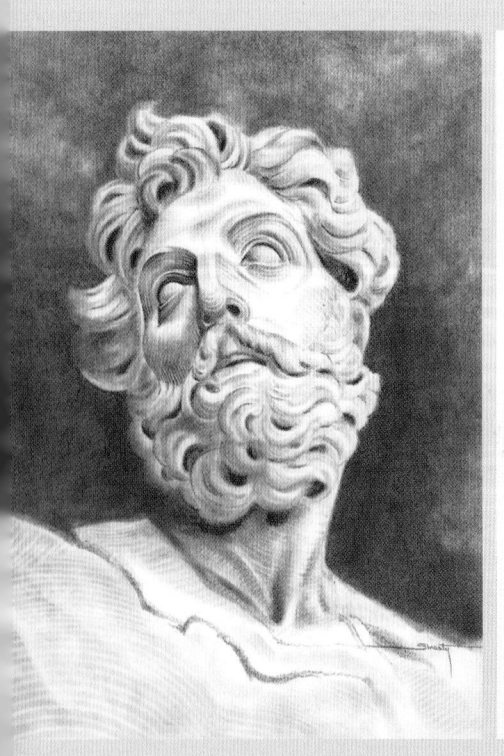
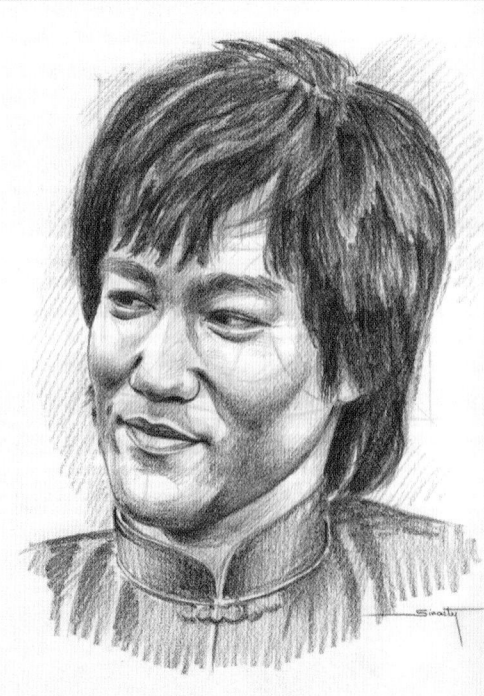
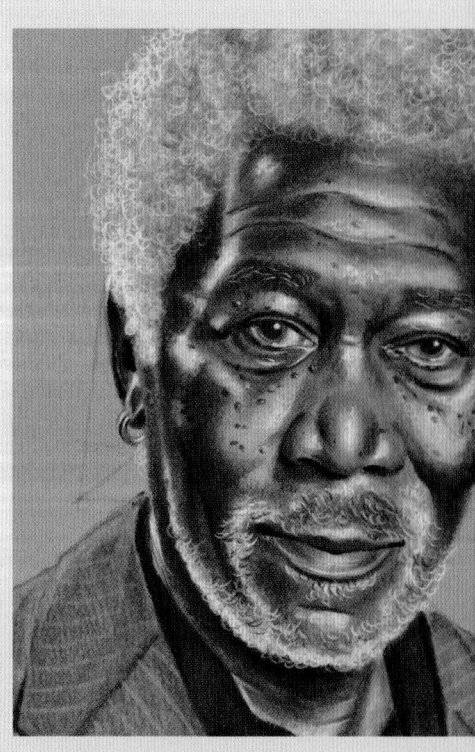

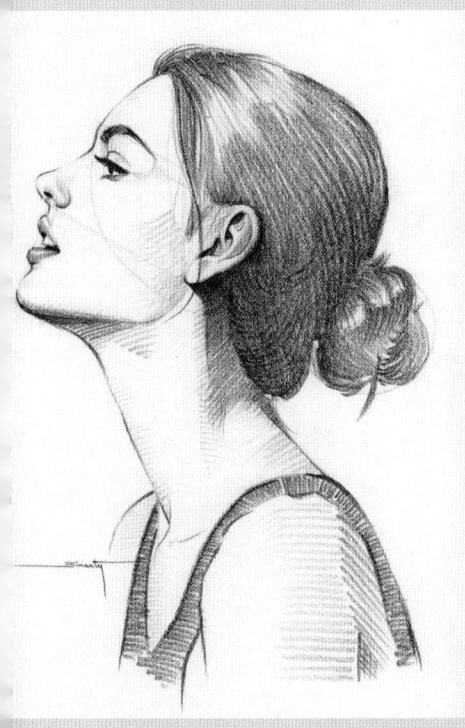

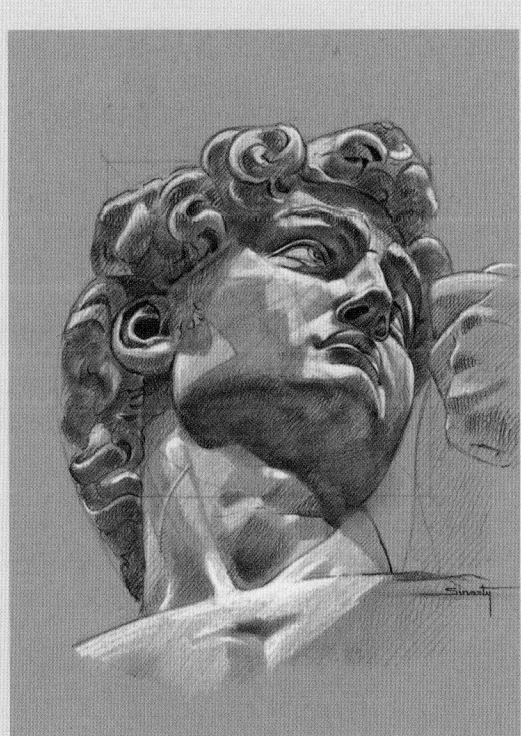

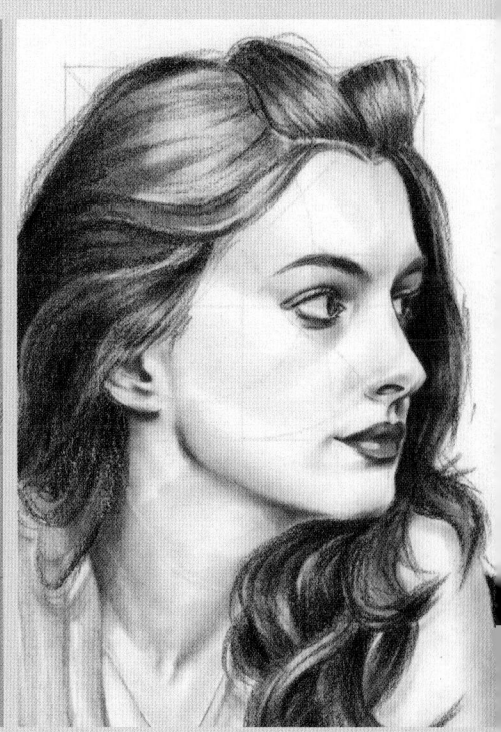

INTRODUCTION

Drawing is a way to express your mind. We all start scribbling at a very young age, with the first coherent shapes that a child can draw being circles and squares. This was the motivation behind my style – each portrait in this book will be built on top of these basic shapes. We will journey through different techniques of sketching, shading and proportions. The aim? To help you draw recognizable portraits from references, starting with very basic shapes.

I was born in the busy city of Mumbai, India, to a family of artists. My parents are both architects and so was my grandfather – consequently, there was no shortage of art supplies at home. I was three years old the first time my grandfather and I sat down together with a brush and watercolour paints. Watching him whip up a watercolour sketch of a small boat on the water, I was fascinated with how the picture came alive with just a few brushstrokes. Shortly after, I started scribbling on any surface I could find. My parents took me to most of the art stores in my city, where I could explore lots of different mediums, from pastel crayons to coloured pencils. They also took me to different art exhibitions around Mumbai. I gravitated towards drawing portraits early on in my life, and remember drawing a live portrait of my grandmother when I was seven years old. My love for portraiture had begun.

Portraiture is exciting to me as there is a "likeness" factor involved which demands close attention to proportions, the relative distance between features and tonal differences. Have you ever tried to draw a portrait and felt that something was missing? Have you felt that individually, all the facial features look perfectly drawn, but as a complete portrait, something is a little off? By sharing techniques that I learnt along the way and still use, I will try to help you identify the problem *and* the solution. Making mistakes while drawing, especially when working with proportions, is very common. Learning to be a good self-critic is vital. This book not only includes a step-by-step process for drawing portraits, but also showcases unedited mistakes I myself made during the process. You will see how I identified the problems and eventually, how I corrected them.

Portraiture makes you an overall observant artist. It is exciting to me that you can communicate with the observer through your drawing. A face can be very expressive – it is fascinating how subtle changes in the shadows can change the expression completely. With this book, I will take you on a journey through my mind to visit all the things I love about portrait drawing. I hope it inspires you to find your own path.

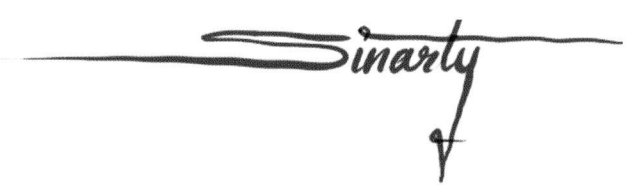

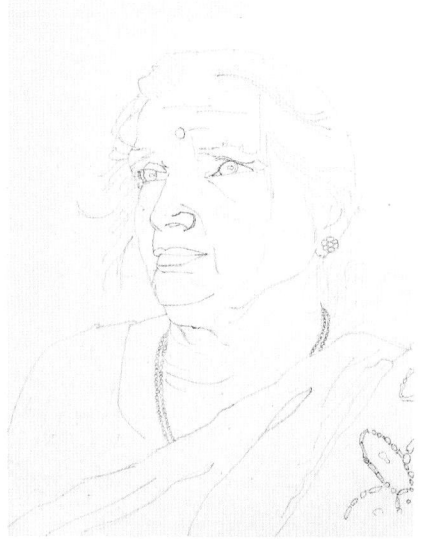

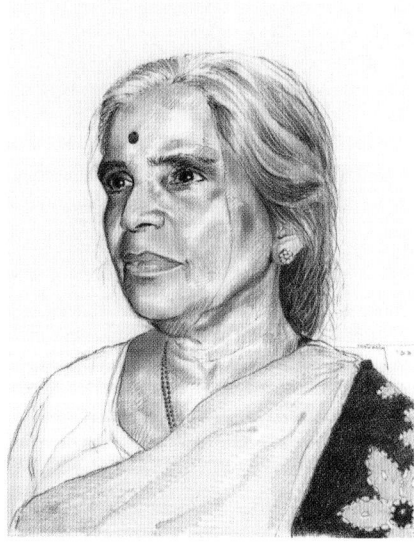

I drew this portrait of my grandmother (top) when I was seven years old – this was my very first portrait. I recreated the portrait (above) while writing this book, applying the techniques I learned during my journey.

HOW TO USE THIS BOOK

To use this book to effectively improve your portrait drawing skills, start by familiarizing yourself with its contents, from tools and materials to techniques and the portraits themselves:

Choosing your materials

The great advantage of starting as a pencil artist is that most of the materials are readily available, but investing in artist-quality materials goes a long way to enhancing the overall look of your drawing. Read the Tools & Materials section to understand what is out there in today's art stores. Experiment with different materials and choose what you prefer.

Putting pencil to paper

The Sketching Fundamentals section provides a hands-on guide to strengthen your drafting and shading skills using the techniques that I have learned. In Proportion Techniques, familiarise yourself with the fundamental methods to draw proportioned portraits.

Drawing the features

Next, the Facial Features section provides a detailed, step-by-step guide to drawing each individual feature. Before moving to the full portrait, practise some of these facial features and get familiar with the techniques used.

On to the projects

Once confident with the fundamentals, we can delve into the main section – The Portraits – which is divided into people portraiture and sculpture drawing. Use the completed sketch on the first page of the project as your reference. These projects cover all the different methods discussed in the previous sections of the book. You will find yourself going back to the previous chapters periodically throughout your drawing process.

Gather the required tools and materials listed at the beginning of each project, and take note of the different skill levels indicated at the top of the same page. As you progress, challenge yourself to tackle more complex portraits and try out different mediums and shading techniques.

Each project is divided into an outlining stage and a shading stage. The outlining stage starts with a basic shape, generally a circle or a square. The first step shows where on your page to make those first marks. Follow each step closely, noting the thought process behind each one. In the shading stage, take your time to observe and replicate the steps shown.

Continued creativity

Each portrait can be drawn multiple times, then referred back to as you track your progress and explore your own creativity and style. The Taking It Further section offers advice on how to elevate your skills and enjoy your artistic development.

HELP IF YOU NEED IT

The final step of the outlining stage of every project has its own page. This allows you to trace the full-page outline of the portrait and skip directly to the shading process if desired. However, I strongly recommended that you build your portraits from scratch. Don't be afraid to experiment and make mistakes – this is all part of the learning process.

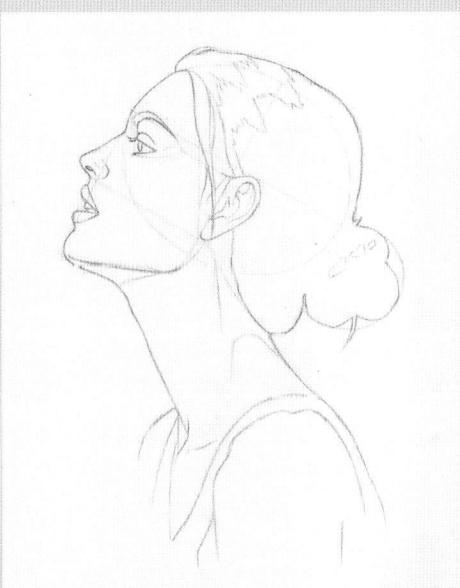

The final outlining stage is shown full-page size in every project.

PAPER

Choosing the right paper for drawing is a crucial decision that can greatly impact the outcome of your artwork. Your choice effects how your mediums interact with the paper's surface, the overall texture and appearance of your drawings, and even the longevity of your artwork. By understanding the different characteristics and qualities of your drawing paper, you can enhance your artistic expression and bring your creative visions to life. Let's look at a few of them.

COLOUR

Throughout this book, I have used both white and toned paper.

White sketching paper

When shading on white paper, I start with the midtones (*see* Sketching Fundamentals: Shading Techniques). You can then use an eraser to move to the lower value extremes, while darker pencils allow you to move to the darker extremes. We can also "stain" white paper with graphite or charcoal to give the effect of a toned paper, enabling us to move to both value extremes.

Toned sketching paper

Shading on toned paper means starting with a mid-value. This gives you the freedom to move in either direction of the value spectrum by using dark and white pencils. It also allows better control of the grade and pressure of our pencils. This method is commonly used by oil painters, who "stain" their canvas with a neutral colour and value before painting. Toned papers are most commonly available in grey and tan – we will use both in this book.

Choosing a colour

This can be based on the reference, your mood, the type of shading you have planned and the mediums used. My reasons for choosing the papers in this book take these factors into account and more! I usually prefer hatching and cross hatching techniques on white paper, since you can clearly see the process. On toned paper, I generally use gradient blending technique.

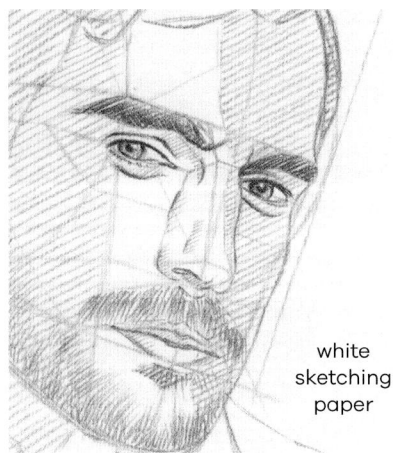

white sketching paper

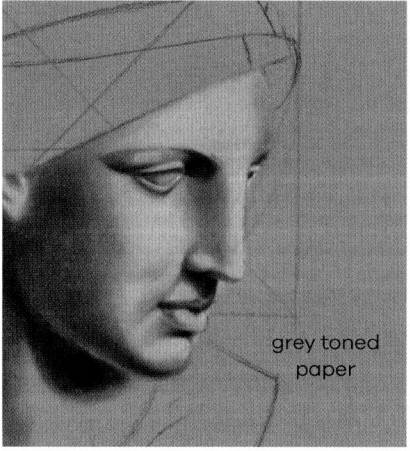

grey toned paper

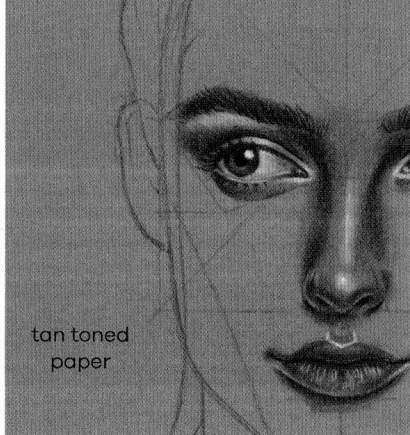

tan toned paper

The hatching techniques used to draw *Henry Cavill* (*see* The Portraits) are effectively rendered on white paper.

The cool marble tones of *Venus* work well with the grey paper, while the tan toned paper brings out the pops of white charcoal in *The Look* (*see* The Portraits for both pieces).

DIMENSIONS

In my experience, 22.9 x 30.5cm (9 x 12in) is a good size of for portraits and general sketching. I also use a smaller size of paper– 18.2 x 25.7cm (7¼ x 10in). Toned paper is usually available in this size.

WEIGHT

Good quality paper has some weight to it, determined by its thickness. Papers with more weight can withstand pencil pressure and erasing better than thinner, lighter types. The heavier paper also provides better support and durability, preventing smudging and ensuring your sketches last longer.

For graphite sketching, I generally prefer a weight of anything between 90–130gsm/60–80lbs. Any lower than this, the paper becomes slightly translucent and cannot effectively capture the nuances of drawing with different grades of pencil.

When sketching with charcoal, I choose a paper weight up to 160–200gsm/100–120lbs.

SURFACE TOOTH

A paper's surface "tooth" describes its texture. Fine-toothed paper is smoother; the more tooth it has, the rougher it gets. Fine-toothed paper is generally used for graphite drawings, and when we need a smooth surface for fine details and seamless transitions in value. While graphite is inherently a finer material that adheres well to paper, charcoal is grainier and can also be dustier. Charcoal needs more help to adhere to the paper's surface, and a larger-toothed paper helps in this regard.

The tooth/texture of the paper can be found on the cover of the sketchbook. In most art stores, there are also sample pages allowing you to test the paper before buying the sketchbook.

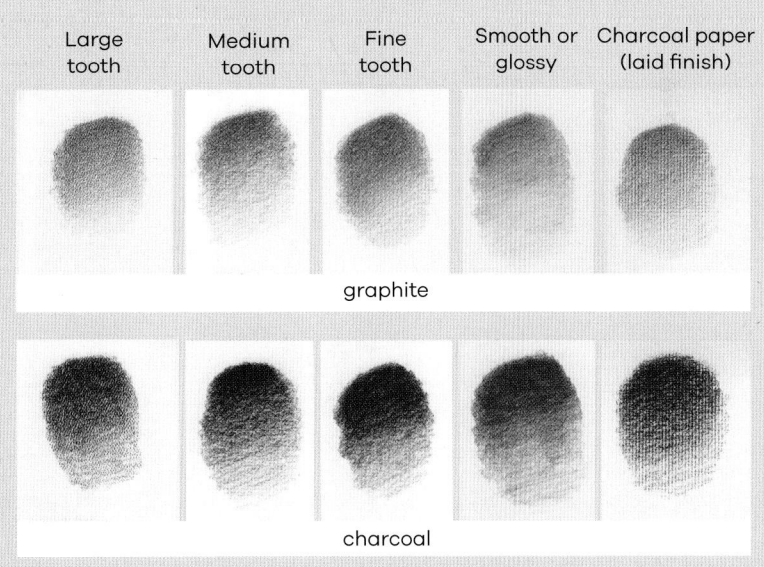

| Large tooth | Medium tooth | Fine tooth | Smooth or glossy | Charcoal paper (laid finish) |

graphite

charcoal

TRYING & BUYING PAPER

Experiment with the colour, texture and weight of sketching paper to find the ones that work best for you. You can buy single sheets of various papers, and some brands and retailers offer sample packs. I usually buy spiral-bound sketchbooks, as you can remove pages and store them as desired. Their perforated lines allow a clean, neat tear.

DRAWING MEDIUMS

We will focus on two basic drawing mediums – graphite and charcoal. Everyone has a pencil lying around the house, so beginners can get started right away. In addition, it is easier to depict a subject quickly and easily using values alone, without colours. These two mediums come in different forms, depending on how you like to draw and shade.

GRAPHITE PENCILS

The very familiar graphite pencil is the main ingredient in this book! Experiment with its tonal quality, darkness and smoothness. Graphite pencils come in a range of grades, from lighter to darker – I use mainly 2B–8B. Graphite drawings generally have a shiny finish.

Mechanical pencils
Also known as lead pencils, mechanical pencils are preferred by artists exploring fine art. They are a great choice for precise lines without constant sharpening (particularly while drawing details such as hair). Different grades of lead are available, from lightest 2H to darkest 2B, but for most purposes, a 2B lead is sufficient. Lead sizes available include 0.5mm, 0.7mm and 0.9mm – I mostly use 0.5mm.

CHARCOAL PENCILS

Compared to the shiny finish of graphite pencils, charcoal pencils are darker, with a matte finish. However, they are softer and more prone to crumbling, making them a little messy to work with. It is also sometimes harder to cleanly erase a charcoal line.

White charcoal pencil
This is a great tool when working on toned papers (*see* Tools & Materials: Paper).

GRAPHITE AND CHARCOAL STICKS

In addition to the commonly available wood variety, woodless stick pencils are made entirely of graphite or charcoal. Like their pencil counterparts, they come in different grades, and provide a broad range of strokes, allowing you to draw more quickly. They can even be used to create quick, broad gradients with the same stroke, so work well for staining the canvas or shading a background.

Drawing freehand
Sticks also allow you to connect more directly with the medium, and can give a rustic feel to your freehand drawings. Try blending it with your fingers to get an idea of how the paper picks up the medium for a fully freehand drawing experience (*see* Sketching Fundamentals: Shading Techniques).

GRAPHITE AND CHARCOAL POWDER

Powder is used along with a tool such as a sponge brush or a paper stump (see Sketching Fundamentals: Shading Techniques) to create soft contours and quickly cover large areas of the canvas. It is also easier to erase.

PENCIL EXTENDERS

To use your pencils until their very end, a pencil extender attachment allows you to continue using them even after they have been used and sharpened down to a much shorter length. Certain types of extenders can also improve the grip compared to a regular pencil, providing a much more comfortable and ergonomic hold.

SHARPENING

As pencil artists, we need to keep that tip sharp at all times! Invest in the best-quality sharpener you can afford to make life easier and keep your pencils in good condition.

Sharpening a longer nib
Use a one-sided blade to sharpen a longer nib (used for finer detailing and to quickly cover large areas of paper). Holding the one-sided blade in your dominant hand, use it to gently peel the wood of the pencil until the lead core is exposed. Do this while constantly rotating the pencil. Once long enough, shape the nib in the same way.

Refining the nib
You can further shape or smooth a longer nib for more even coverage of large areas. After sharpening the nib with the blade, fine-tune it with sandpaper. Lightly run your lead away from you over the sandpaper. Slightly rotate the pencil as you "file" to ensure even sanding on all sides.

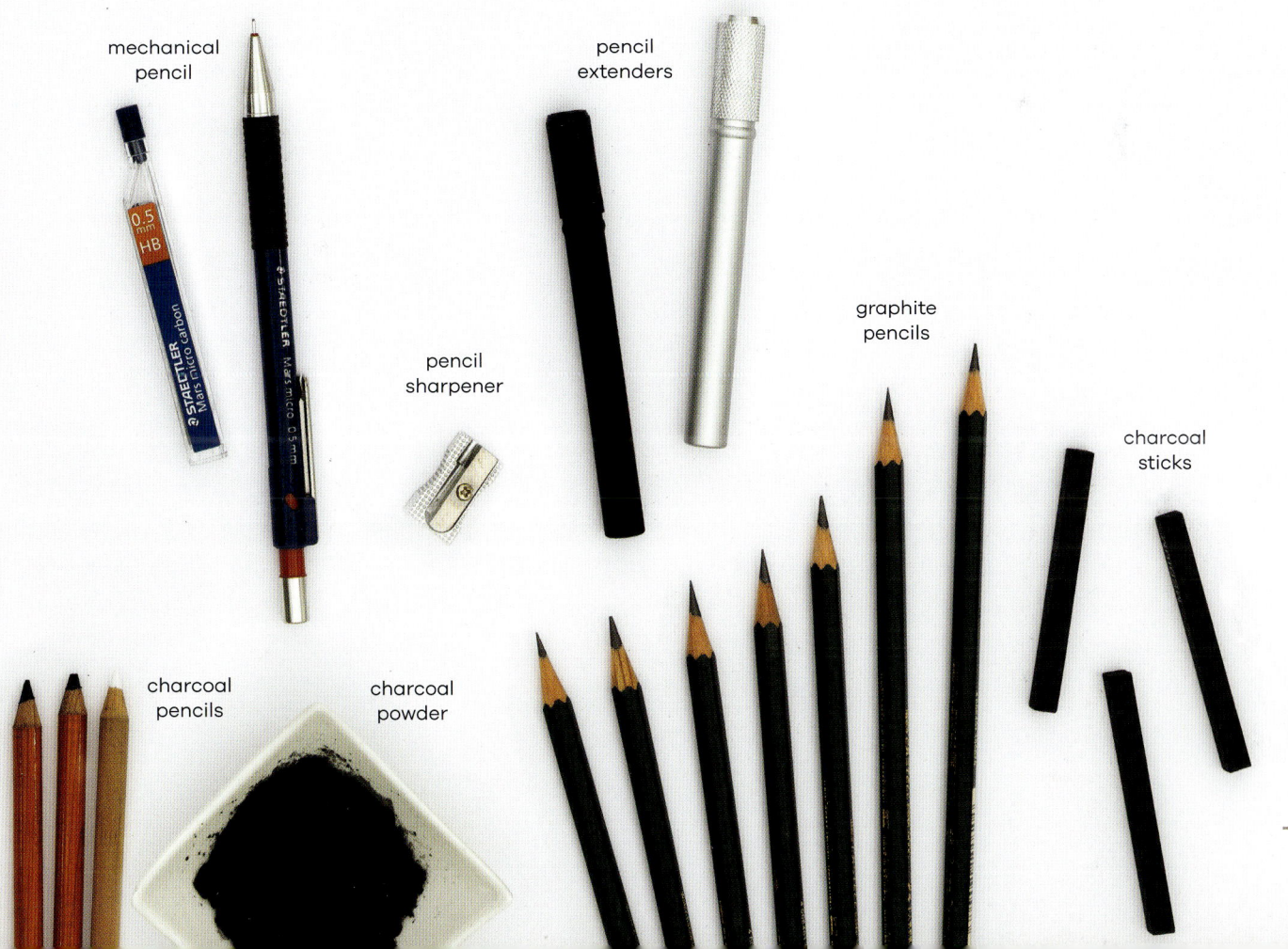

mechanical pencil

pencil extenders

pencil sharpener

graphite pencils

charcoal sticks

charcoal pencils

charcoal powder

BLENDING TOOLS

To achieve depth, texture and smooth transitions, blending tools are essential companions, allowing artists to seamlessly blend tones and lines, create captivating visual effects and enhance the overall quality of their artwork. Whether you work with graphite or charcoal, understanding the range of blending tools available – and how to use them – can significantly elevate your drawing skills. From traditional options like paper stumps and tortillons to more innovative sponge brushes, there is a vast selection to choose from. Let's go into the details of each.

PAPER STUMPS AND TORTILLONS

Paper stumps (made from paper pulp) are used to blend graphite or charcoal over large areas. They come in various sizes and generally have two pointed ends. Tortillons are tightly rolled paper pencils, suitable for blending smaller areas as well as finer details.

Both paper stumps and tortillons can be sharpened and cleaned (using sandpaper). However, the excess medium coating the tip can also be used for shading.

Sandpaper
Small strips of sandpaper usually come with your paper stumps and tortillons. Use these strips to scrape the charcoal and graphite from the tip of the blending tool to make it suitable for use on a cleaner area of your drawing. You can also use the sandpaper to fine-tune graphite pencil points (*see* Tools & Materials: Drawing Mediums).

SPONGE BRUSH

Sponge brushes (or brush pens) are made of dense washable foam and can pick up medium easily. They can be used to achieve a soft edge (*see* Sketching Fundamentals: Shading Basics) to your blending. I used one for shading the soft shadows on the cheek of *Venus* (*see* The Portraits). A very smooth transition in shadows can be depicted with a soft swipe of the brush dipped in a little charcoal or graphite powder.

COTTON BUDS

Cotton buds (cotton swabs) are handy for smoothly blending graphite or charcoal over large areas. They can pick up a good amount of medium to shade contours or backgrounds with texture where needed. Use small circular motions to cover the area with your cotton bud and medium.

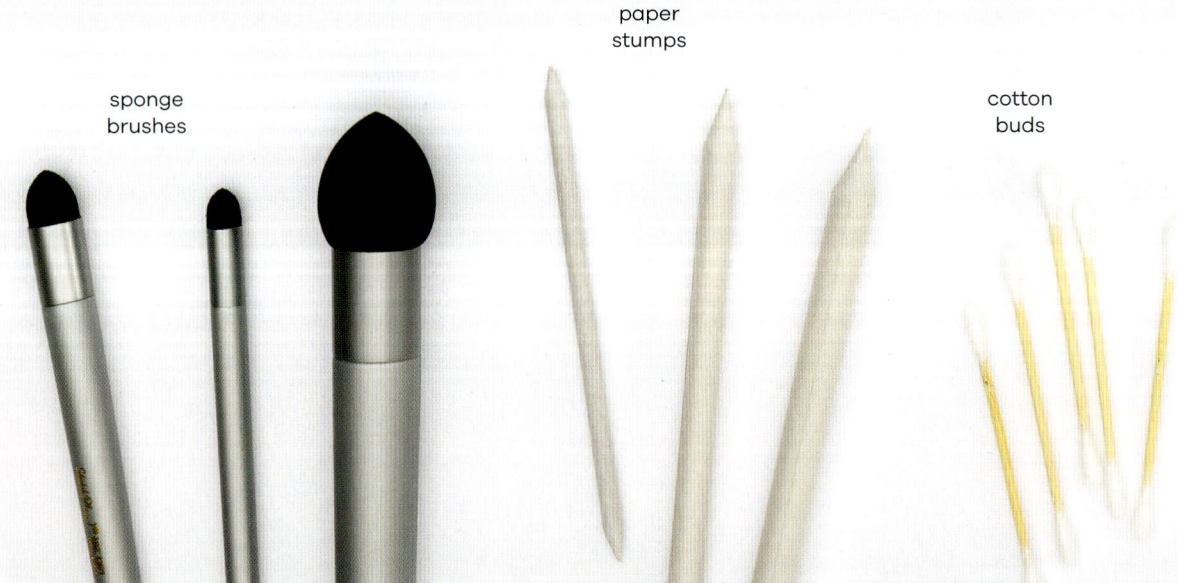

paper stumps

sponge brushes

cotton buds

ERASING TOOLS

Erasing tools are indispensable for an artist, especially when working with graphite and charcoal. They not only provide the ability to correct mistakes, but also help in adjusting and fine-tuning details, and achieving the desired highlights and textures. No matter what your level of skill and experience, understanding the different erasing tools available can enhance the quality and precision of your drawings. In this book, we will explore their characteristics, alongside tips on how to make the most out of each to achieve remarkable results in your artwork.

PENCIL ERASER

Although this eraser can simply erase mistakes (on both white and toned paper), it is widely used by portrait artists to create fine highlights, especially near the eyes.

Hard-edged highlights
A pencil eraser is also a great tool to depict highlights on the hair, and is used to draw hard-edged highlights.

Barrel eraser
A barrel eraser works in a similar way to a mechanical pencil. The difference is that instead of lead, you load the barrel with long, slim pencil eraser refills.

Electric eraser
A battery powered pencil eraser looks much like a barrel eraser, the difference being the circular rotations of the eraser itself that allow you to easily make accurate highlights and details.

KNEADED ERASERS

While a pencil eraser is made from a relatively hard material, a kneaded eraser can be moulded or "kneaded" into any shape to fit the desired form. A kneaded (or "no-mess") eraser will gently lift and lighten graphite or charcoal marks without damaging the paper, allowing for precise, controlled erasing. For example, mould it to create a point for detailing, or a flat edge for erasing large areas of graphite.

Soft-edged highlights
Kneaded erasers are one of my favourite tools to create soft-edged highlights (*see Sketching Fundamentals: Shading Basics*).

SAFE STORAGE & TRAVEL

A good-quality fixative can protect your drawings from smudges, smears and dust. Using a workable fixative allows you to add further layers of any medium over it. To keep your drawings safe for both storage and travel, invest in a good-quality art portfolio.

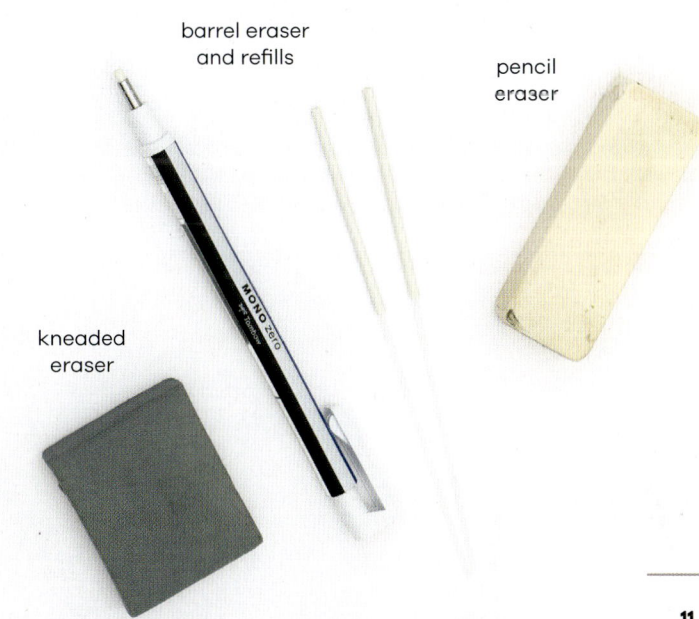

barrel eraser
and refills

pencil
eraser

kneaded
eraser

PENCIL HOLDS

The way we hold the pencil plays an important role in the quality of our linework. There are three main types of holds, and we can alternate between these as required throughout the drawing process. Some of these grips can be awkward to start with, but understanding their benefits – and practising them – will serve you well in the long run as an artist.

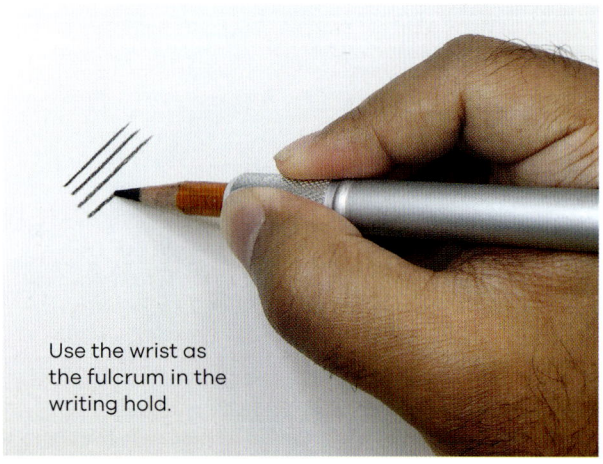

Use the wrist as the fulcrum in the writing hold.

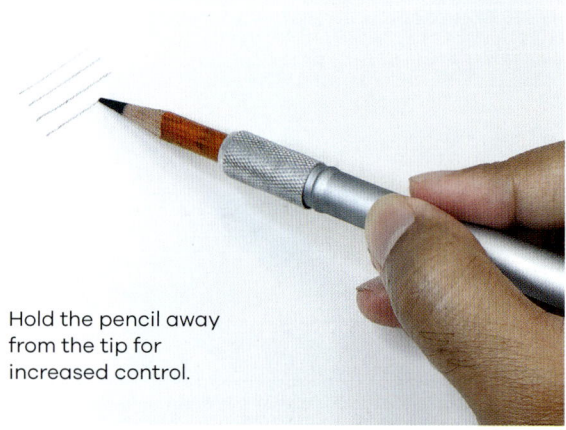

Hold the pencil away from the tip for increased control.

THE WRITING HOLD

The writing hold, also known as the tripod hold, is the most common way of holding the pencil. In this hold, grip the pencil close to the tip between the thumb and index finger, with the middle finger supporting from below. This grip provides stability, control, and precision in executing fine details and dark lines.

The pivot point

When using this hold, a notable difference between writing and drawing is the movement of the wrist. When writing, your wrist is the fulcrum (the pivot point). However, while drawing, it is recommended that the fulcrum should be your elbow or your shoulder – I go into more detail later in this section (*see* Sketching Fundamentals: Pencil Exercises).

Drawing faint lines

To draw faint lines, use the modified writing hold where you hold the pencil further away from the tip. The further away from the tip you hold the pencil, the better control you have over your pencil pressure.

PENCIL PRESSURE CONTROL

Learning how to control the pencil pressure on your paper while drawing is an important skill to master. Variable pressure is used to solidify proportions and create depth in your drawings. Always start a sketch with the lowest amount of pencil pressure to create barely visible lines. Faint lines give us room to correct our mistakes early in the process. We can improve our pencil pressure control by practising the exercises discussed later in this section.

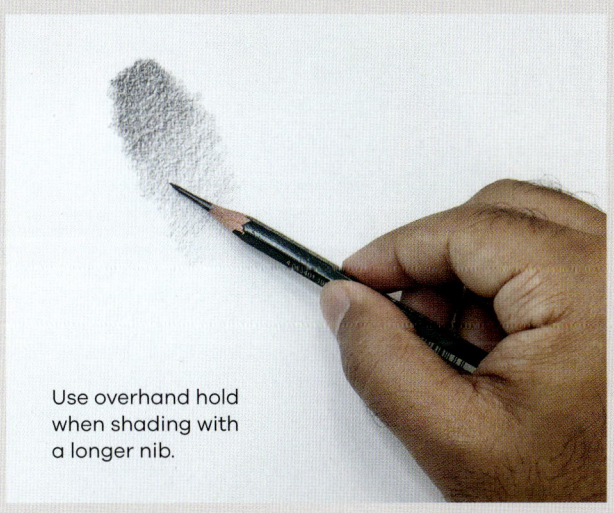

Use overhand hold when shading with a longer nib.

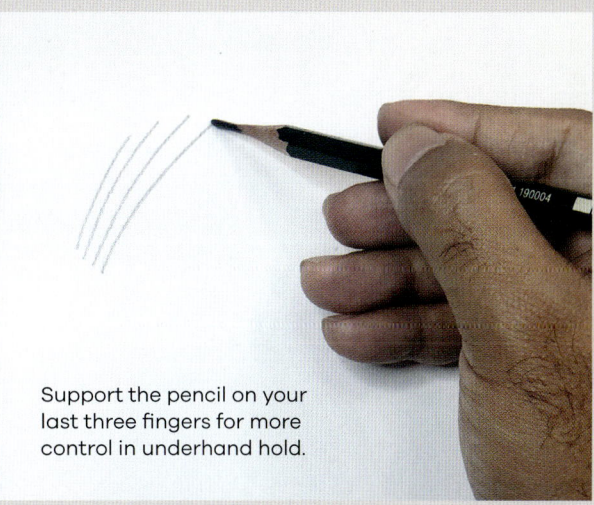

Support the pencil on your last three fingers for more control in underhand hold.

THE OVERHAND HOLD

The overhand hold – also known as the extended or full-hand grip – involves holding the pencil with a looser grip that is positioned towards the end of the shaft. The pencil rests across the palm, allowing for broader strokes, shading, and a more expressive drawing style. This hold is popular due to the freedom it allows to draw on both a horizontal and vertical canvas set-up. In other words, when your canvas is flat on a table, with your wrist supported, or on an easel where your wrist is free to move. This grip helps you to draw longer unbroken lines and smoother curved lines. It also helps your pressure control while shading.

Shading with a longer nib

Overhand hold also allows you to shade with the side of the pencil. The broad stroke of the longer nib exposes more surface area of the lead. It is recommended to use a blade to carefully sharpen your pencil for a longer nib (*see* Tools & Materials: Drawing Mediums).

THE UNDERHAND HOLD

This loose, relaxed grip is useful for exploiting the natural movement of the wrist to draw smooth curves. The underhand hold is similar to the writing hold, but your wrist is tilted to allow the last three fingers to support the pencil from beneath. It provides better control over your pencil pressure over the light-to-medium range.

Gesture drawings

This hold is also predominantly used for gesture drawings where you need strong, bold strokes, most commonly found in figure drawing. However, having a repertoire of holds and mark-making allows you to be versatile and ready to try new techniques.

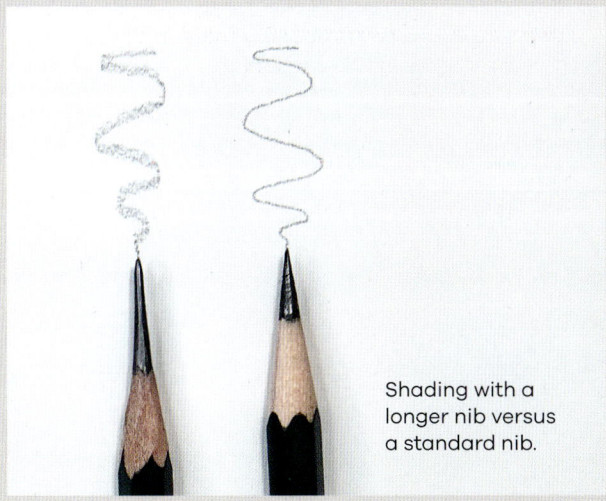

Shading with a longer nib versus a standard nib.

EXPERIMENT WITH DIFFERENT HOLDS

During your drawing exercises (see Sketching Fundamentals: Pencil Exercises) and drawing sessions, it is worth exploring the three holds demonstrated. Notice how each method feels as you draw, and the difference it makes to the results.

PENCIL EXERCISES

We will now explore some basic exercises you can perform to improve your hand steadiness, develop hand-eye coordination and refine your skills as an artist. Whether you're a beginner looking to build a solid foundation, or an experienced artist seeking to sharpen your skills, these exercises can be used as a warm-up before starting any drawing project. Let's look into a few of them.

LINEWORK CONTROL

This exercise is designed to improve your linework, allowing you to draw smooth controlled lines. Use a 2B pencil or mechanical pencil, and the regular writing hold for this exercise (*see* Sketching Fundamentals: Pencil Holds).

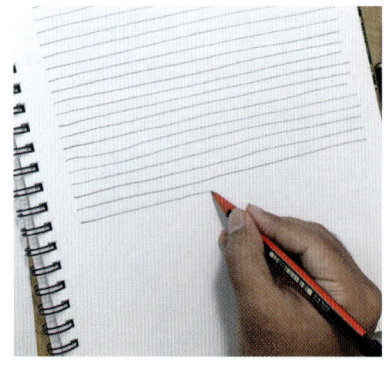

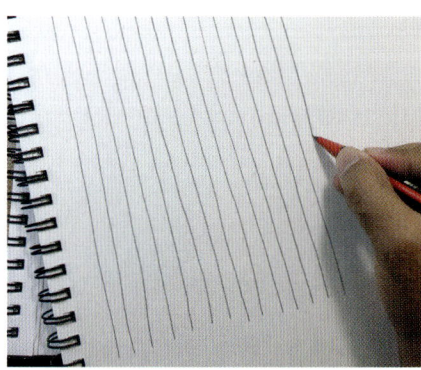

Horizontal line exercise
Start by drawing horizontal lines from one side of the page all the way to the other. Keep the pressure on your pencil constant to achieve a smooth, straight line. Use the same pressure on every line and practise keeping them parallel and equally spaced.

Vertical line exercise
Now move on to drawing vertical straight lines. Starting on the left or right side of a new page, draw a line from top to bottom. You'll notice that you can only use your shoulder as the fulcrum. Again, use the same pressure on every line, keeping them parallel and equally spaced.

Finding the fulcrum
Hold your wrist steady and use your elbow or shoulder to draw the lines without lifting your pencil. Transferring the fulcrum point from the wrist to the elbow while drawing gives a more fluid motion to your hand and doesn't restrict the flow of the line drawn. This will avoid broken or choppy lines as shown.

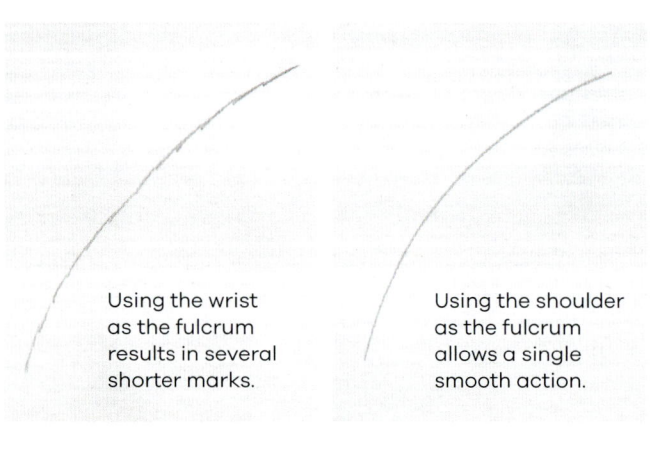

Using the wrist as the fulcrum results in several shorter marks.

Using the shoulder as the fulcrum allows a single smooth action.

PRESSURE CONTROL

This exercise will improve control of your pencil's pressure on the paper, and is also a great warm-up exercise to do before starting a portrait. Use the writing hold and a 6B pencil.

Increasing pressure

Draw sets of four short horizontal lines. Use light pressure on the first set as shown. Increase the pressure slightly and keep it constant for the next set. Continue this way until you reach the darkest value, then perform the exercise in reverse, from dark to light.

Variable pressure

Repeat the same exercise, again in the writing hold, but this time exert variable pressure along the same line in a single stroke. First, begin to draw a line using the maximum pencil pressure, gradually decreasing the pressure as you extend the line. The line will become fainter towards the end. Next, begin drawing a faint line and slowly increase the pressure – the line will get darker towards the end. Draw a few more lines, alternating between dark and light values within each line as you gradually increase and decrease your pressure on the pencil.

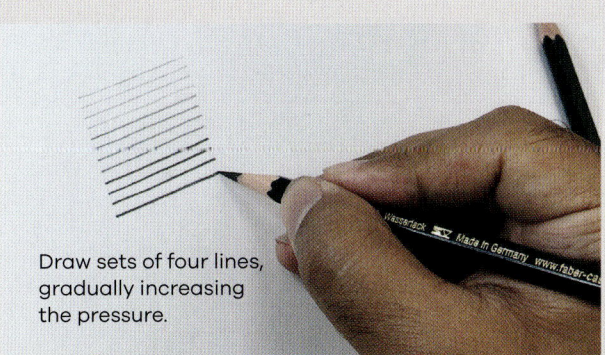

Draw sets of four lines, gradually increasing the pressure.

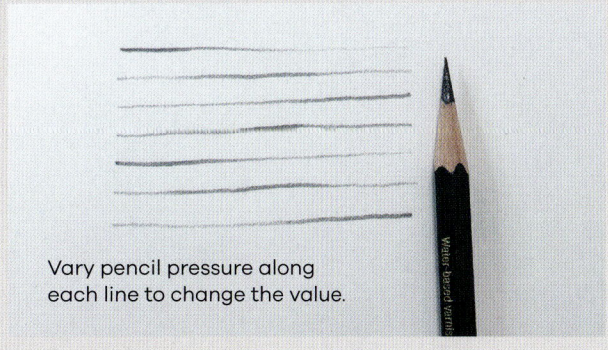

Vary pencil pressure along each line to change the value.

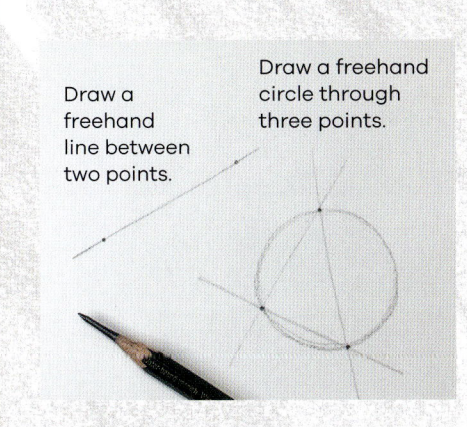

Draw a freehand line between two points.

Draw a freehand circle through three points.

TAKE A PRACTICE SWING

To get an idea of how the line should look, glide your hand over the paper without drawing, just replicating the motion of the lines with your pencil. Think of this as a golf drive visualization – the golfer practises the swing without hitting the ball to get a feel of their drive. Once visualized, they make the actual drive.

FREEHAND CONTROL

This exercise, in the writing hold, will help you visualize your drawings before putting pencil to paper.

Freehand straight line

Mark two random points on your canvas, around 10cm (4in) apart. Draw a line that passes through the two points. The further apart the points, the more difficult this exercise becomes. Try to visualize the line before drawing it. You may not get it on the first try, so keep a very light hand at the start.

Freehand circle

Mark three random points and draw a circle that passes through all three points. It doesn't need to be perfect, but as close as possible.

PRACTISE IN OVERHAND HOLD

Repeat all these exercises with the overhand hold to help you become comfortable with it. As with any variation of hold, you will notice slight differences. For example, you may not be able to achieve the same strength and darkness of line with the writing hold. The first few times might be uncomfortable, especially when drawing a circle and other shapes. But with practise, overhand hold makes it much easier to draw faint lines with control.

SHADING BASICS

Pencil shading is a fundamental technique in drawing that brings depth, dimension and realism to your artwork. By mastering shading basics, you can create the illusion of light and shadow, adding form and texture to your drawings. Understanding the principles of value, contrast, gradation and layering is essential for achieving realistic effects.

WHAT IS VALUE?

Value in art refers to the degree of lightness or darkness of a colour or tone. By manipulating values, artists can create a sense of volume, texture, and spatial relationships. An understanding of value is required for correctly depicting highlights and shadows across an entire portrait.

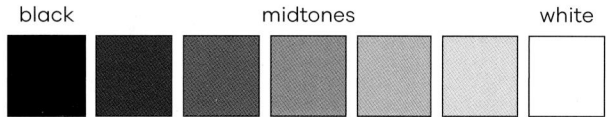

black   midtones   white

Every colour has two key attributes: value and chroma.

- Value is the lightness or darkness of any colour
- Chroma is the strength (or saturation) of the colour

Since we are exclusively using graphite (grey) and charcoal (black or white) throughout the book, we will only be working with the first attribute – value.

THE VALUE SCALE

A value scale in drawing is a visual representation of the range of values from light to dark. It is typically depicted as a series of evenly spaced rectangles or squares, progressing from pure white to pure black, with varying shades of grey in between.

DRAWING YOUR OWN VALUE SCALE

Drawing a value scale with your graphite pencils is the fundamental exercise to improve your shading. It improves your pencil pressure control, observation skills and hand-eye coordination as an artist.

1 Use a ruler to draw a horizontal rectangle about 10.5 x 1.5cm (4¼ x ⅝in) onto white sketching paper. Divide this into seven equal sections (or if you prefer, five to begin with.)

2 Shade the extremes first. Use your darkest pencil with maximum pressure to shade block #1. Leave block #7 blank, containing only the white of the paper.

3 Next, shade block #4 with a midtone using a 4B pencil. The midtone might not be accurate at this stage, but use your best judgement.

4 Slowly, complete the remaining blocks. Use a combination of 4B, 6B and 8B for blocks #1, #2, #3 and #4. Use a mix of 2H, 2B and 4B for blocks #5 and #6.

Refining your scale
Rework the blocks which you observe to have the largest shift in value. Make sure you see a clear transition between the values.

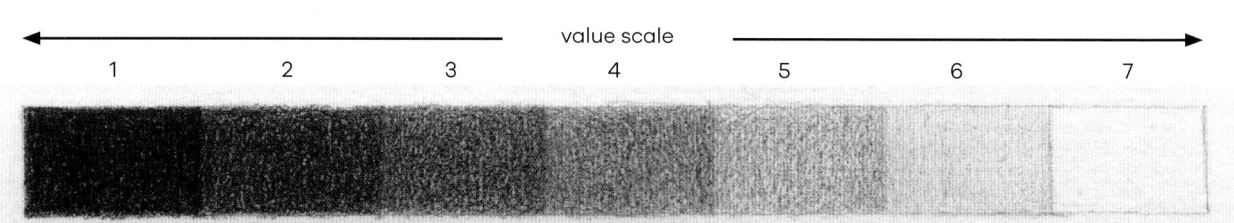

value scale

1   2   3   4   5   6   7

HARD AND SOFT EDGES

There are two types of edges to consider:

- Hard edges have an abrupt transition in value
- Soft edges have a gradual transition in value

Hard edges define a clear boundary between two objects, and determine how sharp and clean your sketch looks. Hard edges can be confused with outlines, but the latter are not that common in realistic portraits.

Soft edges are important when conveying smooth curves and contours. Practising these subtle transitions to create soft edges will give your drawings depth. Use a very light hand with multiple layers of graphite (*see* Sketching Fundamentals: Shading Techniques).

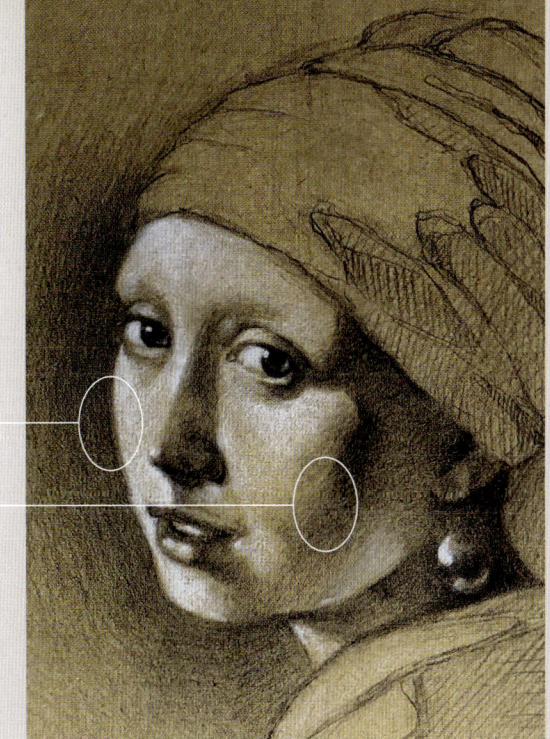

hard edge

soft edge

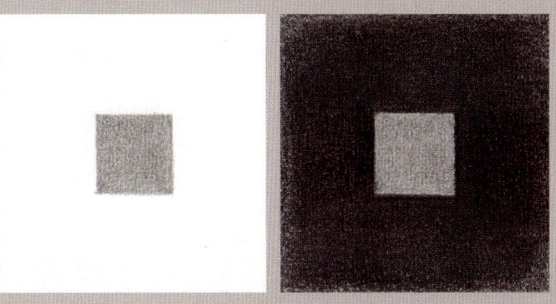

The light source is top left of the canvas, a little behind the subject.

THE ASARO HEAD

Note the location of the light source in relation to the planes of this face. The Asaro head was created to help artists simplify their view of these planes which, combined with understanding value, is key to an authentic looking portrait. The light source is top right of this head, so the lightest values appear on the right-hand side. The darker values are concentrated down the centre and left-hand side.

THE CHEQUERBOARD ILLUSION

This well-known illusion allows us to understand how a single value can appear different depending on its background.

Compare the values of each smaller centre square. The left-hand square appears darker, but in reality, the values of both are identical. So, how does this affect our shading? While shading, we try to replicate the values we observe in our reference by varying the pressure and grade of our pencil. Due to this illusion, it is possible to incorrectly shade certain areas of the sketch, resulting in a portrait with unbalanced lighting and contours.

Being aware of this illusion not only ensures we create values that are accurate in relation to their immediate surroundings, but also in relation to the overall image for more balanced results.

SHADING TECHNIQUES

Understanding and practising shading techniques is fundamental for building creative flexibility. Your choice of technique gives your work individuality and sets the mood. The projects in this book use one or more of these techniques – combining several adds unique textures to your drawings.

SIMPLE SHADING

I have used four shading techniques throughout the book:

Unidirectional hatching
Draw equidistant parallel lines in a uniform pattern. Change values by varying the distance between the lines, your pressure on the pencil, and the grade of the pencil.

Cross hatching
Overlap sets of unidirectional hatching to make a "cross" pattern of perpendicular lines. To give your work depth, overlap two or more sets, following the surface contours. To preserve the distinctive cross effect, limit the number of sets to four.

Squiggle shading
Draw circular scribbles, starting with small and evenly distributed squiggles to fill an area. To create shadows, layer sets of different scales and values.

Gradient blending
Vary pencil pressure to create smooth gradients, as done when you created your own value scale (see Sketching Fundamentals: Shading Basics). Different values are achieved only by changing pencil pressure and/or grade. Blending tools can help smooth transitions between different values.

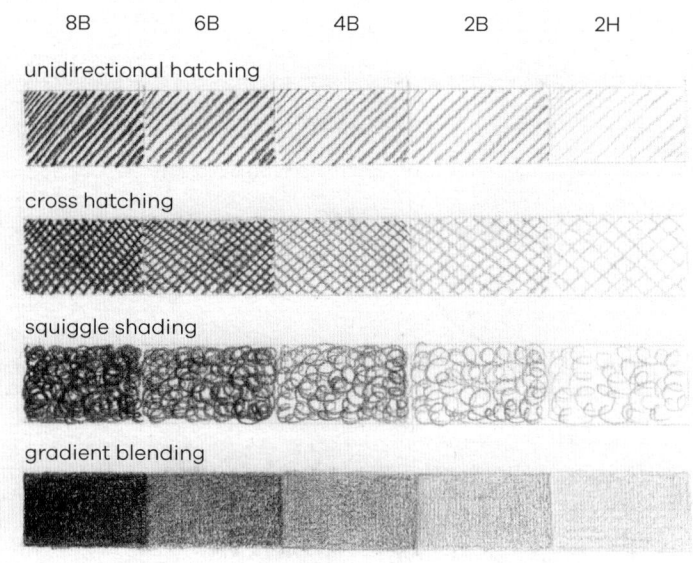

SHADING A SPHERE

Practise these four techniques by shading a sphere with highlights on one side. For each method, try using various pencil grades to create different values.

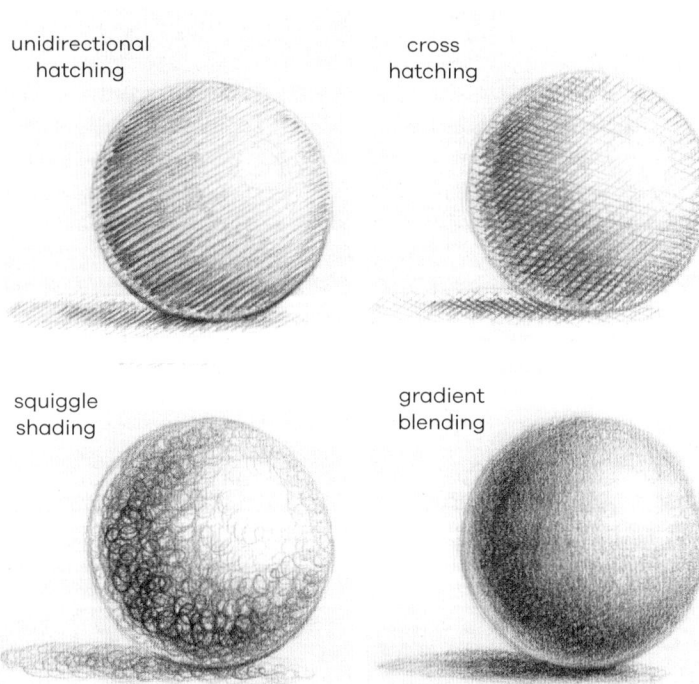

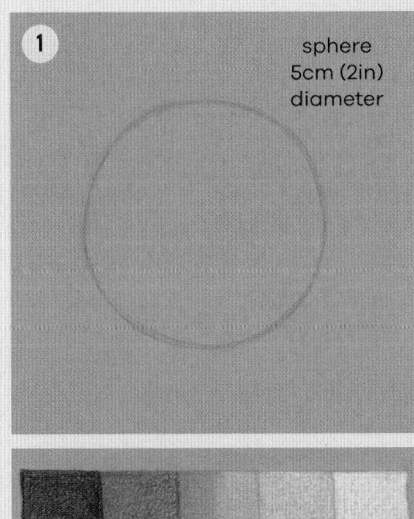

1 sphere 5cm (2in) diameter

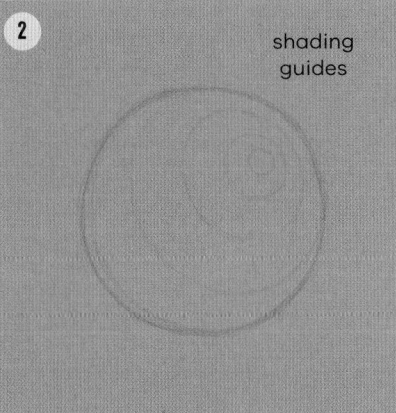

2 shading guides

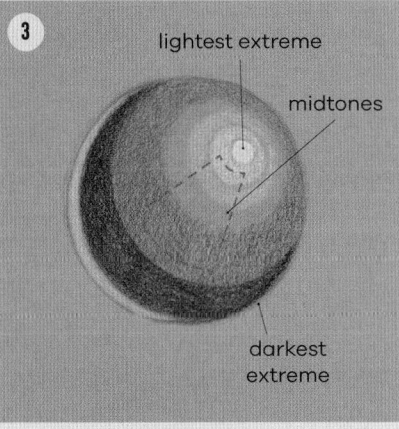

3 lightest extreme

midtones

darkest extreme

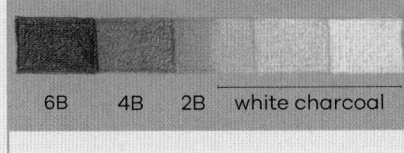

6B   4B   2B   white charcoal

Varied pressure
Gradient blending has been used throughout the steps, varying the pressure of the white charcoal to achieve the different lighter tones.

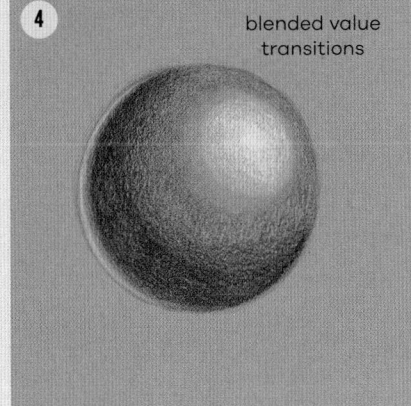

4 blended value transitions

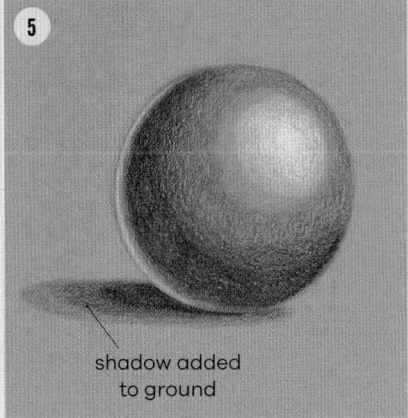

5 shadow added to ground

SHADING ON TONED PAPER

All the techniques discussed so far have been demonstrated on a white paper, but can also be used to shade on a toned paper. We start with midtones and move towards either of the value extremes. I use the 6B or 8B graphite pencils for the dark extreme and white charcoal pencil for the light extreme.

Let's shade a sphere on toned paper using the gradient blending method. We will use 2B, 4B and 6B graphite pencils for the darker values and a white charcoal pencil for the lighter values.

1 Draw a sphere approximately 5cm (2in) in diameter.

2 Next, mark guidelines for the value transitions.

3 Shade the lightest extremes (white charcoal) and darkest extremes (6B graphite) of the sphere. To achieve the lightest extreme, use more pressure with the white charcoal. Add the midtones with a 4B pencil and white charcoal (use medium pressure with the charcoal).

4 Blend the transition edges until you get a smooth gradient. In other words, use variable pencil pressure to convert all the hard edges into soft edges. It is important to use a very light hand to gauge how much further into the value you would need your layer to overlap to achieve a smooth transition. Take your time with this step.

5 Add a shadow beneath the sphere, using the same method of graduated value bands. This grounds the sphere and reinforces the direction of the light source.

REFERENCE IMAGES

In this book, you will learn techniques to draw portraits from reference images. Drawing from life does give you freedom in composition and lighting that may be limited with a photograph. However, a reference image can be easily edited to suit the mood of the subject; professional artists frequently combine both techniques.

WHAT MAKES A GOOD REFERENCE?

A suitable reference photo has a balance of light and symmetry in its composition. Choose a reference that is clear and has a high enough resolution. This is to ensure that the finer details are clearly visible and not blurred. If the image is blurred and too small, you will have to create the "sharpness" in the drawing from your own imagination. This includes creating both the shadows and the highlights yourself, rather than having a reference to study. It is not unusual to "prep" your reference photo before drawing. With a digital image, adjust the brightness and contrast to enhance these properties and bring out otherwise hidden details further. Adjusting in this way can also affect the overall atmosphere and mood of the subject.

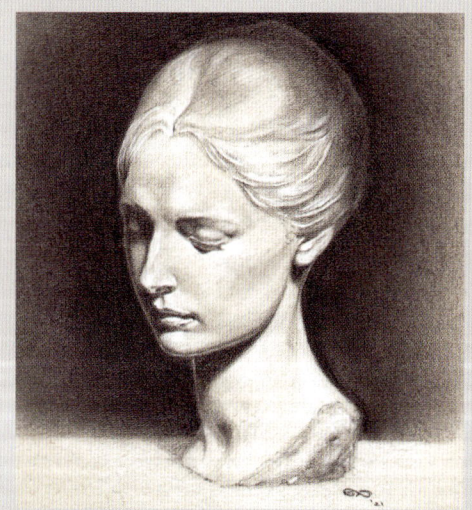

Contrasting values
Notice how the subject is brought into focus by relying on the stark difference in highlights and shadows. Observe the subtlety of the shadows in highlighted areas like the cheek and the neck.

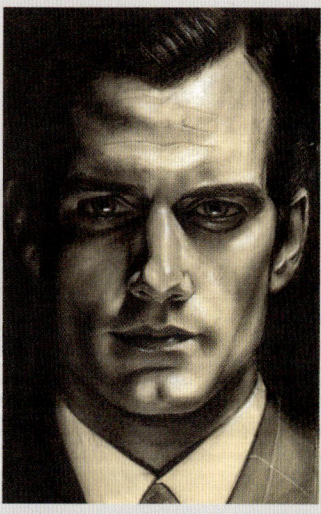

Bold symmetry
The combination of striking lighting and symmetry in the reference photo made this a great charcoal portrait of Henry Cavill.

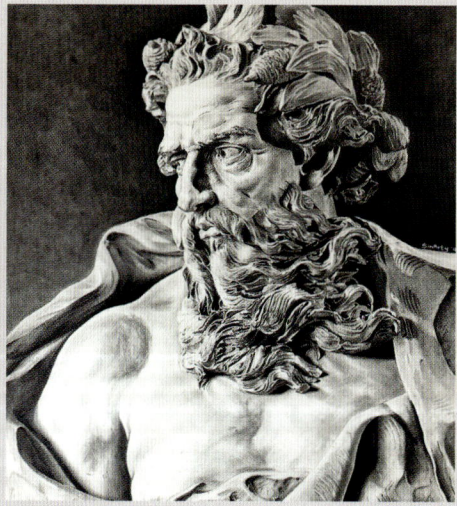

Background balance
I liked the balance of light on this sculpture of Neptune. The composition of the sculpture combines well with the subtle texture and value changes in the background.

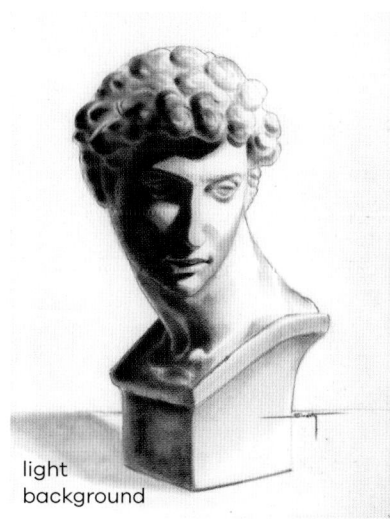
light
background

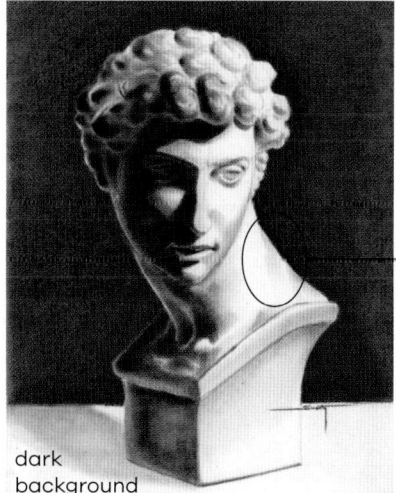
dark
background

Notice that to
accentuate the face,
the background is
darker on the right
of the drawing than
on the left (*see* The
Portraits: *Guiliano*).

CHOOSING A BACKGROUND

The background of the portrait is as important as the portrait itself, but it may not be
ideal in your reference image. Some design choices need to be made to bring focus to
your subject and improve your sketch further. The highlights on the face pop out from
the shadows better if they have a contrasting dark background.

INTERPRETING A PHOTO

My idea of portraiture isn't to capture every single
pixel of the reference image. Keeping the "human
touch" intact is important, and some so-called
imperfections are desirable.

We can control the values we actually sketch. This
could be in relation to the background, or perhaps
you feel that the shadows need to be darker than in
the reference image. We can draw what we "feel" the
subject should look like, instead of copying exactly
what we see. Other creative decisions you might
make include the choice of style, the visible pencil
strokes of your shading, the intentional messy nature
of smudges in certain areas, and so on. All of these
subjective, creative touches distinguish your portrait
from the reference.

GETTING STARTED

Tips for finding and using reference images:

Filter for quality
Reference photos can be sourced online, where
search-engine filters can help you find the desired
size and resolution.

Focus on the values
I like to convert an image to greyscale before
drawing. Removing the chroma element makes
it easier to gauge the values while shading (*see*
Sketching Fundamentals: Shading Basics).

Recognisable faces
Famous people are a great subject for practising
portraiture. Not only is it easier to capture their
likeness, but mistakes in proportions become
glaringly obvious – it is a great way to master
proportion. Many caricaturists start drawing
famous people for practice in order to capture
a likeness of the face rather than the realism.

THE BLOCK-IN METHOD

This is a powerful technique for artists seeking to create accurate, proportionate portraits. It is also used in genres like landscapes, still life and even architectural drawing. We will explore this method in detail – how to analyse and simplify forms, establish proportions, and refine the initial block shapes into a finished drawing.

WHY BLOCK IN?

It is common for artists to focus on the details of their subject, drawing these first. For example, while drawing a portrait, it can be tempting to completely detail the eyes before anything else. However, this approach restricts the proportion of the rest of the features of the portrait, making it quite difficult to draw them correctly.

Imagine writing a sentence on a sign where you need that sentence to fit on a single line. The size and position of the first letter dictates the size and position of each subsequent letter. It is not possible to know if it will fit right at the beginning, but if we lightly "block in" the letters first, we can gauge the fit before committing to the final design. Learning one or more methods for mapping out proportion avoids this problem.

HOW TO IDENTIFY YOUR BLOCKS

Start from the "macro" (blocks) and move towards the "micro" (details). The macro is a light sketch of the overall shape of the subject, without any details. It will take practise at first to identify the basic shapes of your reference. Two helpful ways to identify the macros are zooming out (or stepping back) and squinting.

Zoom out
View your reference from a distance to identify the blocks. If working digitally, reduce the size by zooming out. Simply stand back from a physical photo.

Squint
Alternatively, squint your eyes to blur the reference, filtering out the details and defining the main shapes.

Both of these methods can be used together for even better abstraction of the macro shapes.

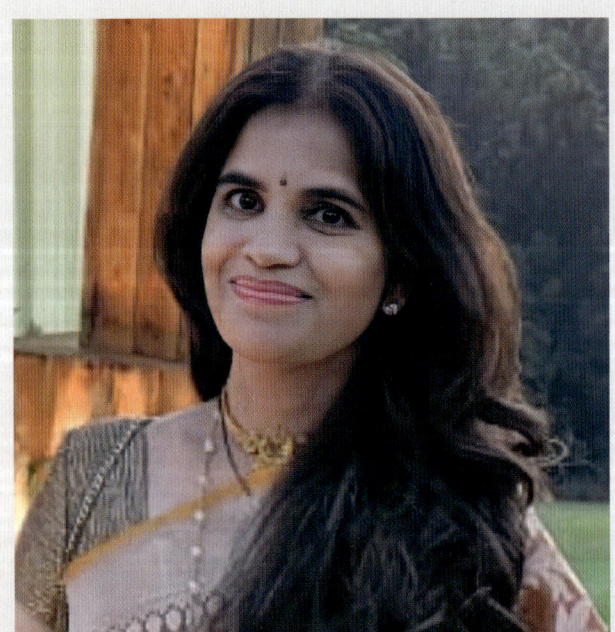

Reference at original size

The reference for *The Smile* (see The Portraits) at its original size, zoomed out to 25%, then 5%, where the details are too small to focus, leaving the main shapes prominent.

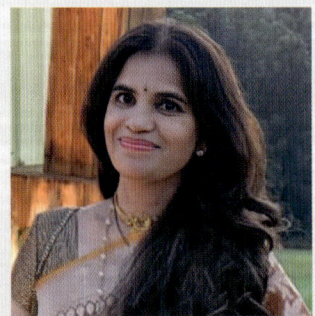

Reference at 25% size

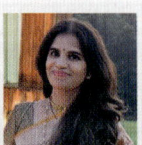

Reference at 5% size

BASIC BLOCKING-IN

In this example, only the key shapes are blocked in, and don't include facial features (*see also* The Portraits: *The Smile* for an example).

1 Analyse your reference to identify your main blocks.

2 Sketch these blocks using straight lines or simple curves. Pixel accuracy is not important at this stage for the garment outline and the curved outline of the face.

3 Once the overall composition is established, gradually add your smaller blocks (fabric across the forehead, eye sockets, shadow around the face, and so on).

4 Once we establish the proportion, we gradually add details and make adjustments for accuracy.

The illusion of proportion

Ignore what you "know" about the face. Instead, look purely at the main shapes forming the image, based only on the edges created by value differences and the shapes they form. For example, the general notion of where the nose sits in relation to the eyes can deviate from a reference. This results in an incorrect measure of proportion, errors accumulate, and even if the nose itself is drawn accurately, the portrait as a whole can look "off".

Turn it upside down

Practise this method by drawing your reference upside down! This forces you to observe the macro shapes without the distraction of familiar micro features. This concept can be applied to any genre where a reference is used, such as landscapes and still-life.

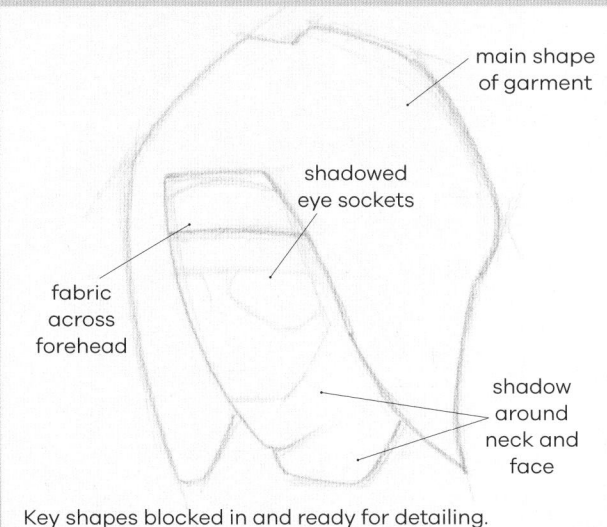

main shape of garment

shadowed eye sockets

fabric across forehead

shadow around neck and face

Key shapes blocked in and ready for detailing.

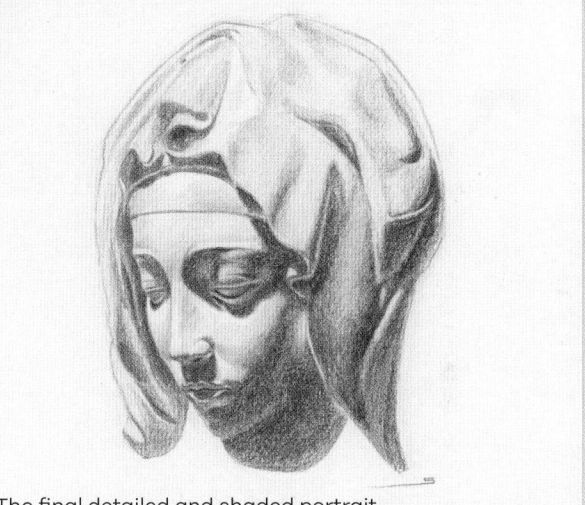

The final detailed and shaded portrait.

From reference to portrait

The resulting blocked-in shapes for *The Smile*. Prominent areas include the hair, the face and neck, and the layers of fabric across the right shoulder. When later adding facial features and other details, it is far easier to gauge the proportions, as the main shapes have already been mapped out to scale.

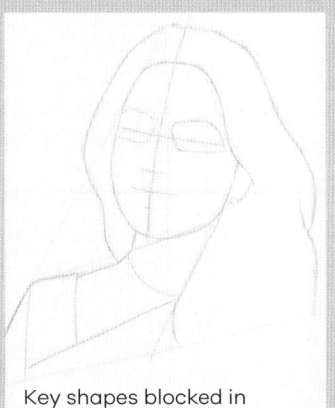

Key shapes blocked in and ready for detailing.

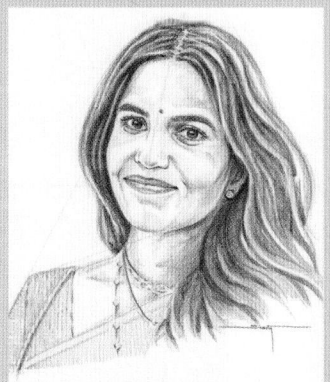

The final detailed and shaded portrait.

THE LOOMIS METHOD

The Loomis method, named after its creator, Andrew Loomis, provides a structured approach to capturing the complexities of the human head. The method focuses on breaking down the head into simple geometric shapes and aids artists in achieving realistic and well-proportioned portraits.

BASIC LOOMIS HEAD

Let's draw the three-quarters angled Loomis head, step by step.

1 Start with a square in the centre, slightly towards the top of the page. Split the square into quadrants and use these guidelines to draw a circle. This circle is the cranium, and the square can be used as a grid to place the facial features.

2 Draw a smaller circle within the first – this will be the side plane of the head – approximately two-thirds of the diameter of the first circle. Position it vertically halfway between the top and bottom of the square as shown. The size of this circle will differ from subject to subject, but here you are working with an average Loomis head.

3 Draw horizontal guides from the top and bottom of the smaller circle out to the edges – these are the nose and chin lines. The horizontal centreline of the square is the browline. Measure the distance between the browline and nose line, and use the same distance below the nose line to mark the chin line. Complete the front plane by drawing two curved lines down from the browline, tapering down to the chin line.

4 Draw a vertical line splitting the side-plane circle in half. Extend the line upwards, curving it towards the middle of the square to create the top of the head. Then extend it downwards, curving it to meet the lower jaw, then the chin.

This completes the construction of the basic Loomis Head. Now you can move on to adding the details.

DETAILING THE LOOMIS HEAD

5 Draw a centreline on the front plane of the face, following the curve of the two outer lines (marked as dashed lines). Position the ear between the browline and the nose line.

6 Create a groove on the front plane for the placement of the eyes. Think of this groove as an inward and an outward plane carved along the width of the front plane of the face.

7 Use the four-plane nose technique to plot the nose, ending at the nose line (*see* Facial Features: Nose).

8 Complete the lips using the bottom line of the square as a guide.

SHADING THE LOOMIS HEAD

9 Finish the Loomis head by shading the different planes with a 2B pencil as described here.

- Imagine the light source from the top left of the head, and use hatching and cross hatching with a 2B pencil (Shading Techniques: Simple Shading).

- Shade the side planes of the nose and face with a midtone – notice the contours added to the cheek.

- Move on to the top planes of the eye socket, the bottom plane of the nose, the upper lip and the shadow area below the lower lip. These features are facing away from the light source, so shade a tone darker using cross hatching (you can use a 6B pencil).

- Shade the ear using the same process.

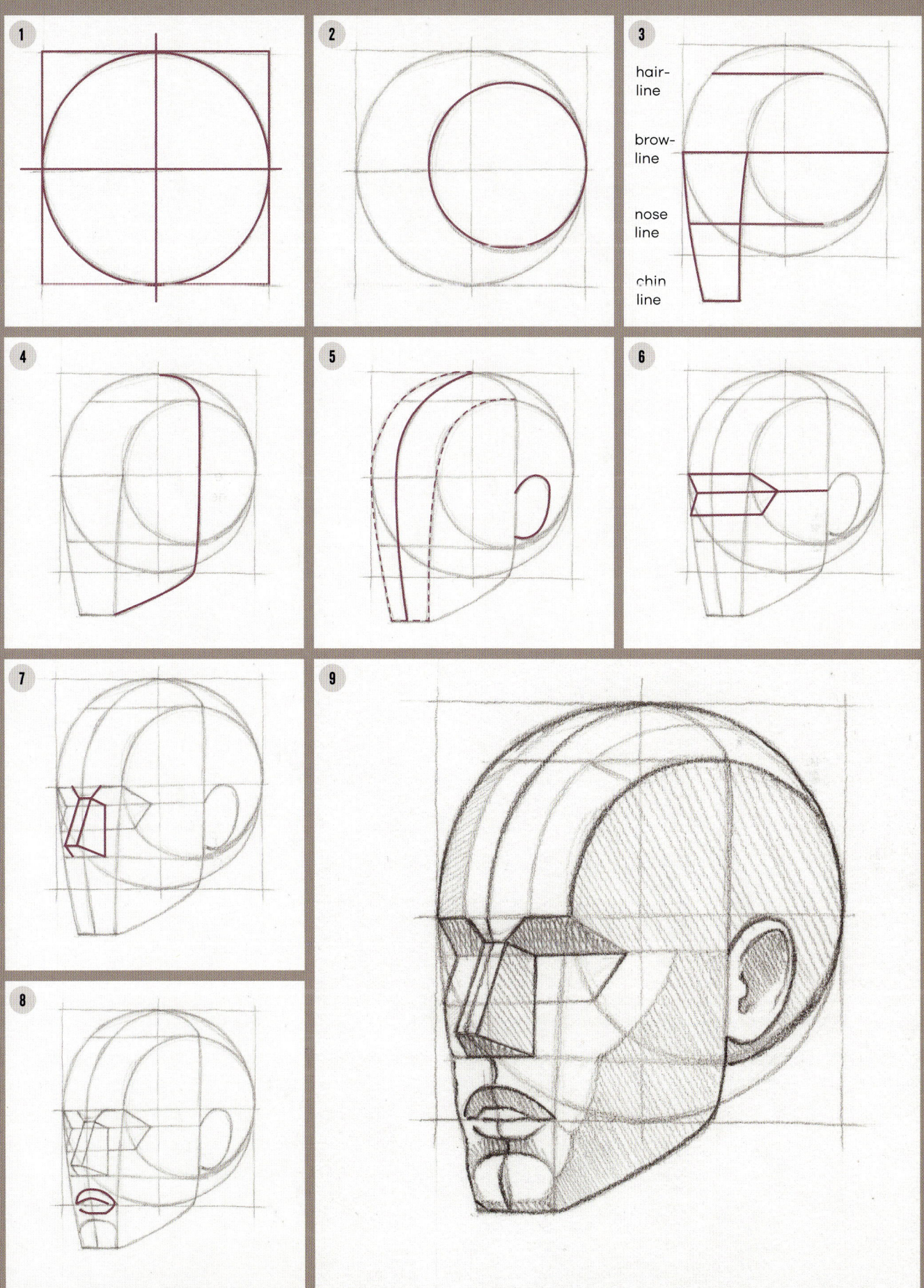

hair-
line

brow-
line

nose
line

chin
line

LOOMIS CUBOID

Loomis cuboid is a revised version of the Loomis Head method, allowing the artist to draw the human head from imagination, as viewed from practically any angle. Since a cuboid can be easily drawn at any angle, practising this method develops a proportion system that can be applied to drawing a head from any viewpoint.

1 Start with a cuboid. Depending on the shape of the head, the cuboid can be elongated (for a narrower face) or squarish (for a broader face). In this case, I am drawing an average oval face. The arrow points in the direction the head is facing – this is the frontal plane. Perpendicular to this plane, split the cuboid into three sections (browline, nose line and chin line).

2 Draw the cranium sphere enclosed in the top two sections of the split cuboid. Then define the frontal plane by extending lines down from the browline tapering towards the chin.

3 Draw the jawline splitting the browline on the side plane of the face.

4 Draw the eye-socket planes, generally splitting the distance between the browline and nose line into thirds.

5 Finish the head by drawing ears between the browline and nose line.

WORK BACKWARDS

Practise drawing a cuboid around a reference portrait (use a drawing app or printed reference) to further understand how the cuboid forms the basis of the head.

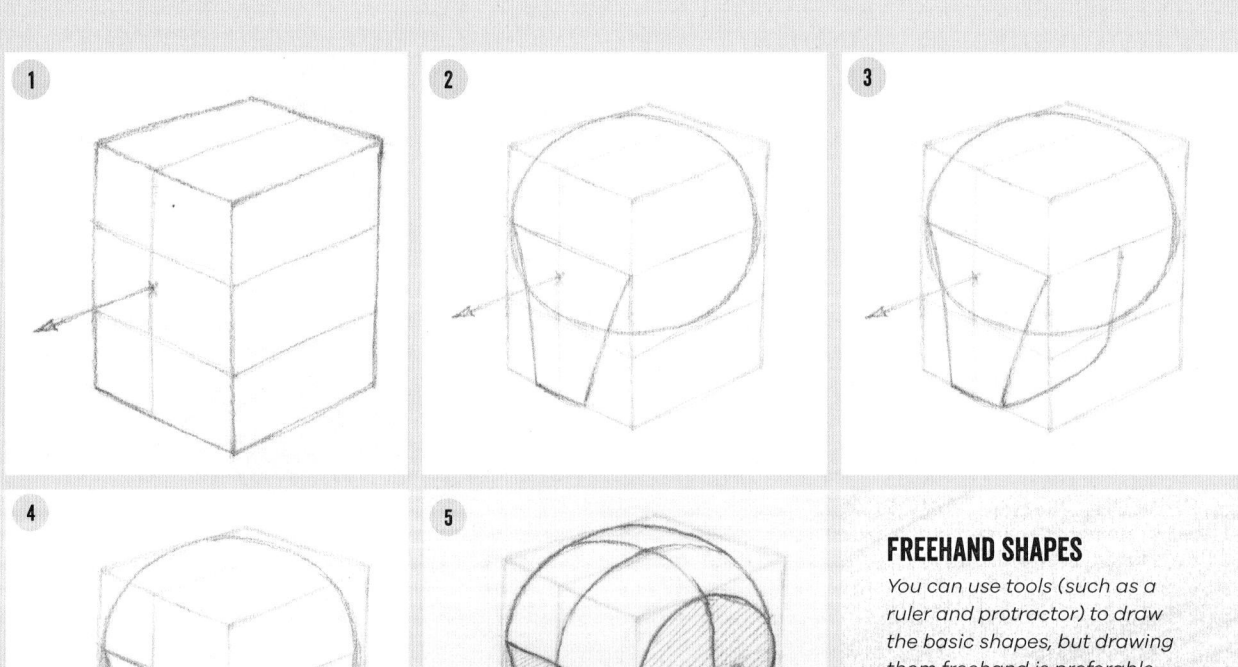

FREEHAND SHAPES

You can use tools (such as a ruler and protractor) to draw the basic shapes, but drawing them freehand is preferable – minor imperfections make the drawing feel more real.

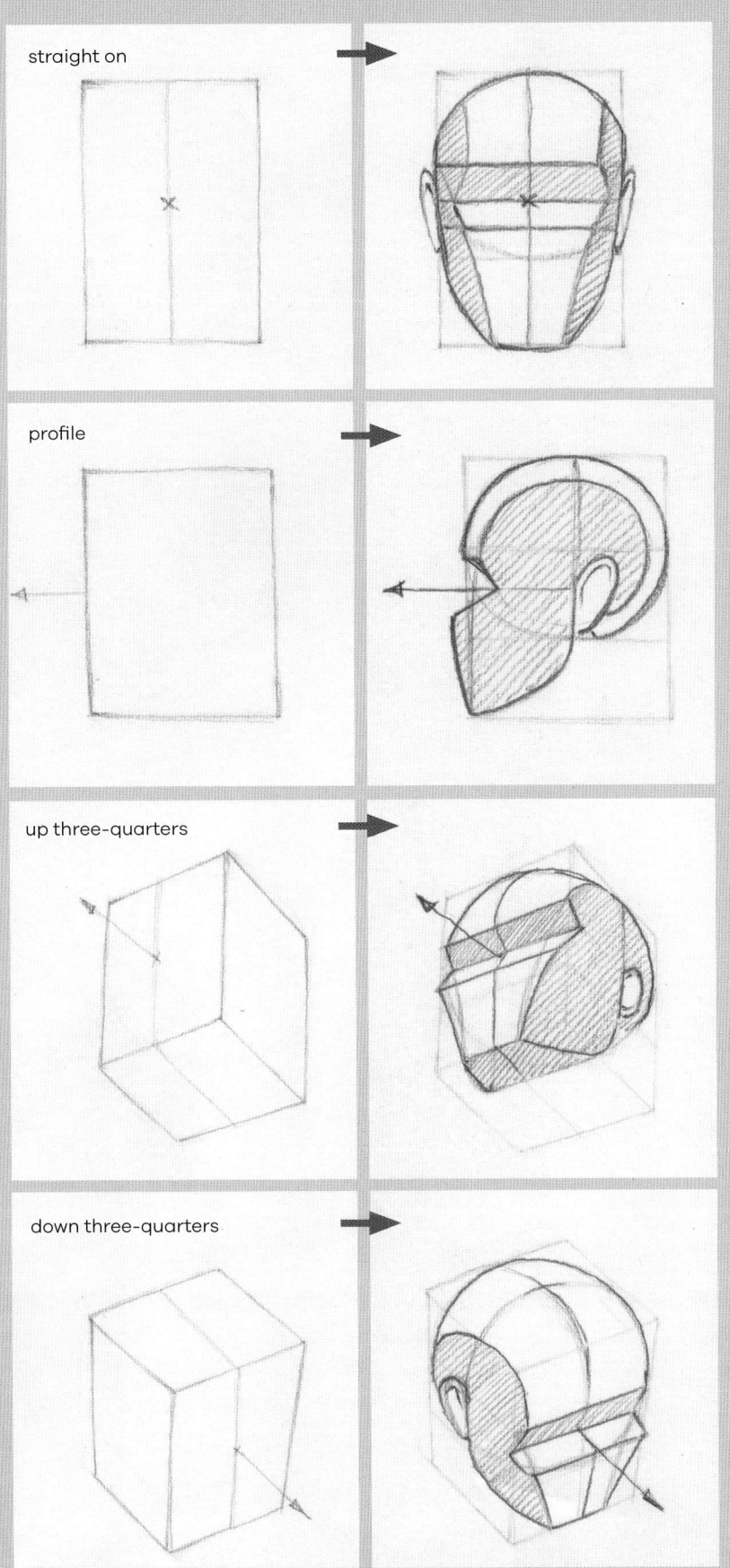

straight on

profile

up three-quarters

down three-quarters

CUBOID VARIATIONS

The following examples show you how the Loomis head can be drawn at any angle when positioned within the cuboid.

Straight on
In this front view, we only see the front plane of the cuboid. In the centre, the "X" is the arrow pointing directly out of the plane of the paper.

Profile
The head viewed from the side. Draw the side plane of the cuboid, which is slightly broader than the front plane.

Up three-quarters
We see the front, bottom and one side plane. The bottom of the chin is visible. The size of the forehead is reduced. We see more of the top plane of the eye sockets than the bottom plane.

Down three-quarters
We see the front, top and one side plane. The forehead is larger compared to previous angles as it is closest to the viewer. We see more of the bottom plane of the eye sockets than the top.

USE YOUR IMAGINATION
A combination of this technique and a knowledge of perspective brings us one step closer to drawing human faces (or figures) from imagination.

GRID METHODS

Grid methods are popular drawing techniques that can help artists achieve greater accuracy, proportion and realism. Two variations are shown here.

THE REGULAR GRID METHOD

First, we draw an equally spaced grid over the reference image, then draw the same grid scaled to the size of our canvas and replicate the reference one square at a time. This method can be effectively used to draw hyper-realistic portraits, when the artist has to replicate every minute detail on the reference image. Tackling the details systematically, one square at a time, is recommended. Grid method is also useful when the size of the canvas is relatively large. Oil painters use this method on life-sized canvases.

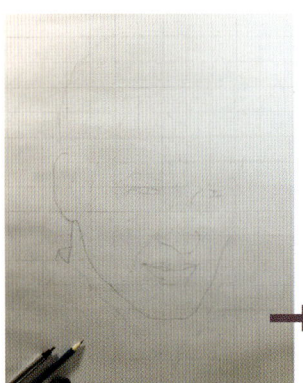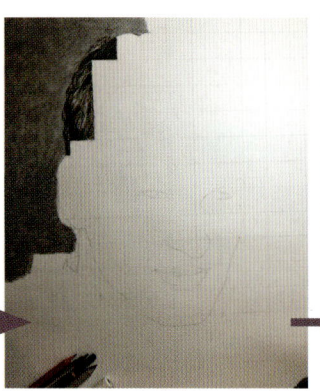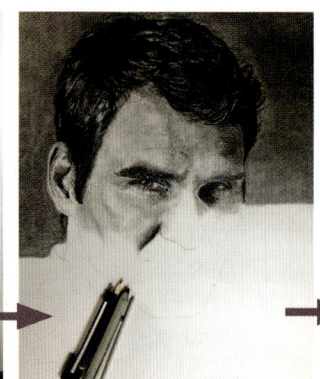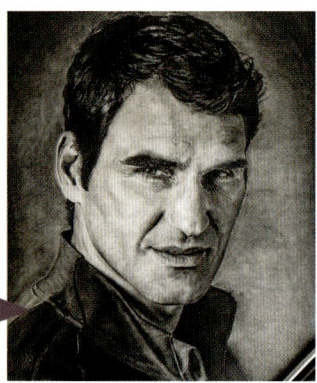

THE DYNAMIC GRID METHOD

The dynamic grid method is a quicker alternative to the regular grid method. Unlike the regular grid method, the grid lines in the dynamic grid are not equidistant from each other. Instead, they are dependent on the features of the portrait drawn, or "dynamic" in nature. Draw these lines directly on your reference image. The grid will form itself depending on the reference. Each subject will have a unique dynamic grid. Note the occasional slanting 45-degree grid line. This is generally to give an idea about the positioning of the rest of the gridlines relative to the slant line when we transfer it to our canvas. Since we don't use a ruler or measurements, this is a quick method to plot accurate guidelines to help with proportions.

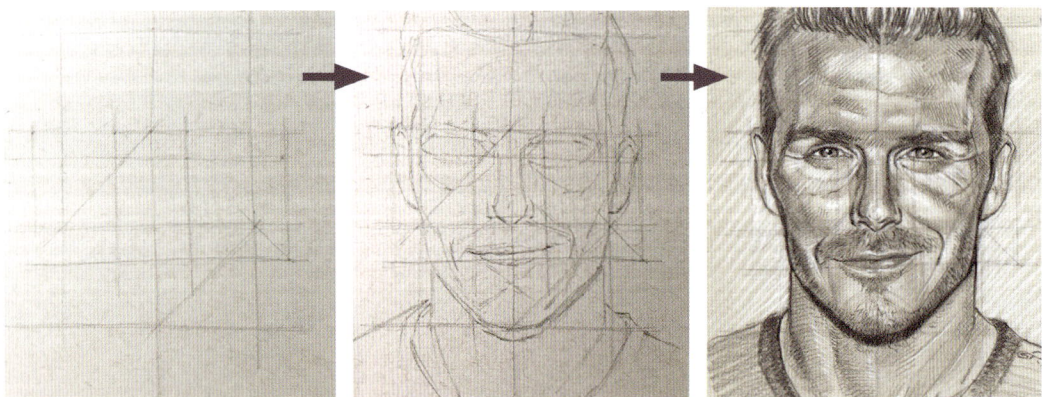

FREEHAND & TRACING

Freehand drawing allows for spontaneous and personal interpretations whereas tracing is a method to accurately copy the reference exactly, with all its details.

THE FREEHAND METHOD

This is a liberating and expressive way to draw without relying on tools like rulers or grids. Instead, we use the approximate positioning of shadows and highlights to gradually sharpen our portrait. It follows the same principle as the block-in method, going from macro to micro, the difference being that this method is more fluid. Its additive and subtractive nature can be compared to sculpting with clay. We use the eraser to remove (subtract) parts of the graphite (clay), adjusting proportions and slowly adding details as we work.

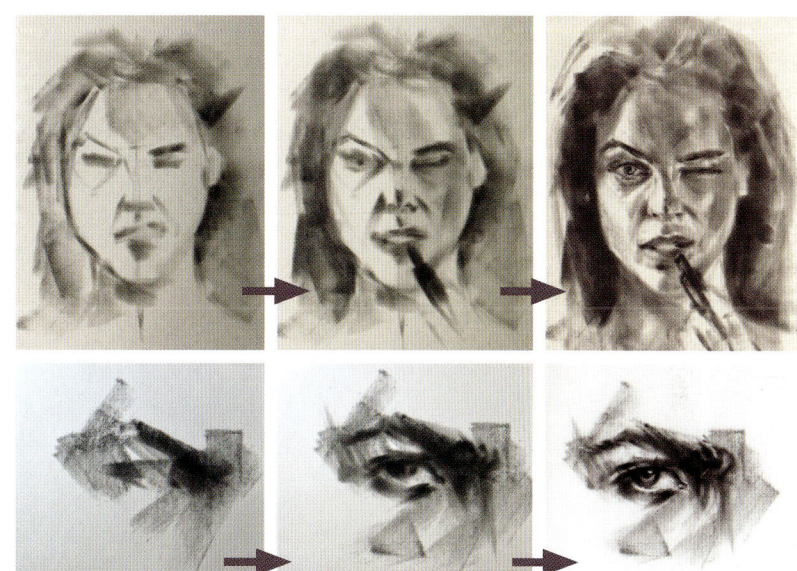

TRACING THE REFERENCE

A powerful way to learn about proportions, tracing allows you to skip straight to shading if you want more practise. There are a few ways to trace the reference onto your sketch paper:

Tracing paper
Place the tracing paper over your reference and copy the edges and outlines of the reference on to the tracing paper. Turn the tracing paper over and redraw the sketch on the back using a dark (6B) pencil. Turn the tracing paper back over and place it over the sketch paper. Transfer the 6B graphite on to the sketch paper by going over the traced lines with your pencil for a third time. When working with multiple layers of paper, tape them to the drawing board to stop them moving as you trace.

Graphite paper
Layer the graphite paper (graphite side down) over your sketch paper, then layer the reference image over the graphite paper. Trace the lines on the reference using a sturdy pencil (such as an HB) – the pressure will transfer graphite from the graphite paper to the sketch paper. (Put tracing paper over the reference if you don't want to work directly onto an original image.)

Bright backdrop
Use a window or light box to illuminate the reference, making it visible to trace through your sketching paper.

Projector
A projector will enlarge your reference straight on to the canvas, and scale it to fit. This method is generally used for large-scale artworks such as murals and wall paintings.

PERFECT IMPERFECTIONS

To become an observant artist, trace only when necessary. It is a great way to copy the reference exactly, but it is desirable to capture human nuances and imperfections. The sense of achievement that comes from drawing freehand is unparalleled.

EYES

The eyes serve as windows to the soul, reflecting the innermost thoughts and secrets of a subject. The careful study of anatomy, shape, and proportion allows us to convey a wide range of feelings, from joy and curiosity to sorrow and intensity. Whether it's realistic, stylized or abstract, drawing eyes is an opportunity to bring life and emotion to the canvas.

BASIC OUTLINES

Starting with basic shapes, we can simplify the process of sketching the eye.

Throughout this example, we are drawing the right eye.

1 First, draw an outer circle slightly larger than the eye – this is a construction sphere that will contain the eyeball. Then draw a smaller circle to position the iris. Draw two curved centrelines to split the larger circle into four parts through the iris, keeping in mind the curvature of the eyeball.

2 Draw the basic outline of the eye enclosed in the outer circle. Use the horizontal curved line as a guideline to position the corners of the eye. Where the line bisects the vertical curved line, draw the pupil. The line above the upper eyelid is the upper eyelid fold. The line below the lower eyelid is the lower eyelid fold.

3 Draw the inner plane of the top eyelid, then the outer plane of the bottom eyelid. Artists often omit these details, rendering the eyelid as a completely flat surface. Draw the general outline of the eyebrow. Finally, using faint lines, we can depict the contours surrounding the inner and the outer parts of the eye.

You are now ready with the basic shape of the eye and can move towards shading it in any style you want (*see* Sketching Fundamentals: Shading Techniques).

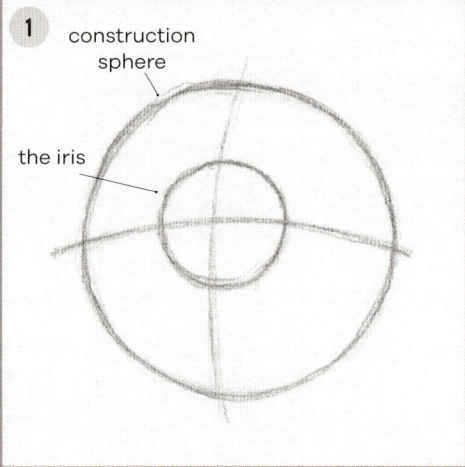

1 — construction sphere — the iris

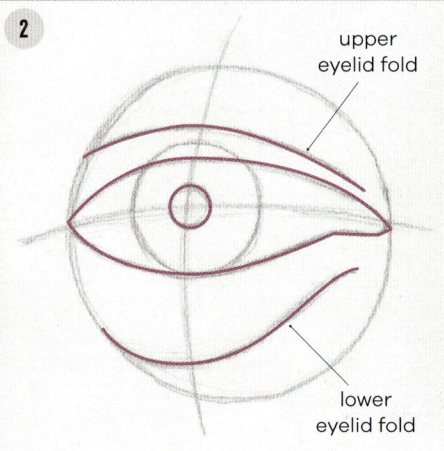

2 — upper eyelid fold — lower eyelid fold

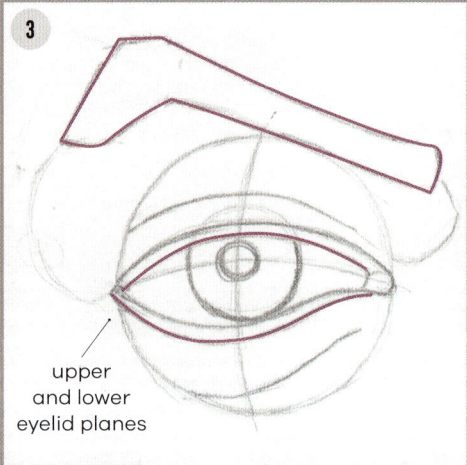

3 — upper and lower eyelid planes

IRIS AND PUPIL

The iris is the part of the eye that gives the portrait its character. Pay close attention not only to the values and textures, but also to its shape, as it changes based on the viewing angle of the eye. Let's practise drawing one as viewed from the front.

1 Draw a circle for the iris.

2 Add a smaller circle within the iris for the pupil. Add a placement upper right for the highlight.

3 Use a 4B pencil to shade the midtone of the iris.

4 With an 8B pencil, shade the pupil with the darkest value extreme (*see* Shading Basics: The Value Scale). Remember to leave the small square of the highlight unshaded.

5 Create a gradient using the 4B and 6B pencils – darken the top of the iris and gradually transition towards the lighter part at the bottom. You can also use a blending tool.

6 To make the iris more realistic, add texture details around the pupil, and the reflection of the eyelashes on the highlight.

GRADIENT SHADOW

This gradient running down the iris is due to the shadow cast by the upper eye lid. The transitions might change based on the lighting and the perspective.

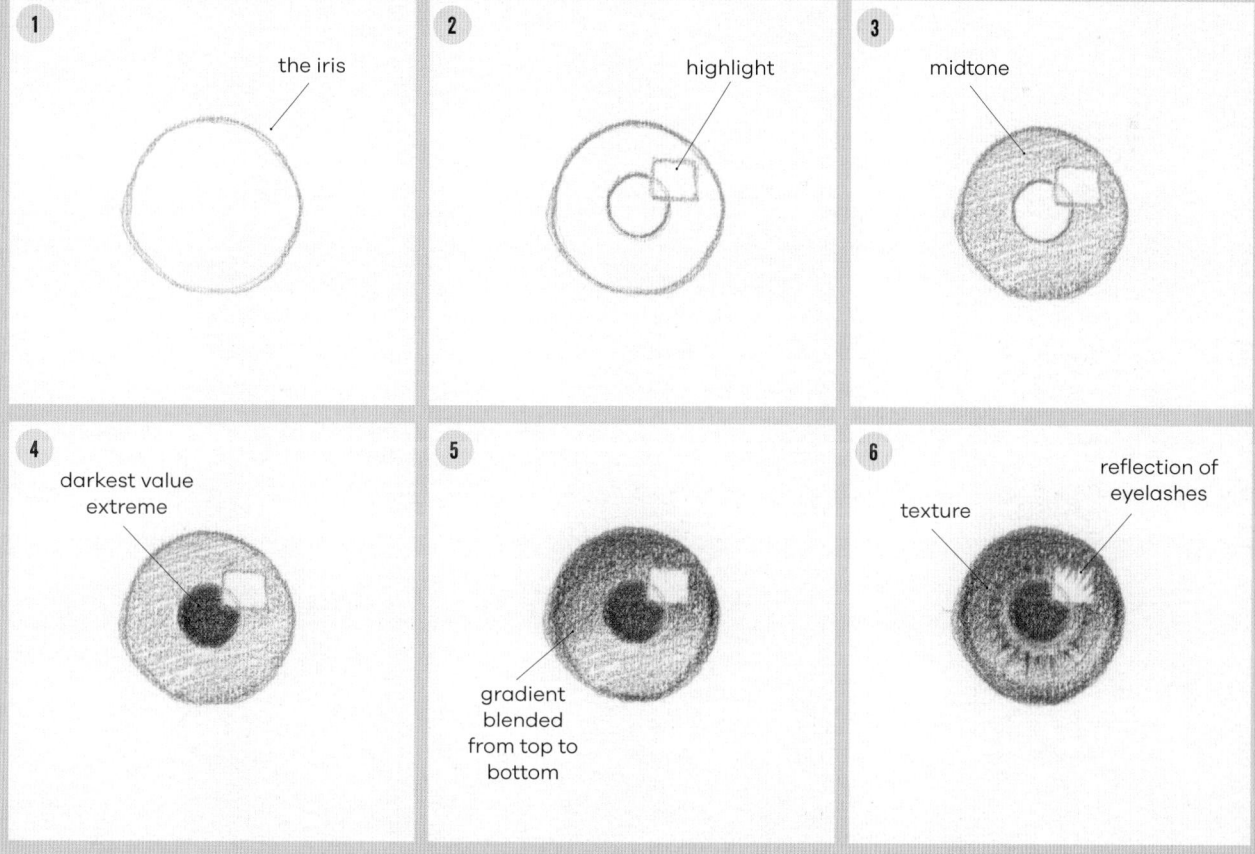

1

the iris

2

highlight

3

midtone

4

darkest value extreme

5

gradient blended from top to bottom

6

reflection of eyelashes

texture

EYELASHES

In my opinion, the eyelashes are the trickiest part of the eye. Drawn incorrectly, they can make the eyes look unrealistic and lifeless. To give them a more natural appearance, it is important to maintain a direction for the lashes, as well as some randomness. Drawing them in a series of "sets" will help you to create this look.

1 Begin with your basic sketch of the eye. The starting point of each eyelash is the upper edge of the top-inner eyelid. Using a sharpened 6B pencil, draw the first set of eyelashes. Observe how each lash on the upper eyelid curves slightly down and inwards towards the eyeball before flicking upwards. Your pencil stroke should follow this motion. Think of it as drawing the rays of the sun.

Use a similar technique for the lower eyelashes. These start at the lower edge of the bottom-inner eyelid, and are smaller than the upper eyelashes.

2 To add realistic density, add a further set of eyelashes alongside the original set, maintaining the general direction. Note how the eyelashes are split into separate groups, with each group roughly converging to a single point at the tips.

3 With a 2B pencil, draw some lighter eyelashes, maintaining the same direction. Continue this way to make the eyelashes as dense as desired.

4 Finally, use an 8B pencil to rework a few eyelashes, which adds depth to the sketch.

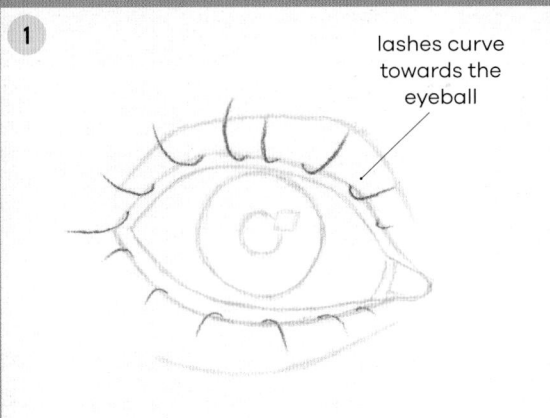

lashes curve towards the eyeball

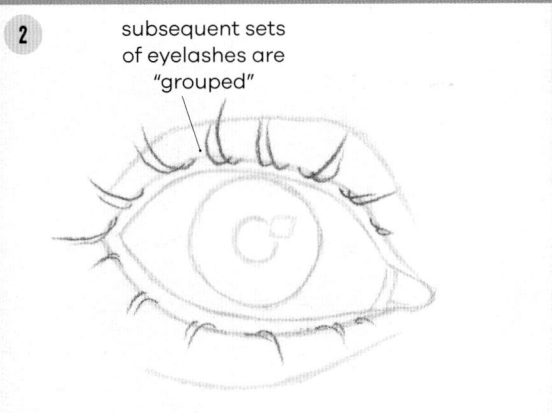

subsequent sets of eyelashes are "grouped"

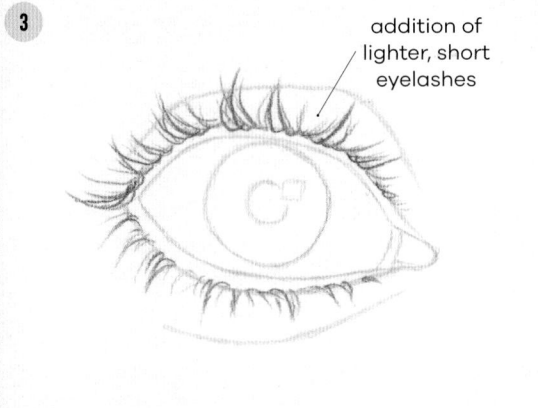

addition of lighter, short eyelashes

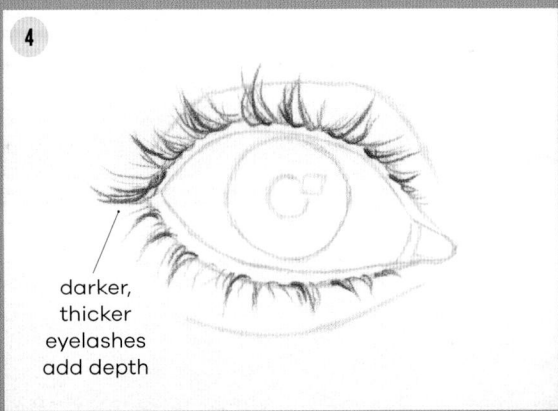

darker, thicker eyelashes add depth

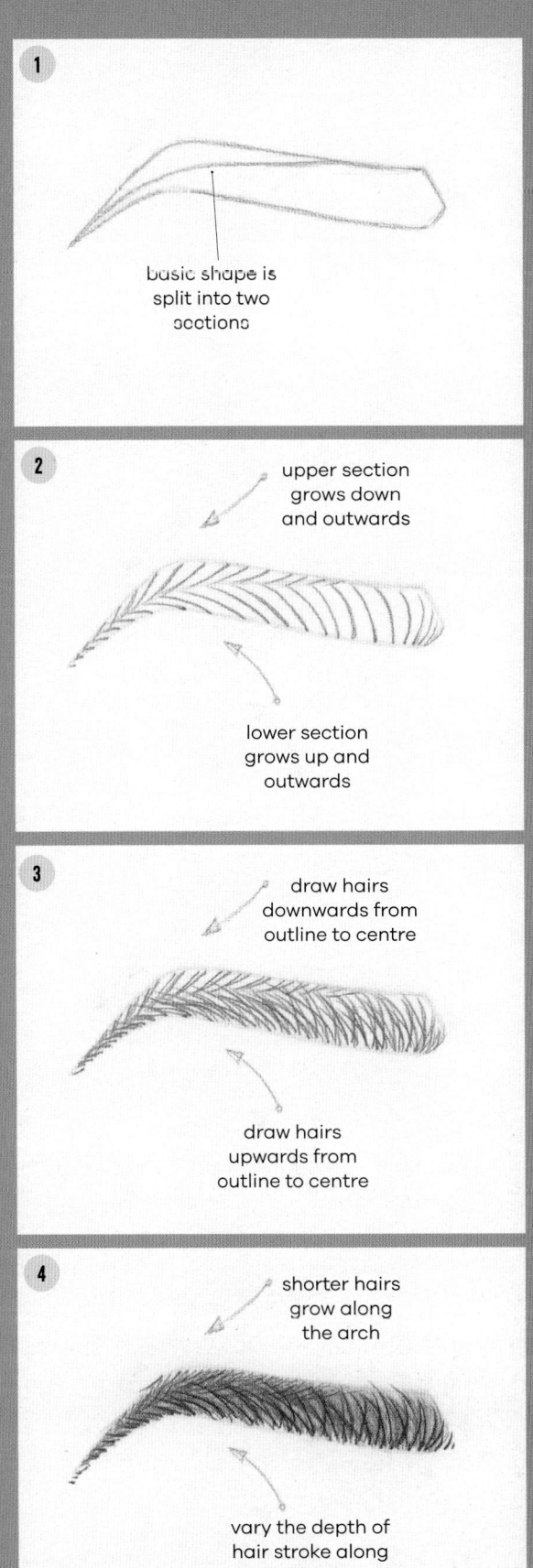

1 basic shape is split into two sections

2 upper section grows down and outwards

lower section grows up and outwards

3 draw hairs downwards from outline to centre

draw hairs upwards from outline to centre

4 shorter hairs grow along the arch

vary the depth of hair stroke along the whole brow

EYEBROWS

The shape of eyebrows will differ from person to person. Some brows may be thin, carefully shaped and precisely groomed, with defined edges. Others are bushy and thick, surrounded by stray hairs and generally ungroomed. Or a combination of both!

For this exercise, we will draw an average eyebrow, showing the general shape and direction of hair growth.

1 Draw a basic shape of the eyebrow. Use a guideline to split it into two sections to define the two different growth directions of the hair.

2 The first movement of hair is an upward curve. Your pencil stroke should start from the bottom and follow an upward curved motion to end in a flick at the top. The second movement of hair is a downward curve which meets the guideline we plotted in Step 1.

3 Begin adding depth to the brow by adding more hairs. Adhere to the general direction of growth of each section, but also incorporate some randomness to make it look natural.

4 Continue in this way until you achieve the desired effect of depth and value. You can use blending to give the brow more volume, making it look fuller.

BLOCKING IN AND SHADING

In addition to blocking in the entire head, individual features such as the eyes can be blocked in. In this example, I have used graphite pencils and toned tan paper to clearly demonstrate the highlights with white charcoal pencil.

Blocking in

Construct the outlines with simple shapes using the block-in method (see Proportion Techniques: The Block-in Method).

1 Draw a pentagon to encompass the whole eye socket, including the eyebrow. The top and upper left side of the pentagon will be the upper edge of the eyebrow. The right corner of the pentagon will determine the shadow along the inner corner of the eye. The bottom corner simply locates the start of the cheek contouring outwards. This can be thought of as the eye-socket pentagon.

2 Draw the outline of the eyebrow following the upper two sides of this pentagon (see Eyes: Eyebrows). The ends of the eyebrow should still be level with each other – this will depend on the reference and the expression of the subject.

3 Draw the basic shape of the eye including the upper and the lower eyelids, and the eyelid folds (see Eyes: Basic Outlines). Note how all these lines finish at the vertical inner corner guide. The lower eyelid fold sweeps along the side of the pentagon.

4 Draw the basic circular shape of the iris and the pupil. Don't forget to mark the small highlight on the iris. It is also important to draw some of the details in this step, particularly the lower plane of the upper eyelid and the upper plane of the lower eyelid. Mark the small triangular shape at the corner of the eye, also known as the caruncle.

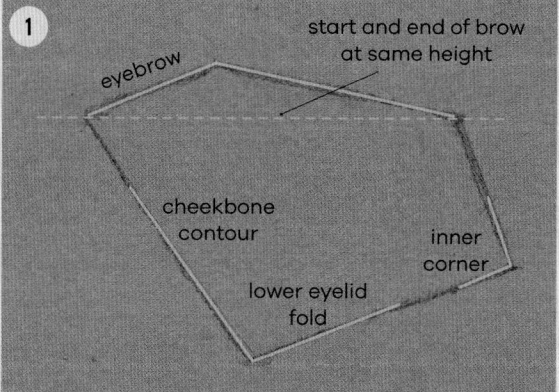

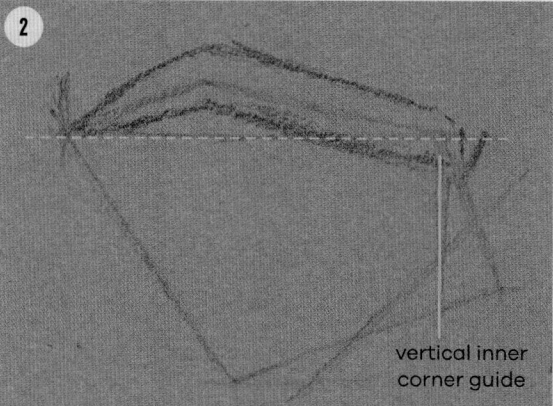

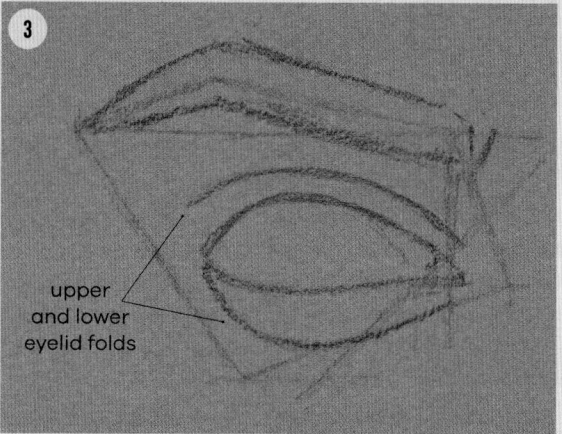

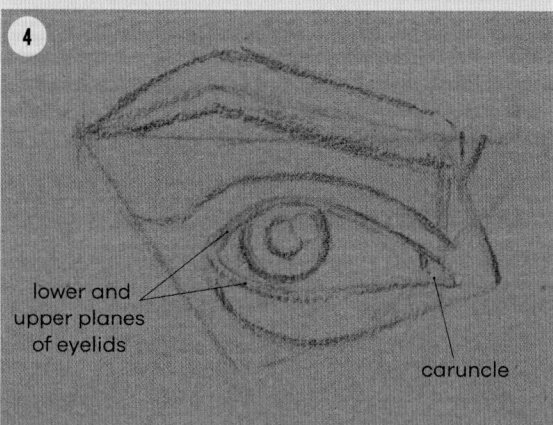

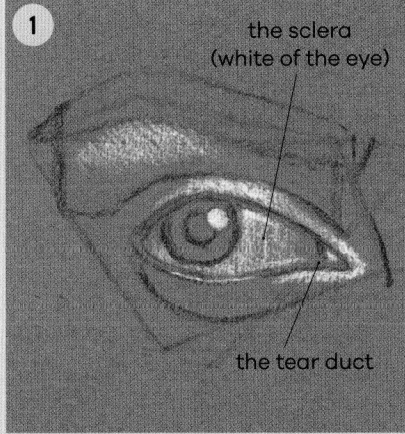

1 · the sclera (white of the eye) · the tear duct

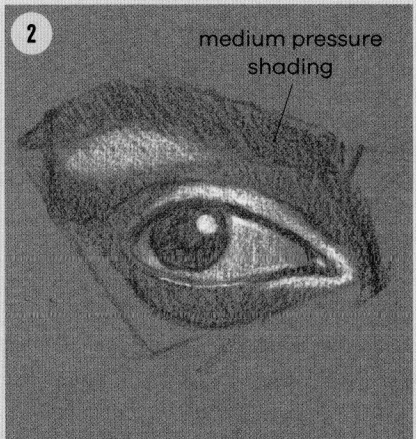

2 · medium pressure shading

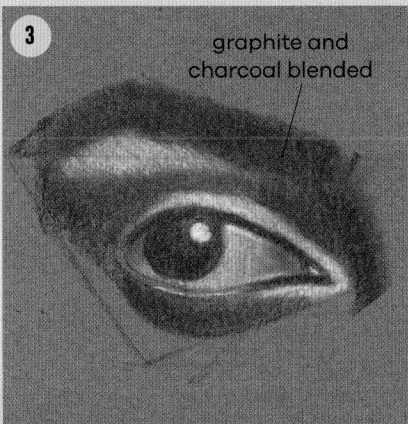

3 · graphite and charcoal blended

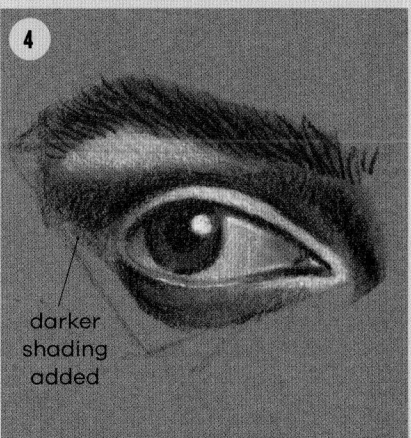

4 · darker shading added

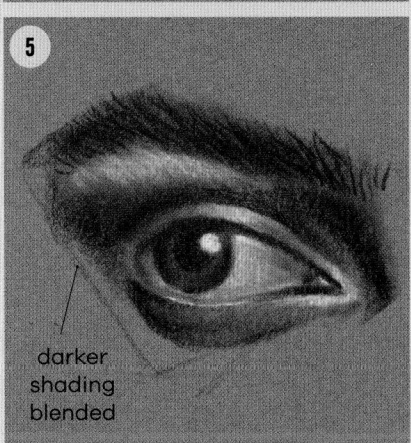

5 · darker shading blended

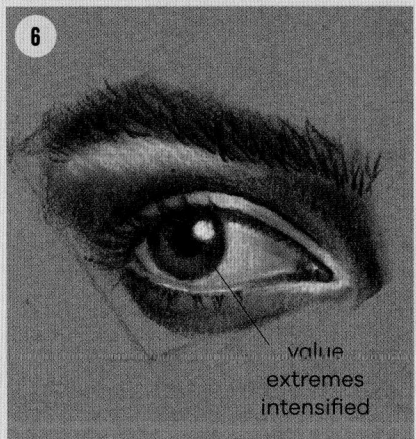

6 · value extremes intensified

Shading

You will need your white charcoal pencil and graphite pencils.

1 Use the white charcoal pencil to shade the highlights: the shine on the iris, the sclera and the skin near the tear duct. There is also a highlight under the arch of the eyebrow.

2 With the 4B pencil, use medium pressure to shade the rest of the eye.

3 Blend the graphite and white areas together, using a paper stump. Then use a clean blending tip to blend the whites.

4 Use a 6B pencil to shade darker regions such as the brow hair, pupil and the fold at the top of the eye lid.

5 Now blend the dark regions using a tortillon or other small blending tool.

6 Finally, focus on the value extremes. Use an 8B pencil to shade the darkest value regions like the pupil, eyelashes and eyebrows. Go over the lightest value regions with your white charcoal to pop the highlights even further.

LIGHT SOURCE

The light source is above the subject, so darken the lower plane of the upper eyelid with a 6B pencil. Use white charcoal to shade highlight on the upper plane of the lower eyelid.

NOSE

Drawing the nose requires keen observation and attention to detail – this prominent feature can greatly affect a portrait's overall likeness. The nose can be split into four planes – the bridge (front plane), two side planes and the bottom plane. We'll draw it from two angles.

THREE-QUARTER VIEW

Draw basic planes to construct the nose.

1 Begin by drawing a quadrilateral for the front plane of the nose, slanting in the direction the head will face.

2 Draw the two side planes. Think of the side planes as being folded away at an angle from the front plane. The bottom edge of each side plane will be larger than the upper edge as the nose protrudes from the face. The angle of the bottom edge depends on the shape of the nose, and will be different for different people.

3 Draw the bottom plane of the nose, and the vertical centreline running down the bridge of the nose. The horizontal line at the back of the bottom plane should be parallel to the top and bottom edges of the front plane.

4 Add details to the tip of the nose, using the guidelines plotted in the previous steps. Notice that the right nostril is tear drop shaped. The other is hidden behind the columella, the part of the nose that separates the nostrils.

5 Extend the tip of the nose upwards along the front plane of the nose to the bridge – note the slight outward protrusion of the bridge. Draw a circular highlight on the tip. The small plane on the side of the tip is known as the facet. Split the front plane into three sections. The top part is the bridge. The middle, called the dorsum, slightly protrudes. The bottom part becomes the bulge at the tip of the nose.

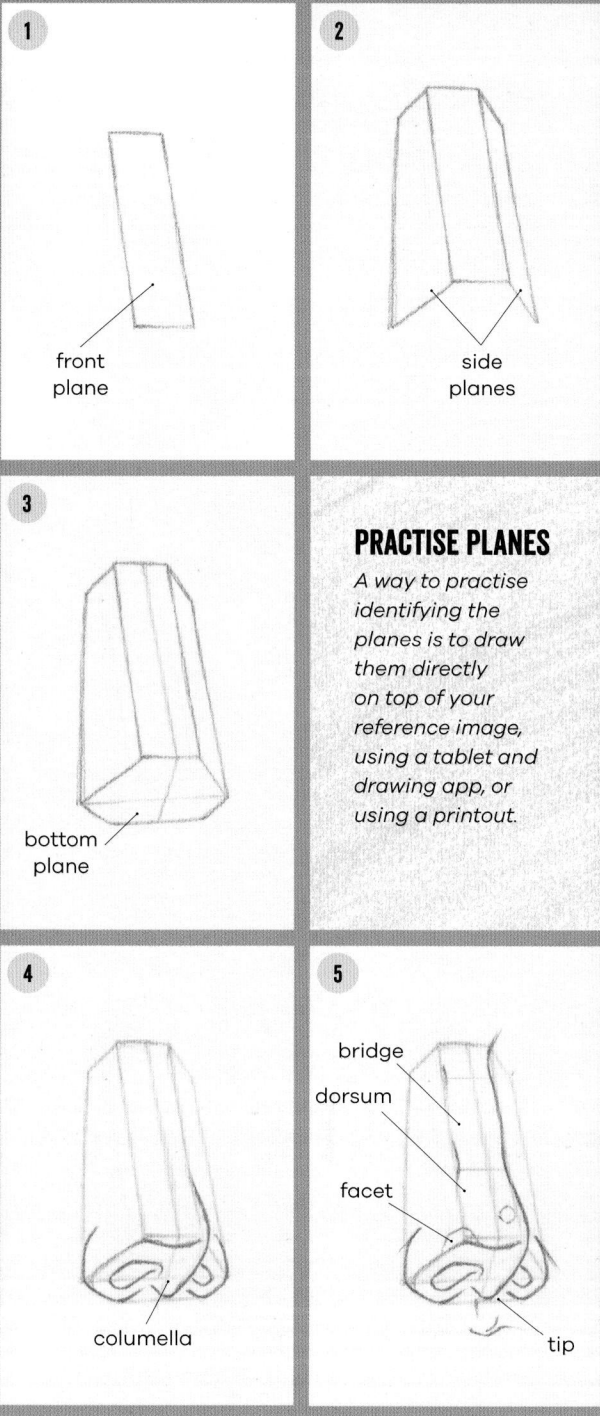

1 front plane

2 side planes

3 bottom plane

PRACTISE PLANES

A way to practise identifying the planes is to draw them directly on top of your reference image, using a tablet and drawing app, or using a printout.

4 columella

5 bridge / dorsum / facet / tip

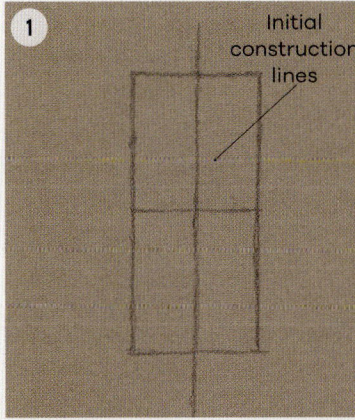

1 Initial construction lines

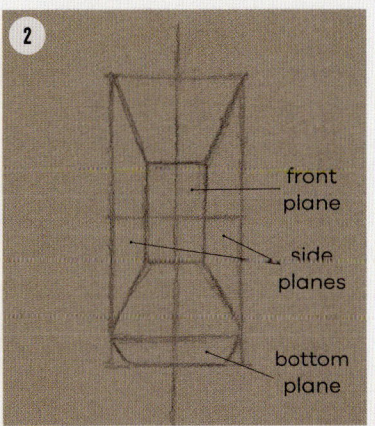

2 front plane / side planes / bottom plane

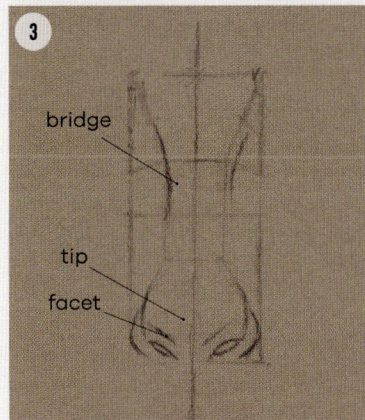

3 bridge / tip / facet

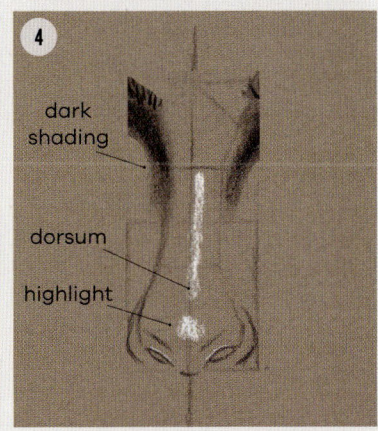

4 dark shading / dorsum / highlight

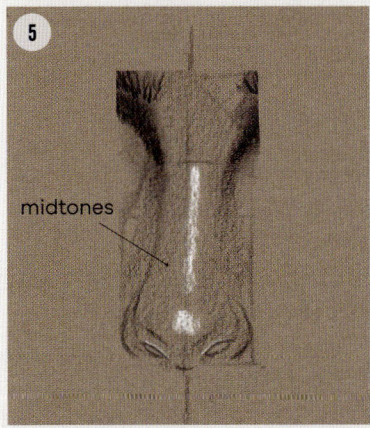

5 midtones

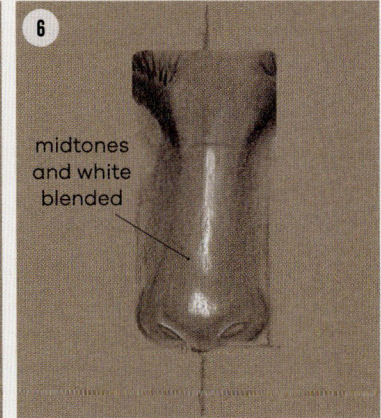

6 midtones and white blended

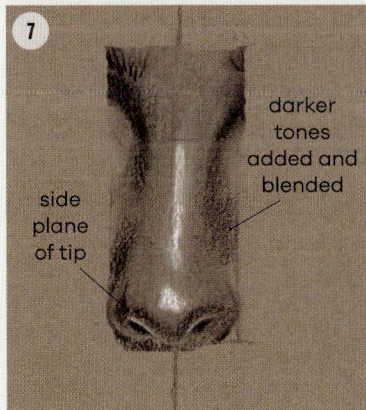

7 side plane of tip / darker tones added and blended

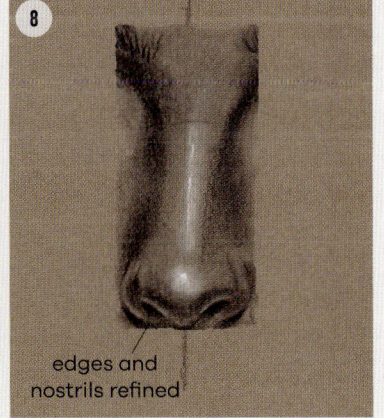

8 edges and nostrils refined

FRONT VIEW

Draw the nose using basic shapes.

Basic construction

1 Draw a vertically elongated rectangle with vertical and horizontal centrelines.

2 Draw the basic planes of the nose including the side and the bottom planes.

3 Draw a simple outline of the nose including the nostrils. Don't forget to mark the planes over the nostrils.

Shading

4 In this step, we simply darken the side planes of the upper bridge of the nose to give it some depth using a 6B pencil. We also use a white charcoal pencil to draw the highlights on the dorsum and the tip.

5 Shade midtones using a 4B pencil.

6 Blend the midtones with the white highlights using a blending tool such as a paper stump.

7 Use a 6B pencil to slightly darken the side planes, nostrils and the bottom of the nose. Don't forget to darken the small side planes of the tip of the nose. Blend these darker tones with the midtones to get a smooth gradient using a smaller blending tool like the tortillon.

8 Finally, use an 8B pencil to sharpen the edges and darken the shadows of the nostrils and the bottom of the nose.

LIPS

Lips are a vital part of the face and a key feature in depicting emotion. Minor variation in the shapes and shadows can completely change the facial expression of the subject. Again, we will look at drawing lips as seen from two different angles.

THREE-QUARTER VIEW

Draw basic guidelines to construct the lips in three-quarter view.

1 Draw a horizontal and vertical centreline for the lips, intersecting slightly to the left of the centre of the horizontal line as you are drawing the lips in three-quarter view.

2 Draw a kite shape, with the smaller sides on the left. The angle of the lips mean the right side of the lips will be smaller and less visible.

3 Using the kite shape as a guide, draw the basic outline edge of the upper and lower lips. This line is also known as the vermilion border.

4 Divide the upper lip into three sections to help us draw a realistic bottom edge. These areas bulge outwards, creating particular highlights and the shadows.

5 Following the three sections, darken the lower edge of the upper lip. Note the wave-like pattern of this edge.

6 Add further details including like highlights and shadows to create the basic structure of the lips.

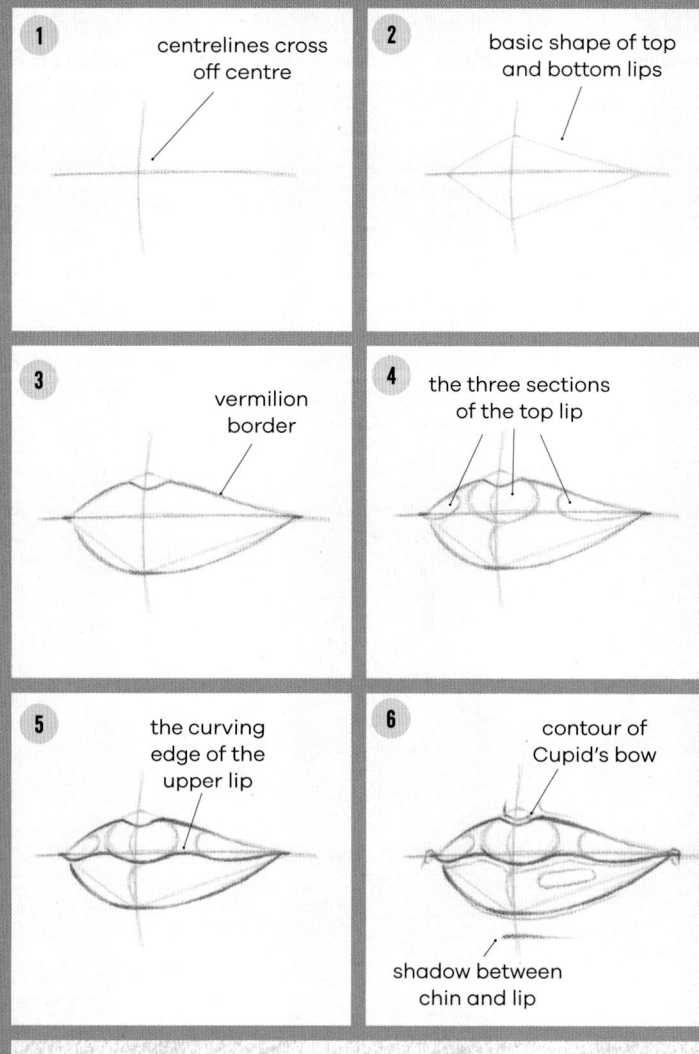

1 centrelines cross off centre

2 basic shape of top and bottom lips

3 vermilion border

4 the three sections of the top lip

5 the curving edge of the upper lip

6 contour of Cupid's bow / shadow between chin and lip

MONA LISA SMILE

The smile of Leonardo da Vinci's Mona Lisa continues to be the most enthralling depiction of subtlety centuries after it was painted. It is a perfect example of how lips play a crucial role in conveying sentiment and capturing the observer's attention.

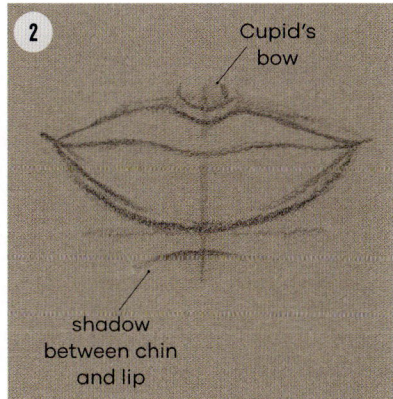

1

lower lip line

vertical centreline

2

Cupid's bow

shadow between chin and lip

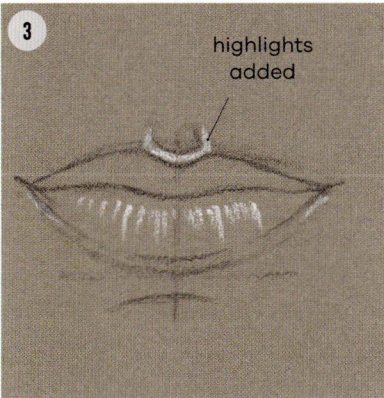

3

highlights added

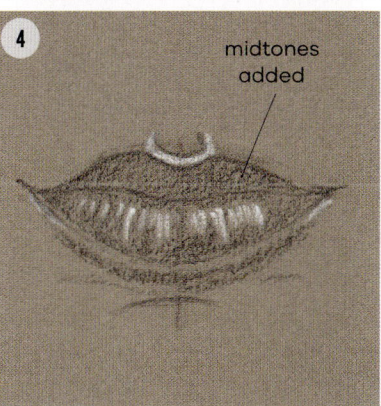

4

midtones added

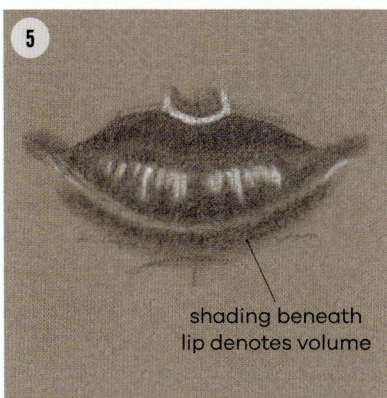

5

shading beneath lip denotes volume

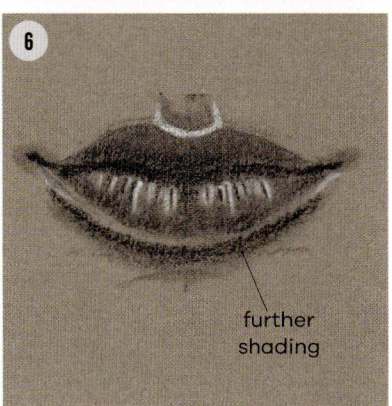

6

further shading

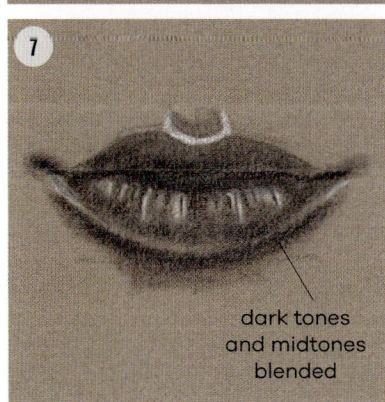

7

dark tones and midtones blended

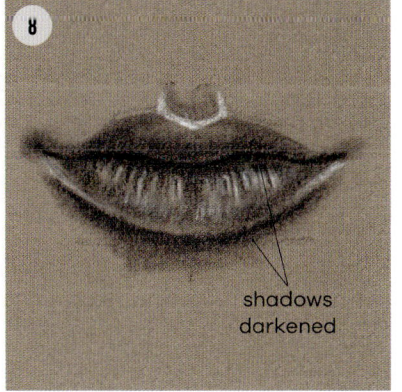

8

shadows darkened

FRONT VIEW

Draw the lips in front view using basic shapes.

Basic construction

1 To begin, draw a vertical centreline. Using this line as the centre, draw a basic outline of the upper and the lower lips.

2 Draw details along the outlines following the previously discussed wave-like structure of the lips.

Shading

3 Add highlights to both lips with a white charcoal pencil.

4 Shade the entire lip with a midtone. Use a 4B pencil with medium pressure.

5 Blend the midtones and add some soft shadows using the graphite on the blending tool itself. The small gap between the bottom lip and the shadow above the chin depicts the thickness of the lips. Small details like this give the face dimension and authenticity, making the lips pop out.

6 Use a 6B pencil to shade some darker tones on and around the bottom lip.

7 Blend these darker tones with the midtones you added in Step 5.

8 Finally, darken the shadows along the middle and the bottom of the lips using an 8B pencil.

HAIR

Drawing hair definitely requires patience. There are lots of ways to draw it, but the key is to understand the flow of the hair, breaking it down into sections as you draw. The volume, the flow and the highlights are the three key aspects of drawing convincing hair. It can be drawn using a minimalistic or a realistic approach.

MINIMALISTIC APPROACH

These are two examples following the minimalistic approach. Notice that the movement of the hair is captured without going into too much detail. The individual strands of hair are not shown, but we still see volume due to the placement of shadows and highlights.

The detailing style of the hair should match with the detailing style used for the rest of the face. It is important to remain conscious of not adding more details than needed, all the while preserving the characteristic of the hairstyle.

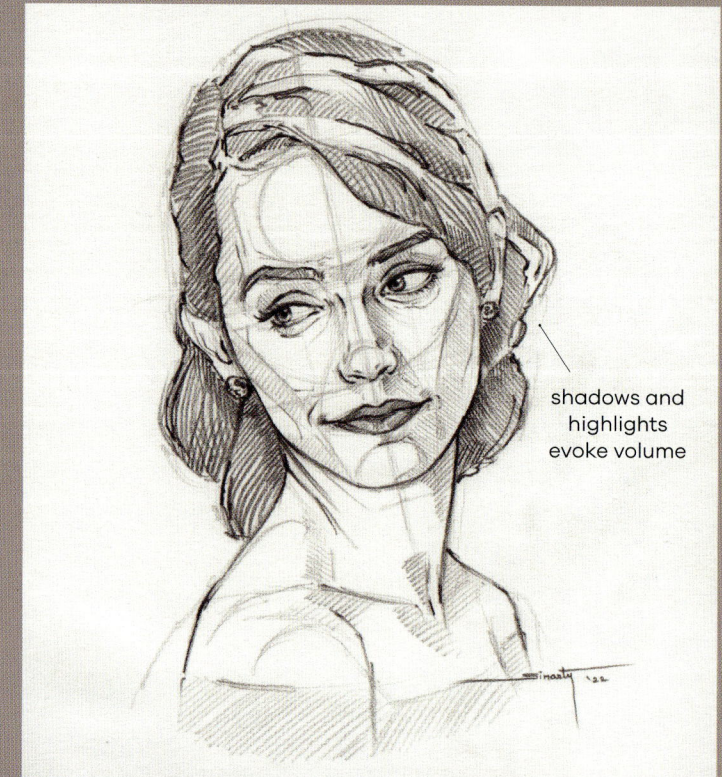

shadows and highlights evoke volume

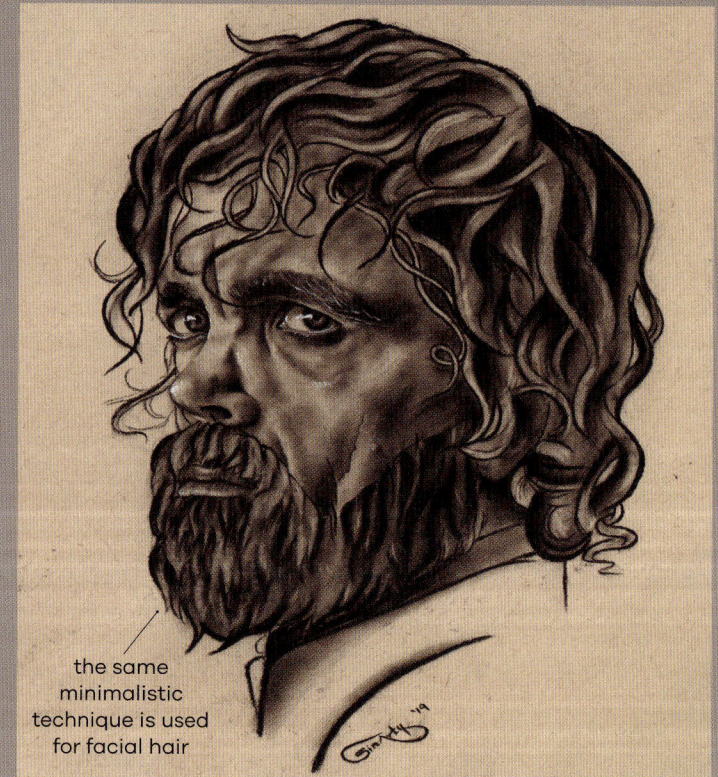

the same minimalistic technique is used for facial hair

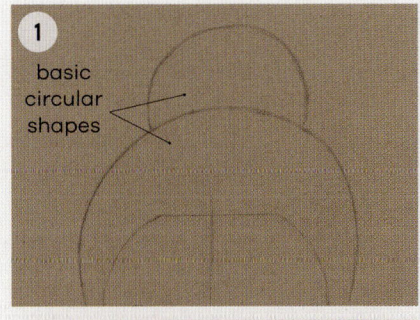

1 basic circular shapes

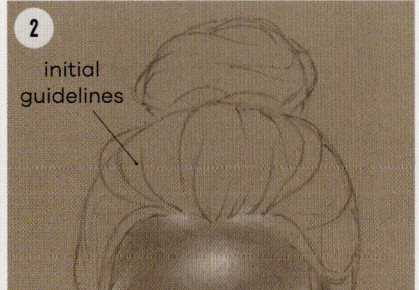

2 initial guidelines

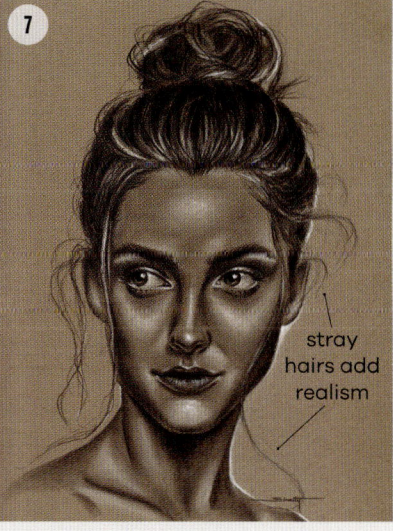

7 stray hairs add realism

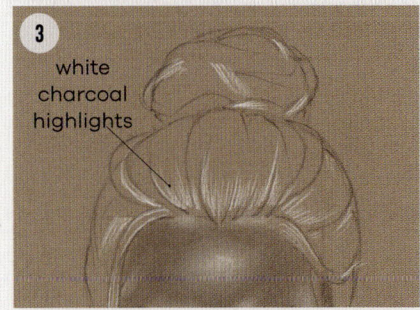

3 white charcoal highlights

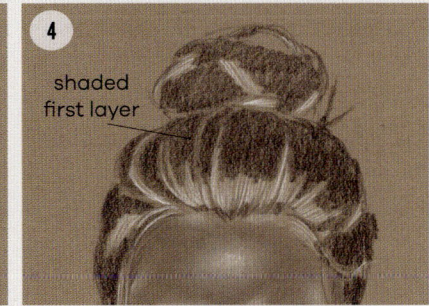

4 shaded first layer

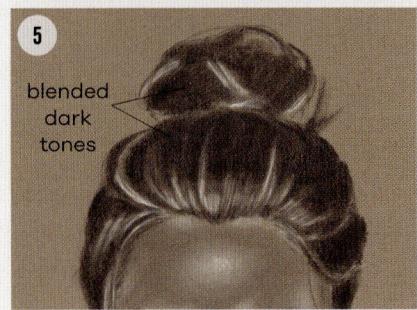

5 blended dark tones

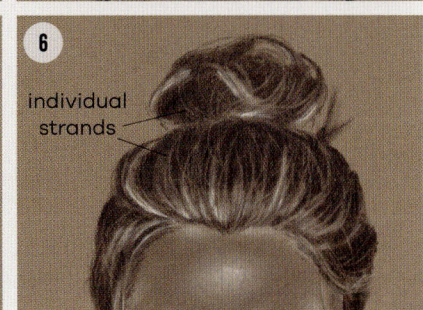

6 individual strands

BREAK IT DOWN!

Drawing hair can be intimidating due to it's complex appearance in the reference image. Try to break it down into layers and sections as shown, building it up gradually.

REALISTIC APPROACH

Drawing realistic hair requires observation of the flow, texture, and direction of strands. Layering and shading techniques bring depth and realism.

Basic construction

1 Begin by drawing a simple outline of the hair using basic circular shapes.

2 Following the hair's direction of flow, add guidelines, keeping details to a minimum for now. Focus on collective chunks of hair rather than individual strands.

Shading

3 Add white highlights along the guidelines with a white charcoal pencil.

4 Select a 6B pencil with a flat tip. With medium-to-hard pressure, shade the rest of the hair leaving some gaps along the guidelines. This will be your first layer.

5 Blend these dark tones using a tool such as a tortillon or cotton bud (*see Tools & Materials: Blending Tools*).

6 With a pencil eraser, draw individual strands of hair. Follow the movement of the hairstyle, drawing a few random strands to add realism. Since we blended the dark tones in the previous step, working with a pencil eraser becomes easier, and you can get a clean erase.

7 Use an 8B pencil to darken some of the individual strands and darken the shadowy areas of the hair. Notice the stray hairs drawn along the outer border of the hair. Use a mechanical pencil to draw these to avoid frequent sharpening.

Repeat Steps 6 and 7 as many times as needed to achieve the desired effect. Take your time with these steps – the result will be worth it.

THE PORTRAITS

Having learnt the basics, we will move on to the portraits themselves. Before you begin, here is a brief overview of how each project will guide you from start to finish.

TOOLS AND TECHNIQUES

At the beginning of each project, you will find a list of the paper, tools and techniques you will be using. The project will also tell you which proportion and shading techniques are used. Prompts throughout the steps direct you back to the basic techniques sections to refresh your memory.

OUTLINING AND SHADING

Each project is split into an outlining stage and a shading stage. For the outlining stage, I recommend using a 2B pencil with a light grip. You will see that the final outlining step has been enlarged. This gives you the option to trace the completed outline, skip the outlining steps and go straight to shading. It is particularly useful if you want to skip the outlining and focus on your shading skills.

SKILL LEVELS

The skill level of the outlining and shading stages indicated at the start of each project is only a guide. If you like the look of a portrait, but are not sure you have the skills, don't worry. Have a go and refer back to the basic techniques sections. Whichever portraits you choose, they will all help you to carry on learning, practising and experimenting.

WARM-UPS

Going into a project directly may result in your linework looking (and feeling) rigid. Warming up with exercises such as simply gradient shading a rectangle can loosen your hand in preparation for the portrait. Even if you don't have a project in mind, warming up can get your creative juices flowing.

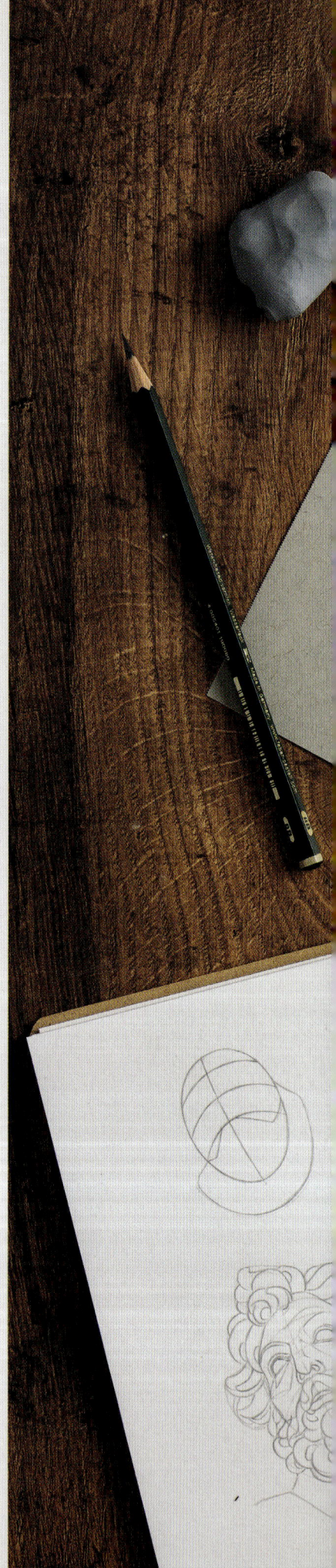

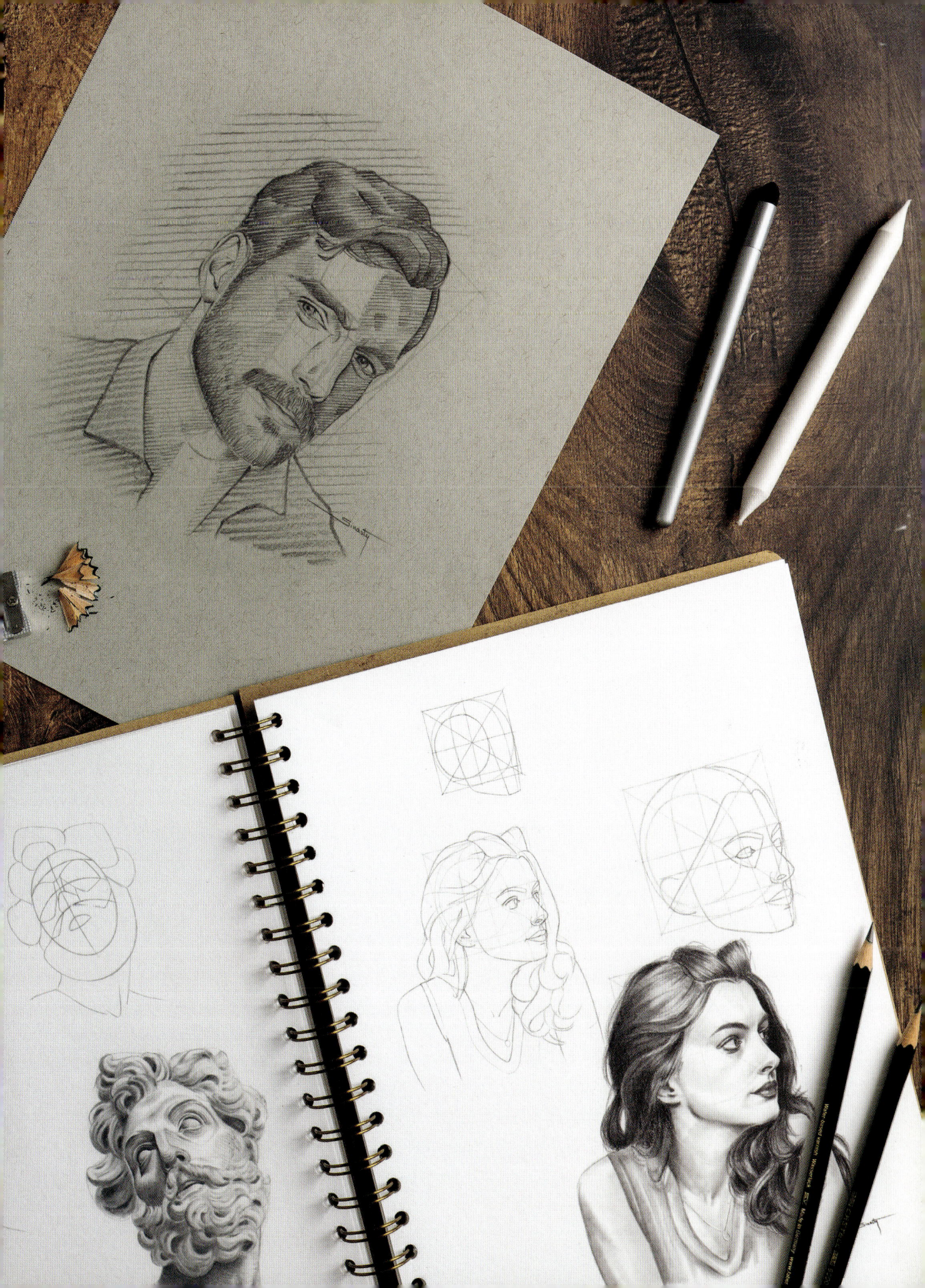

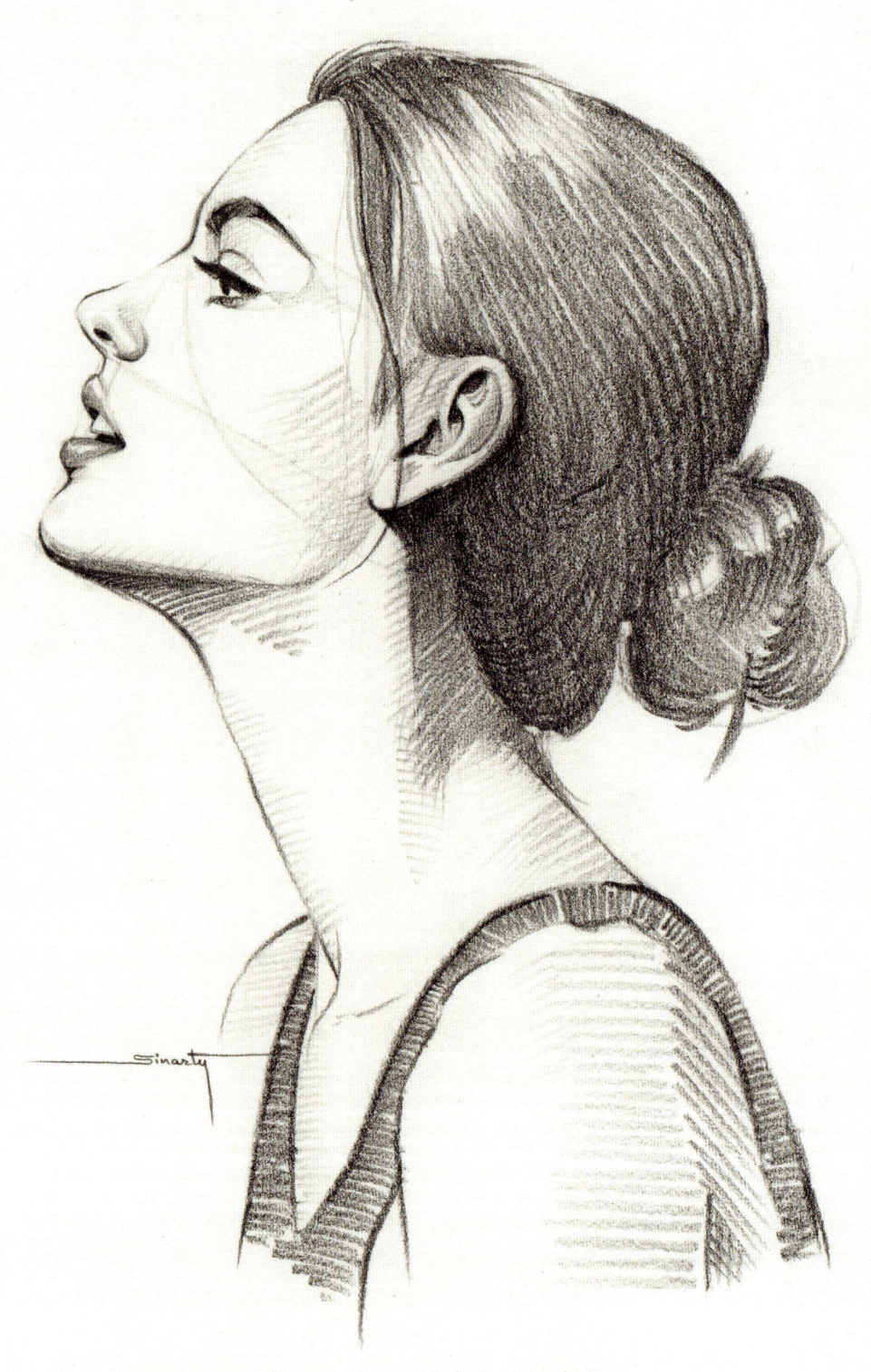

THE PROFILE

We start our journey with this portrait of a beautiful model in profile view. Some of the exercises and techniques covered in the previous sections will be applied to draw the features. We will take a minimalist approach and maintain a "sketch" feel to this portrait. Let's begin!

Materials

- White sketching paper, 22.9 x 30.5cm (9 x 12in)
- Graphite pencils: 2B, 6B, 8B
- Kneaded eraser, pencil eraser
- Good-quality pencil sharpener

Techniques

- Proportion: Block-in
- Shading: Hatching

BASIC OUTLINING

1 Above the centre of the page and slightly to the right (see the inset thumbnail for guidance), draw two perpendicular segments – note that one line is slightly longer than the other.

2 Draw an ellipse passing through the end points of these segments (*see Sketching Fundamentals: Pencil Exercises*).

3 The line passing from the top left to the bottom right is the browline. Draw a nose line below parallel to the browline, and mark the chin line. In this portrait, the distance between the browline and the nose line is approximately the same as the distance between the nose line and the chin. From the left side of the ellipse, draw a vertical line for the front plane of the face, and complete the jaw.

4 Draw the bottom of the chin and extend the line downwards to form the neck.

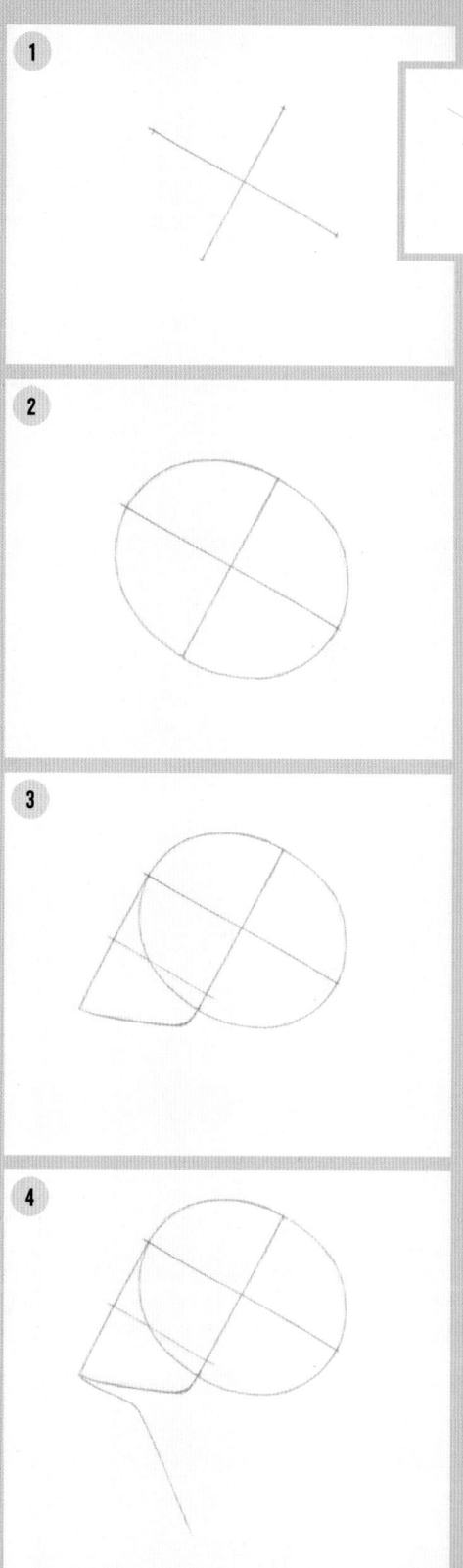

5 Draw a basic outline for the ear between the browline and nose line. Mark the outline of the hair, back of the neck, and shoulders.

6 Block in the eye socket area and nose. Then draw a line extending from the underside of the nose to the chin. This is a guideline for drawing the lips as these tend to protrude slightly ahead of the front plane.

7 Complete the details on the nose and lips.

8 Draw the basic outline of the eyebrow and eye. The shape of the nose is further refined by adding roundness to the tip. The chin and the neckline have also been reshaped, following the previously drawn guidelines.

9 Lighten the background guidelines using a kneaded eraser (*see* Tools & Materials: Erasing Tools) then draw the details of the hair and ear.

10 To finish the outlining stage, mark highlights on the hair (the light is falling from the top left of the canvas) and finish the neck and the shoulder area. The nose is corrected – the bridge is slightly straightened and the tip sharpened.

GO STRAIGHT TO SHADING

Simply tracing the final outline drawing – Step 10 – provides an opportunity to jump ahead to practise shading (see Proportion Techniques: Freehand & Tracing).

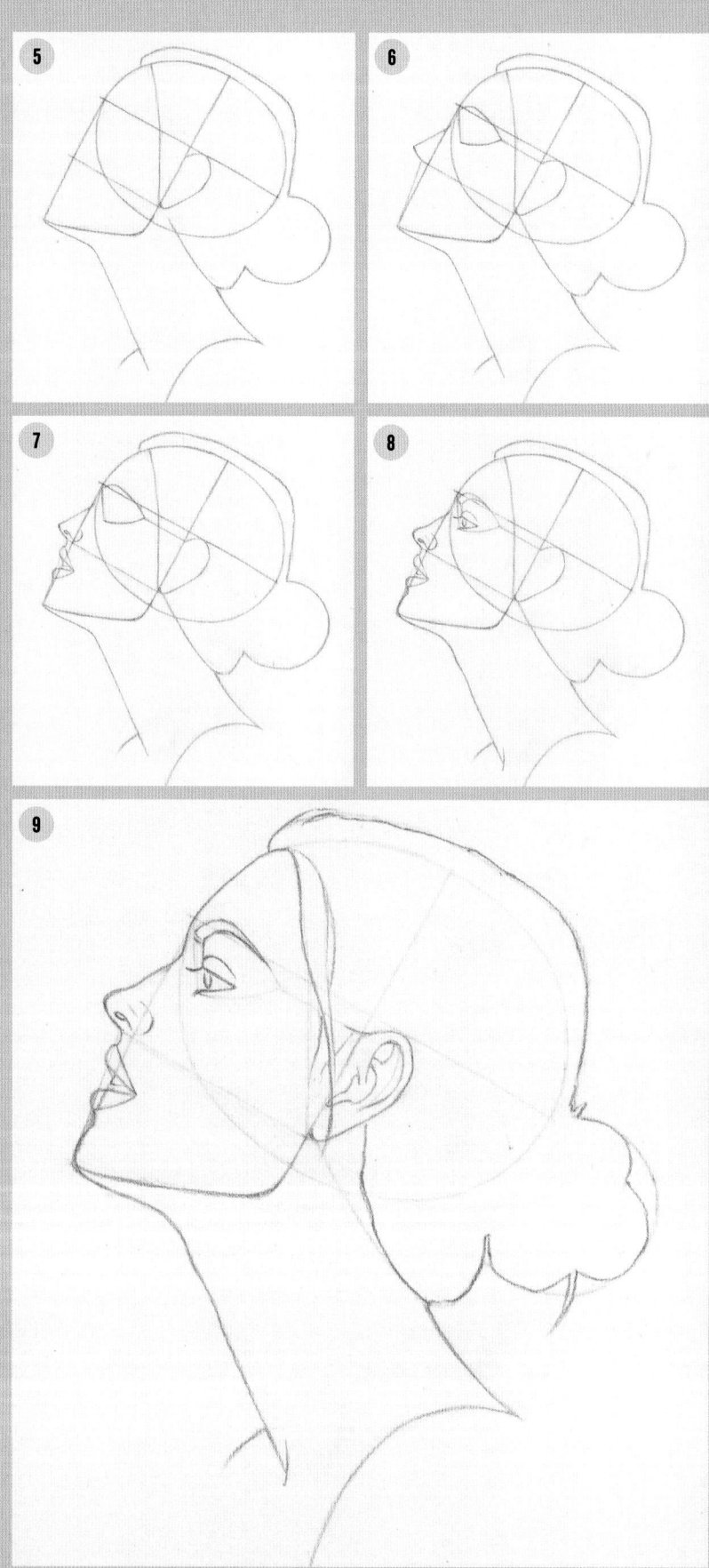

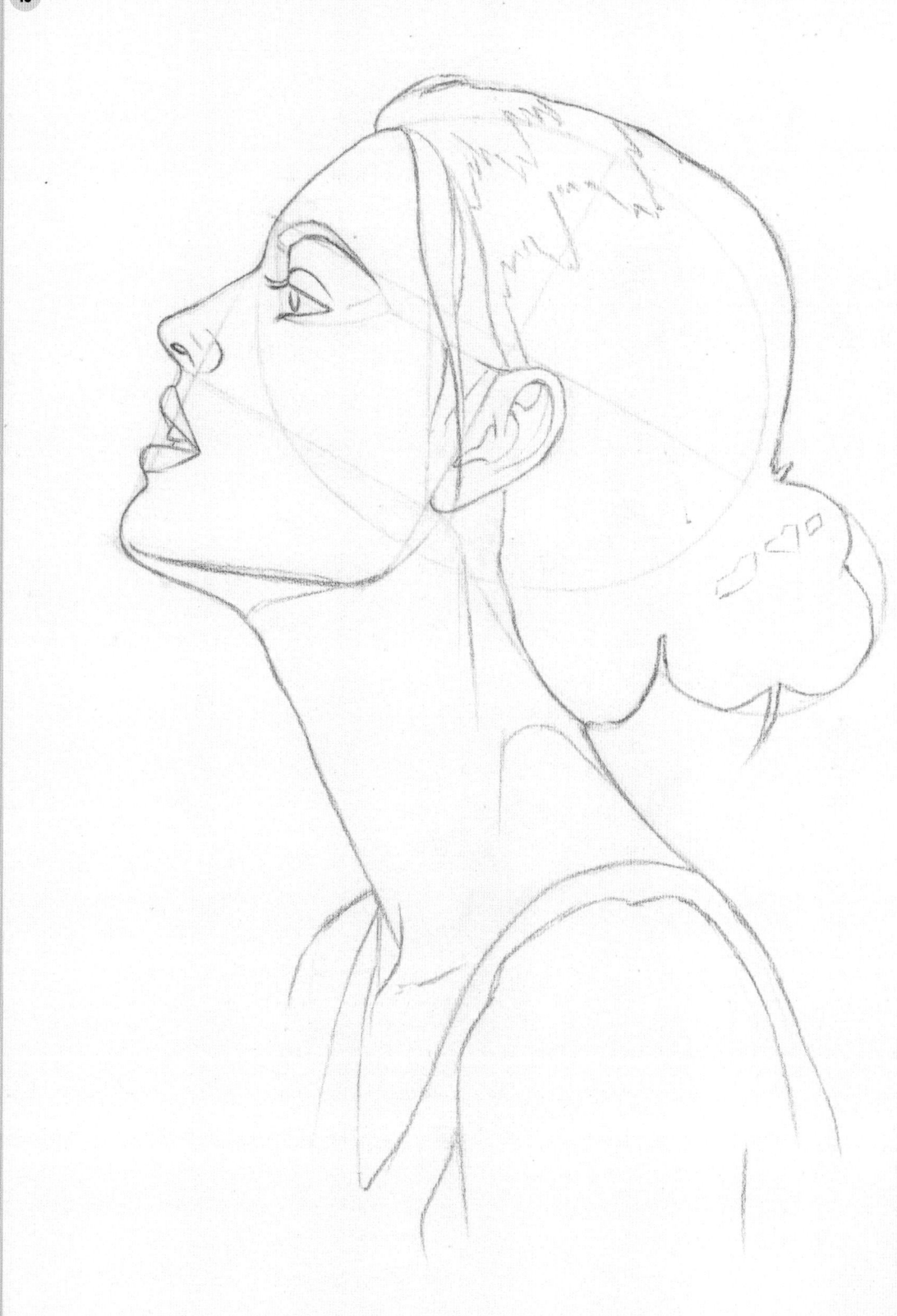

SHADING

At this point, you have completed the portrait construction and outline (either by following the previous Steps 1–10 Basic Construction, or by simply tracing the image for Step 10).

1 We will shade the portrait use basic hatching and some gradient shading. For most of the hatching, use the longer nibbed sharpened pencil (*see Tools & Materials: Drawing Mediums*) to create blunt hatches and cover plenty of area. This is a style choice. Begin by using a 6B pencil to shade the darker shadow regions of the face, including the eyebrow, eye, nose, mouth, jaw and ear. Also shade the back of the neck

2 Using the same pencil, hatch the hair, following the flow of the strands. Leave the highlighted areas unshaded.

3 Using a 2B pencil and medium grip, hatch the areas near the jaw, neck and shoulder.

BOLD PENCIL STROKES

This is a portrait where your hatching strokes should be clean and confident. Warming up with linework exercises (see Sketching Fundamentals: Pencil Exercises) is recommended to help you create bolder, more confident strokes.

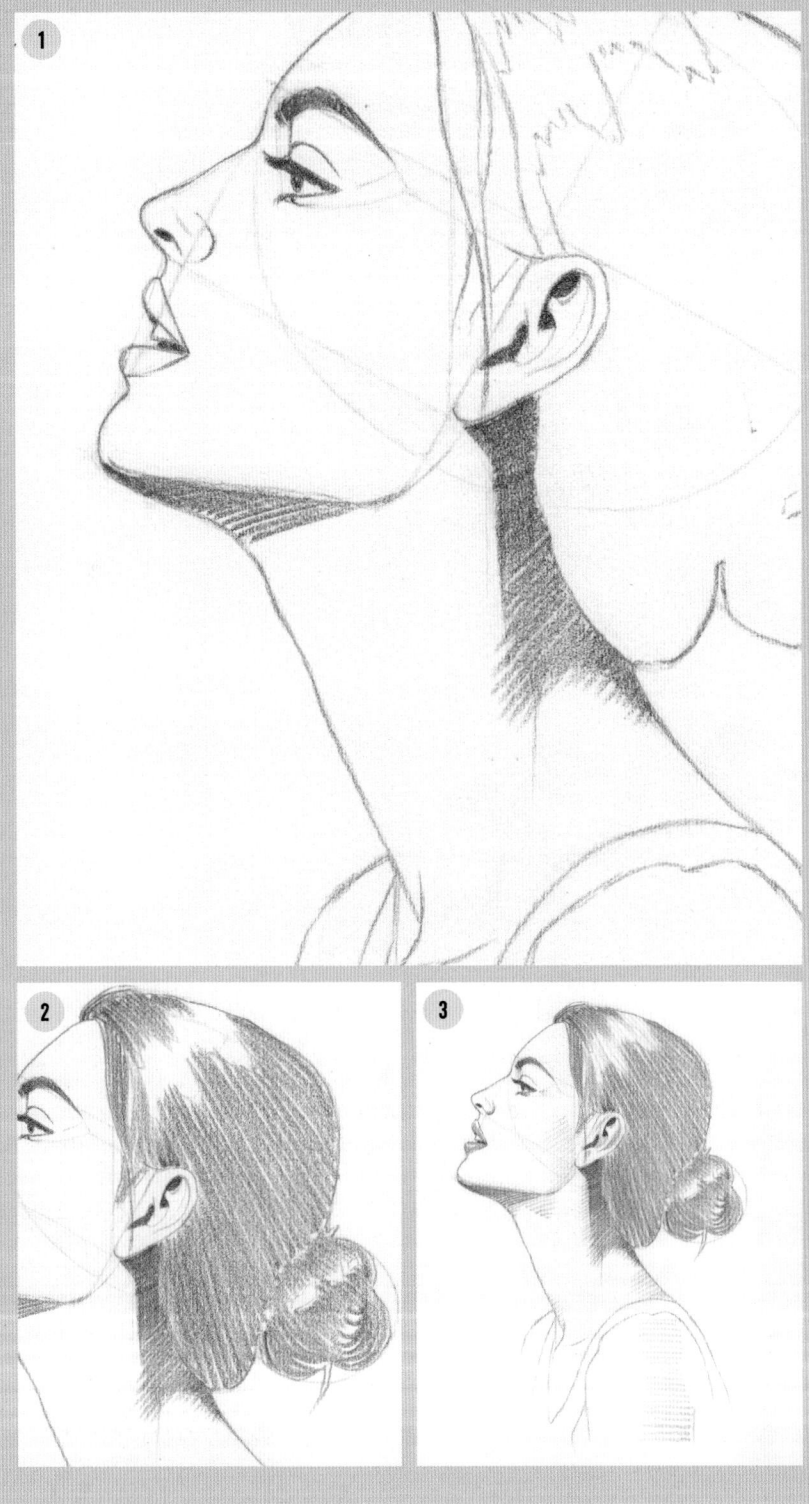

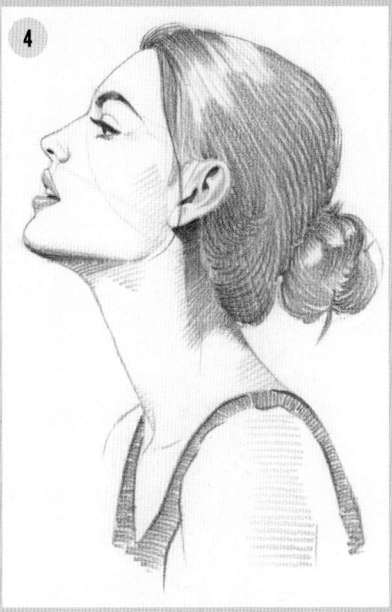

4

LINEWORK STYLE

Notice the change in line depth while drawing the outline of the profile. In my final assessment of the portrait, I erased some outlines, including the top of the nose and the chin, to create an illusion of shine and add a sense of minimalism to the profile. This is a style choice.

4 Using a darker pencil – the 8B – rework some areas to create more depth. Shade the eye, eyebrow, mouth, jaw and neck. Rework the hair, focusing on the changes in values depending on the shadows. Shade the top she is wearing.

5 In this final step, go over the entire portrait once again – step back and look at your work from a distance. Is there any area that needs to be reworked? Do any of the shadows need to be darker? Notice the small correction made to the tip of the nose, which points slightly upwards compared to the previous step. Noticing and improving such small details makes a huge difference to the final result!

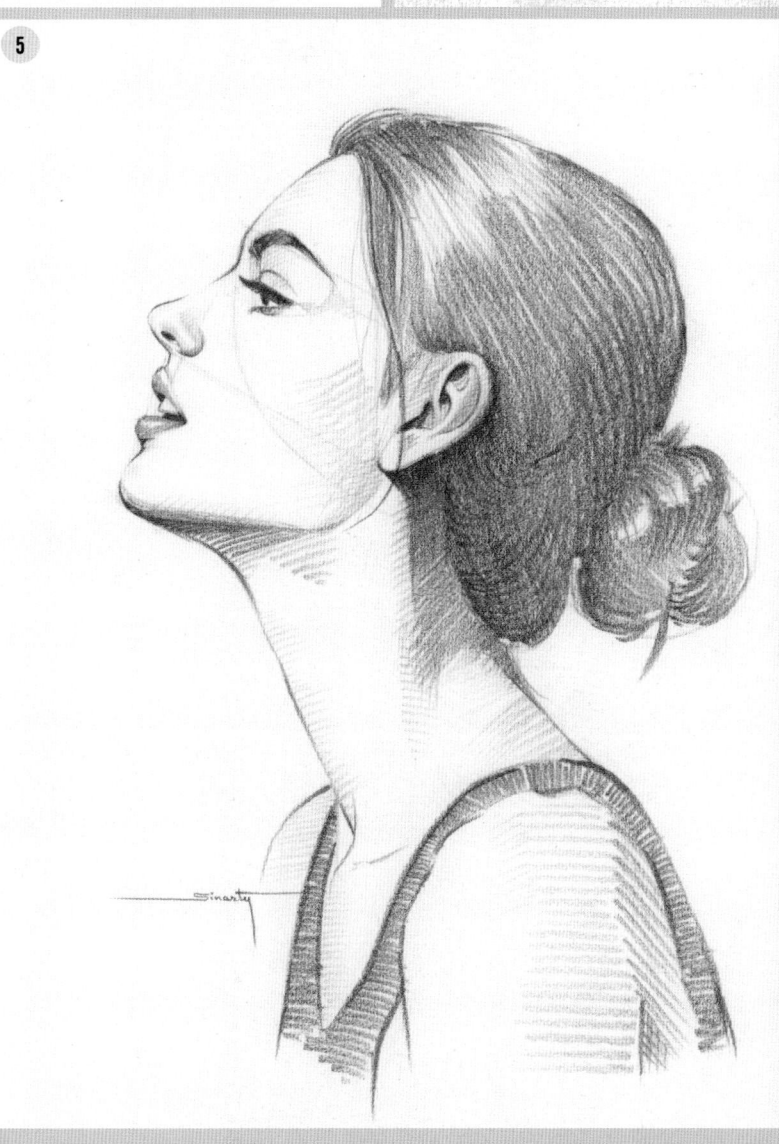

5

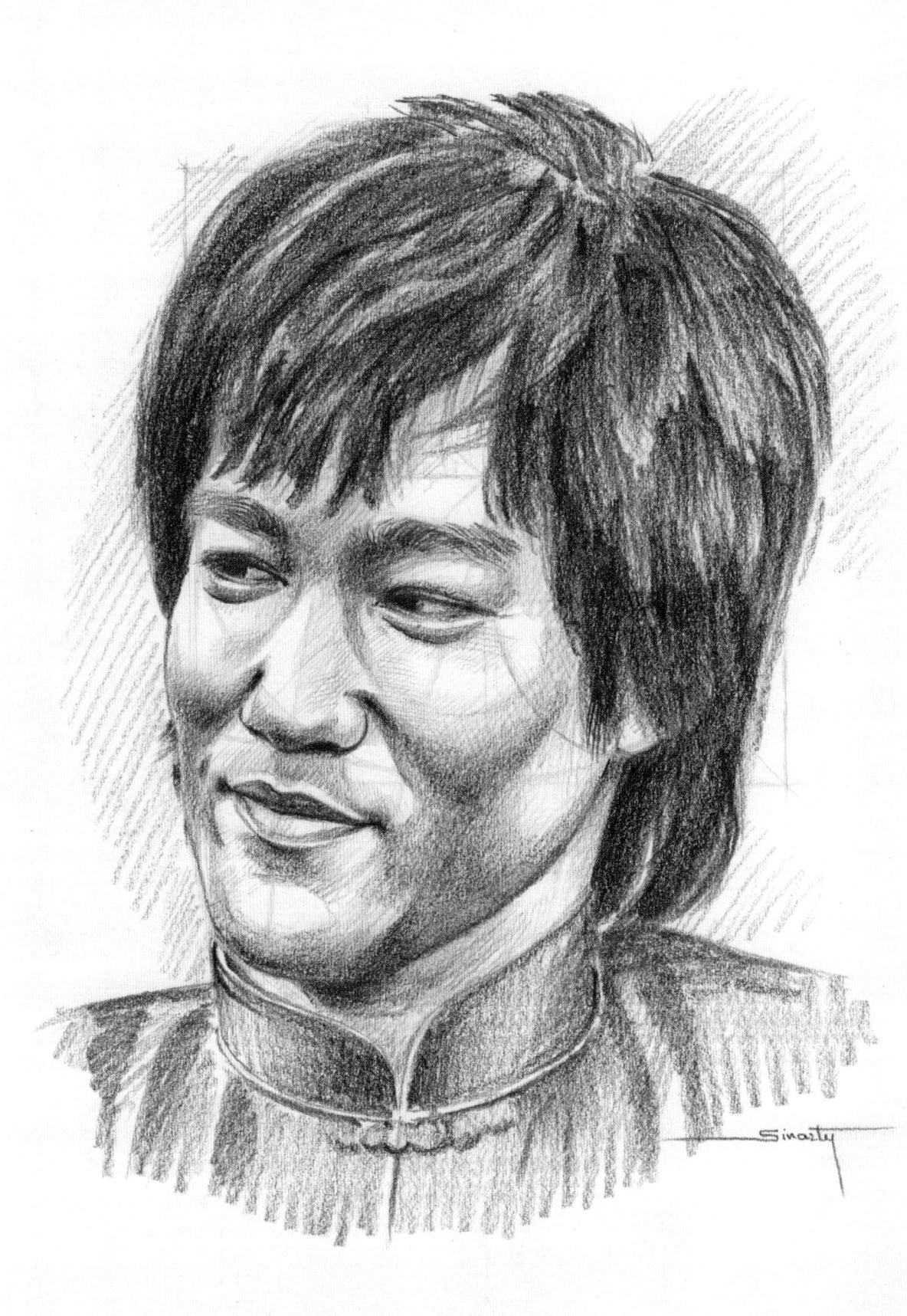

BRUCE LEE

An iconic martial artist and actor, Bruce Lee has captivated generations with his skill and charisma. Drawing this portrait allows artists to capture his subtle smile and intelligence. The expression, chiselled features and iconic hair make for a compelling drawing challenge – capturing this legendary presence on paper.

Materials

- White sketching paper, 22.9 x 30.5cm (9 x 12in)
- Graphite pencils: 2H, 2B, 4B, 6B, 8B
- Kneaded eraser
- Good-quality pencil sharpener

Techniques

- Proportion: Loomis head
- Shading: Hatching and gradient blending

BASIC OUTLINING

1 Begin by drawing the Loomis head. Draw a square slightly to the top-right of the white sketching paper (see the inset thumbnail for guidance), big enough to fit the cranium. Split it into eighths and use this to draw a circle.

2 Draw the centreline and extend it downwards. Now draw the side plane on either side of the centreline (see Proportion Techniques: The Loomis Method).

3 To complete the front plane of the face, mark the browline, nose line and chin line. On this subject, the distance between the browline and nose line is slightly further than the distance between the nose line and chin line. These measurements are the basis of the proportions, so study the reference carefully before drawing them.

4 Draw the jawline and extend it up and along the middle of the side plane. We now have a basic Loomis Head.

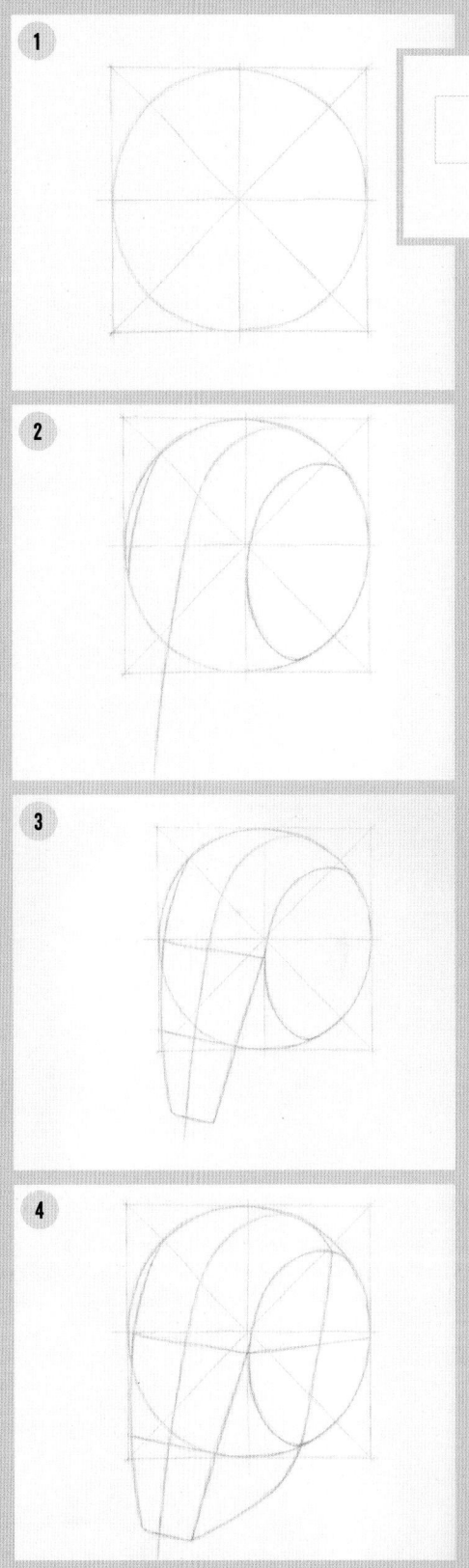

OUTLINE DETAILING

When drawing the following steps, use a 2B graphite pencil and a light-medium hand (*see* Sketching Fundamentals: Pencil Exercises).

5 Mark the eye level on the front plane slightly below the browline and extend across the side plane to plot the ears. Use the square and its intersecting lines (refer back to Step 1) as a grid to determine proportions and placements of the features.

6 Draw a basic outline to mark the silhouette of the hair. This hairstyle is instantly recognizable, so pay attention to the reference.

7 Sketch the eyebrows and eyes based on their guidelines. This is a basic outline, so there is no need for too much detail at this stage.

8 Sketch the basic outline of the nose based on its guidelines.

9 Sketch the outline of the lips, keeping in mind that the lower edge of the lips would be approximately halfway between the nose line and chin line.

10 Start adding detail around the eyes and nose. Focus on drawing some of the shadows and highlights that are visible in the reference – we will use these guides to help us shade.

11 Draw details of the hair, which is split into different sections. Focus on the highlights and the shadows of the reference to identify these sections. You do not need to be accurate here – just add enough detail to get the feel of the flow of hair. We also detail the collar and draw the shoulder line. We are done with the outlining!

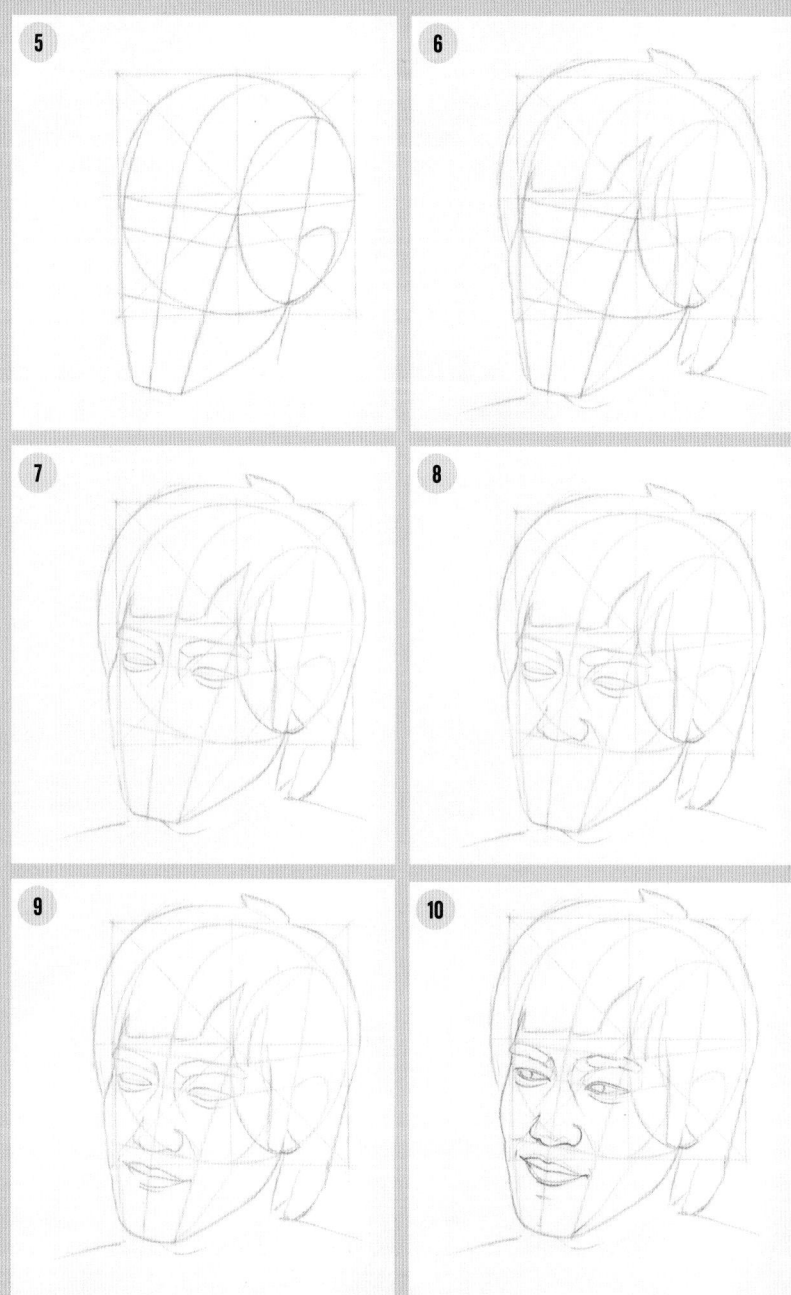

GO STRAIGHT TO SHADING
Simply tracing the final outline drawing – Step 11 – provides an opportunity to jump ahead to practise shading (see Proportion Techniques: Freehand & Tracing).

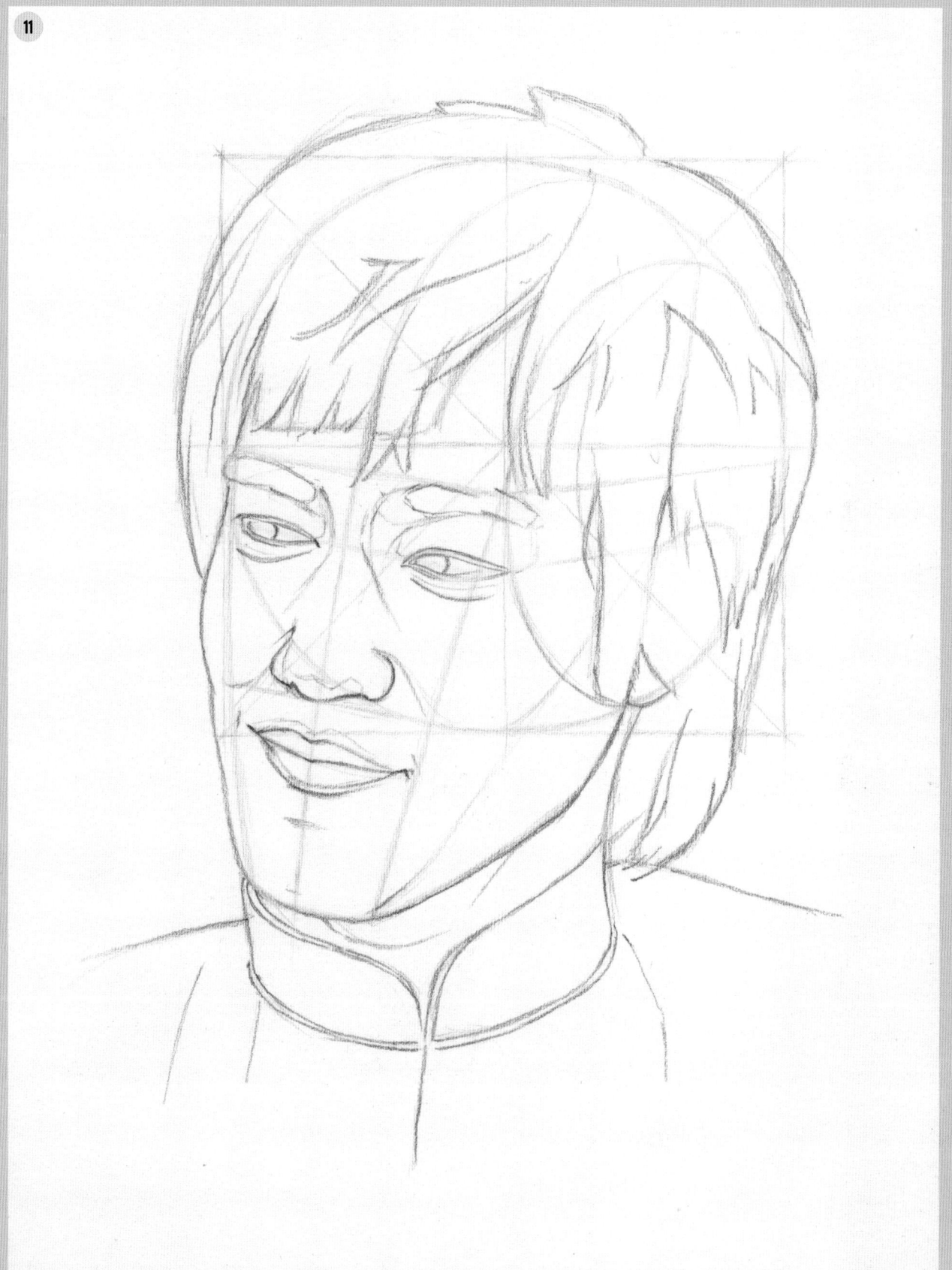

SHADING

At this point, you have completed the portrait construction and outline (either by following the previous Steps 1–11, or by simply tracing the image for Step 11).

1 To begin, use a 2B pencil to render a basic hatch pattern on the face, leaving out some areas for the highlights.

2 Now move towards the darker shades. First, use a 4B pencil to gradient shade the midtones.

3 Then go slightly darker with the shading. Use a combination of 6B and 8B graded graphite to shade the dark value extremes: the iris, the eyebrows and the darker shadowy areas near the eyes and the neck.

4 It's time for blending. To preserve the texture of the paper, avoid the use of blending tools for this stage. Instead, use only pencil grades and pressure variations for blending (*see Sketching Fundamentals: Shading Techniques*). Use neutral 2B and 4B pencils to gradually transition between the lights and the darks, also making the darks darker.

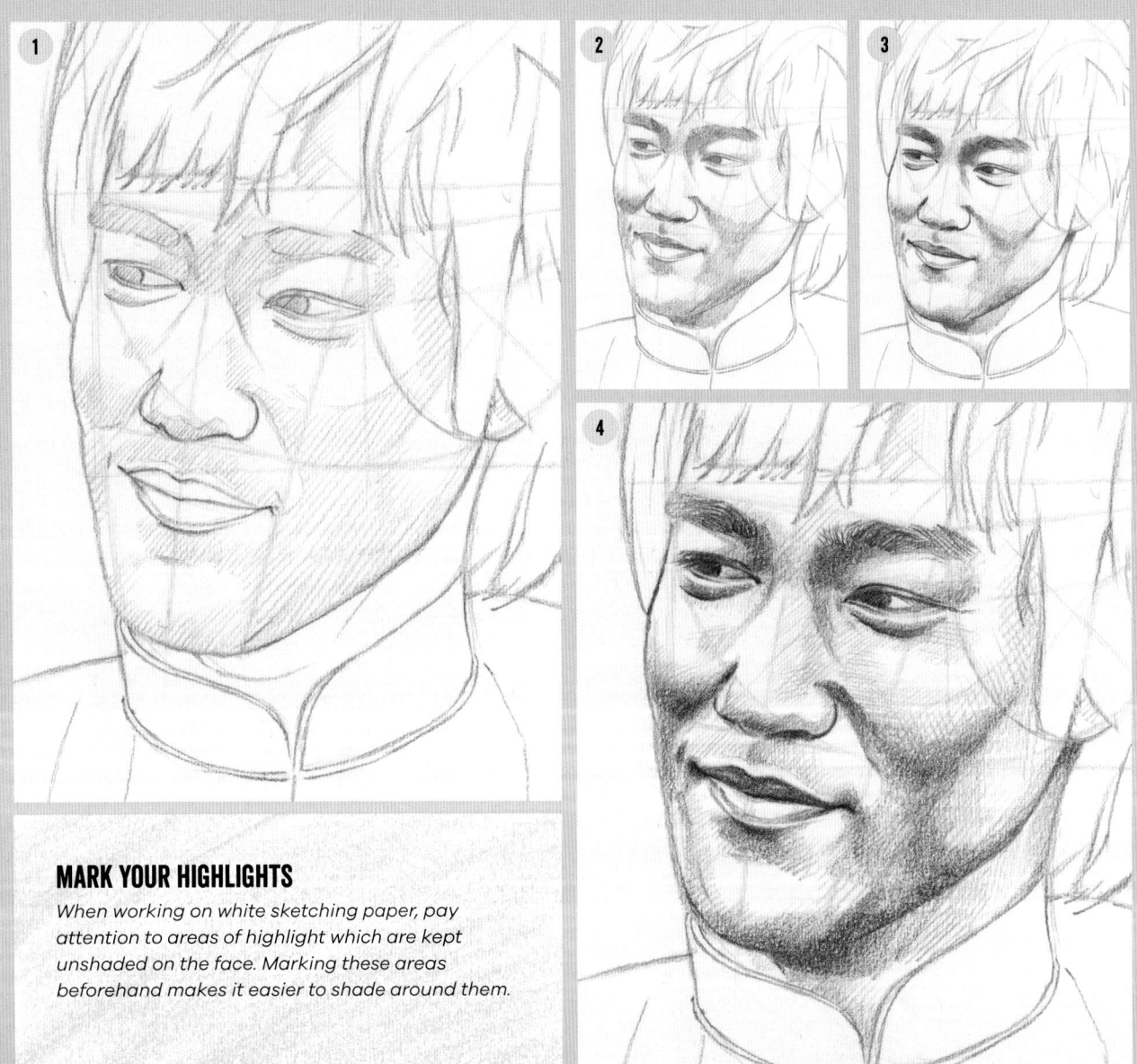

MARK YOUR HIGHLIGHTS

When working on white sketching paper, pay attention to areas of highlight which are kept unshaded on the face. Marking these areas beforehand makes it easier to shade around them.

5 Shade the hair using a 6B pencil with a long sharpened tip. Using the side of the pencil in overhand grip (*see* Sketching Fundamentals: Pencil Holds), create broad strokes along the sections outlined in Outline Detailing, Step 11.

6 Combine 6B and 8B pencils to shade the rest of the hair. Make the shadows directly below the sections of hair darker. Leave areas white to create highlights.

7 Use a flat-tipped 6B pencil to shade the clothes. I used a minimalistic approach without too much detailing to retain focus on the face.

8 Finally, go back and view the drawing as a whole, comparing it to the reference. Work any areas you think need refinement and sharpen the edges. Use a 2H pencil to shade the faint transitions on the face and pop the highlights. I found the top of the eyes needed a bit of shadow to make them look natural, and darkened the shadows on the clothes. To finish, shade a little bit of the background with broad, rustic strokes.

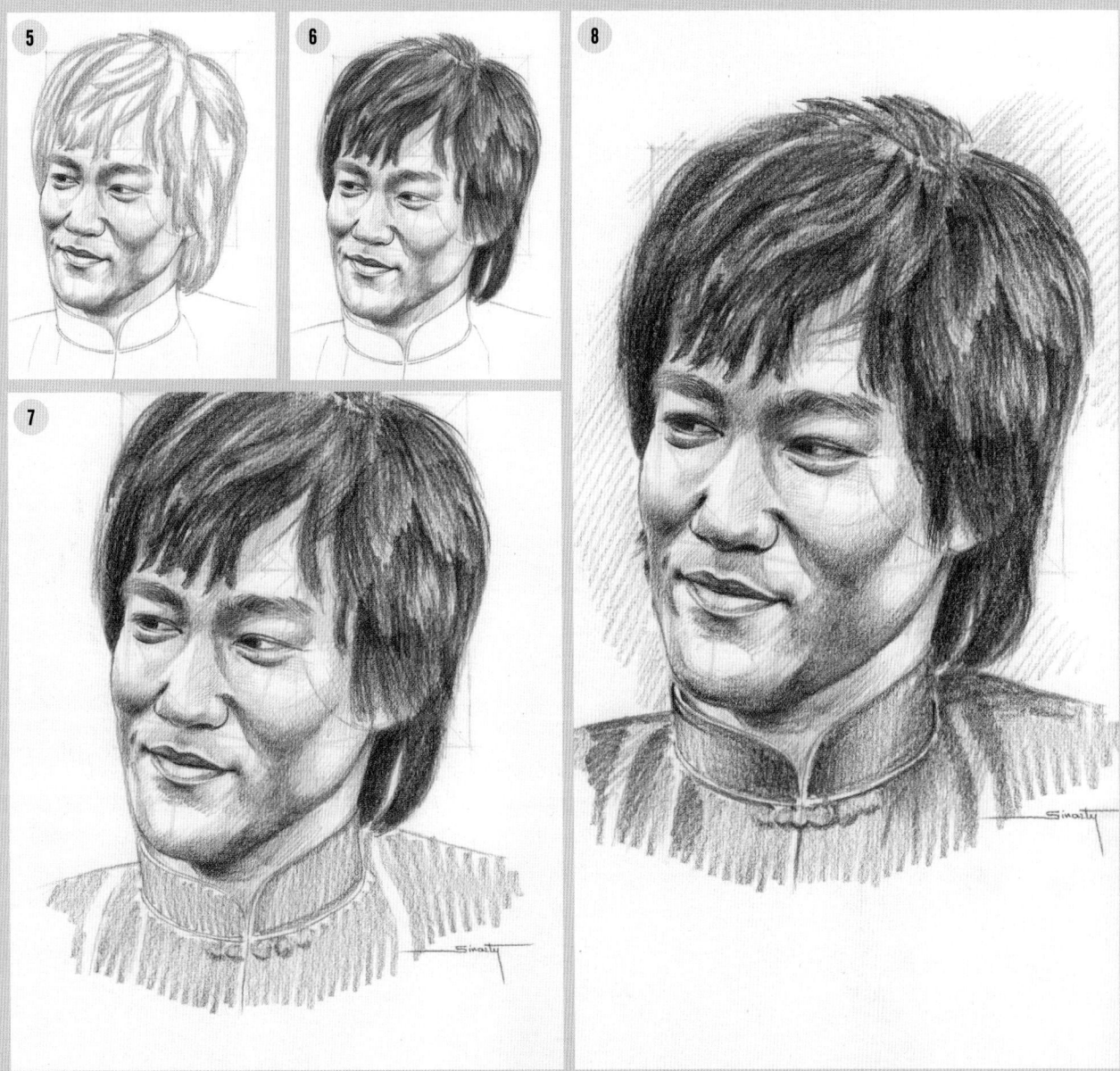

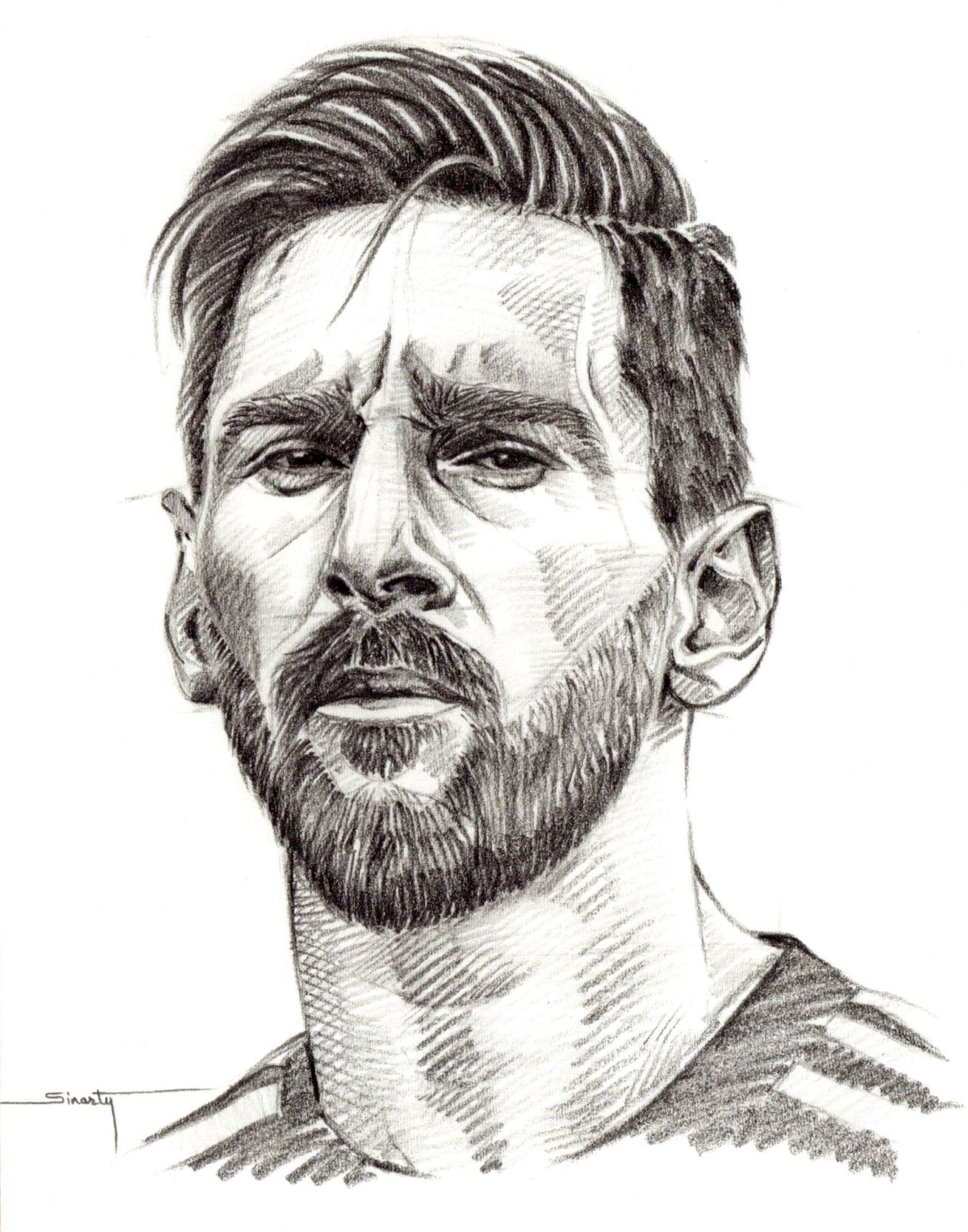

LIONEL MESSI

There are several reasons why Lionel Messi is a great subject for a portrait. Not only is he considered one of the greatest to ever play the game of football, but he also has distinctive features which are fun to draw. You will notice as we progress through the outlining, that we recognize him around Step 3! I particularly liked this reference as it showed the focus on Messi's face – we will try to capture that emotion the best we can. Let's begin.

Materials

- White sketching paper, 22.9 x 30.5cm (9 x 12in)
- Graphite pencils: 2B, 4B, 6B, 8B
- Kneaded eraser, pencil eraser

Techniques

- Proportion: Block-in
- Shading: Hatching and gradient blending

BASIC OUTLINING

1 Draw a vertically oblong ellipse in the top two-thirds of the page (see the inset thumbnail for guidance) as the basis of our block-in. Draw a vertical centreline slightly to the left for the face, and a horizontal line slightly above the middle of the oval for the eyeline. Notice that the curve in these lines creates the initial dimension of the face.

2 Take measurements of the features and mark them using curved lines. Starting at the top and moving downwards, these lines represent the hairline, browline, eyeline, nose line and the lip line.

3 Draw an outline of the ears between the eyeline and the lip line, then the basic outline for the hair. Mark an outline of the neck and draw the shirt. The proportions of the face already make this subject recognizable!

4 Draw a basic outline of the facial hair, including the space where the mouth will be positioned directly below the lip line.

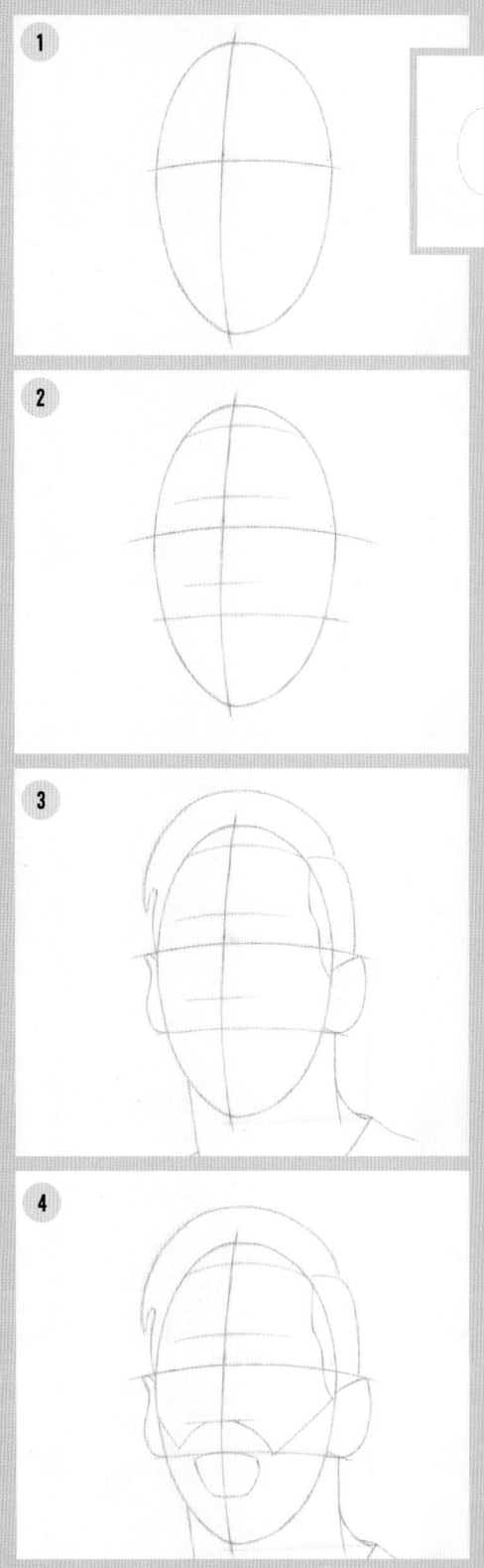

5 Block in the right eye socket and the nose, using the horizontal lines to place them.

6 Block in the left eye socket and detail the nose plane.

7 Use a kneaded eraser to lighten the top of the ellipse to reveal the proportions of the face more clearly. Mark the eyebrows, eyes, lips and gap in the facial hair below the lips.

8 Slightly to the left of the main construction centreline, create a centreline on the nose. Use this to detail more of the nose, including the nostrils.

9 Detail the ears, then lighten the outline of the hair. Detail the hair using lines sweeping from right to left on the top of the head to follow the flow of the hair. Add the stray strand over the forehead.

10 Lighten the blocked-in lines around the eyes. Detail the right eye and the highlight on top of the right cheekbone.

11 Detail the left eye, then the nose. Lighten the beard to prepare this area for detailing in the next step.

12 Add detail to the beard, lips, neck and shirt. Let's start shading!

GO STRAIGHT TO SHADING

Simply tracing the final outline drawing – Step 12 – provides an opportunity to jump ahead to practise shading (see Proportion Techniques: Freehand & Tracing).

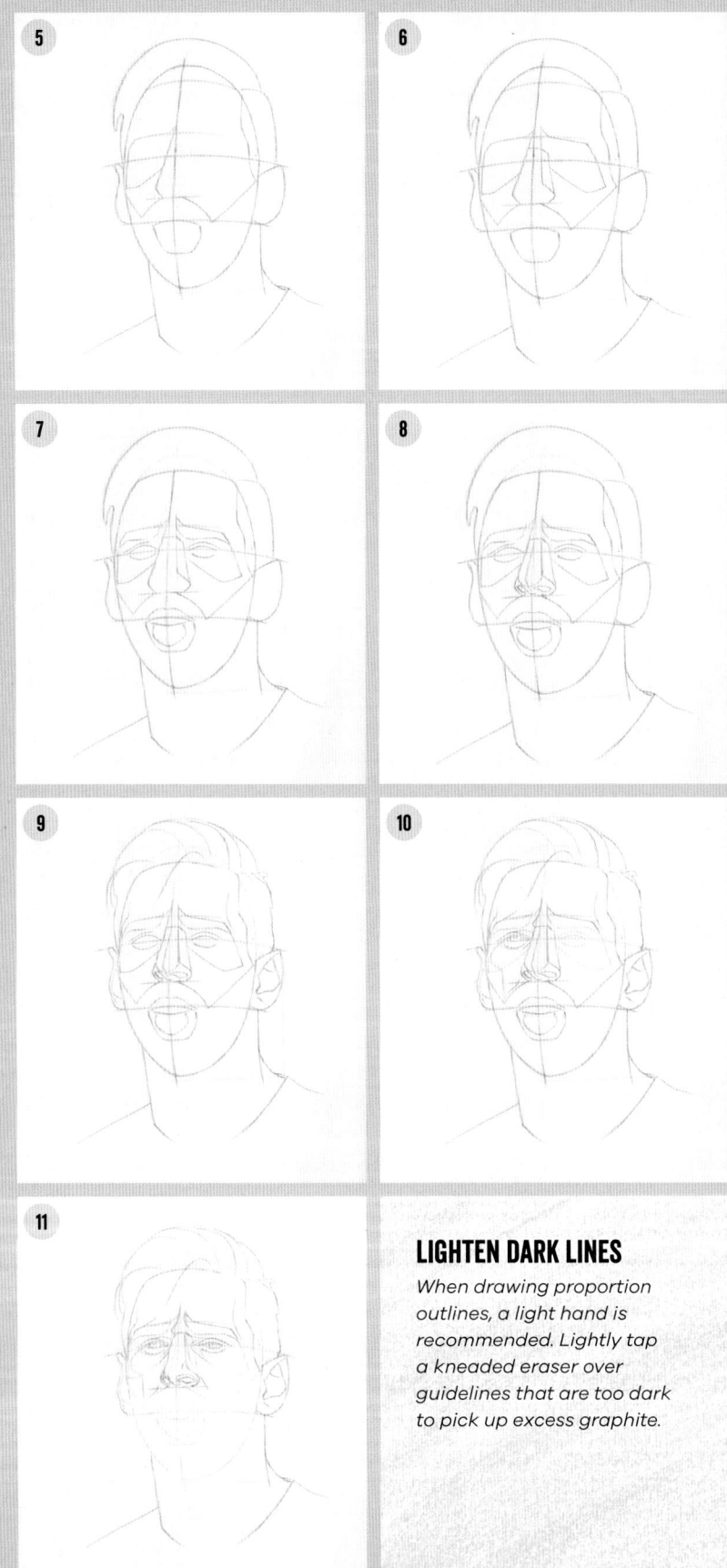

LIGHTEN DARK LINES

When drawing proportion outlines, a light hand is recommended. Lightly tap a kneaded eraser over guidelines that are too dark to pick up excess graphite.

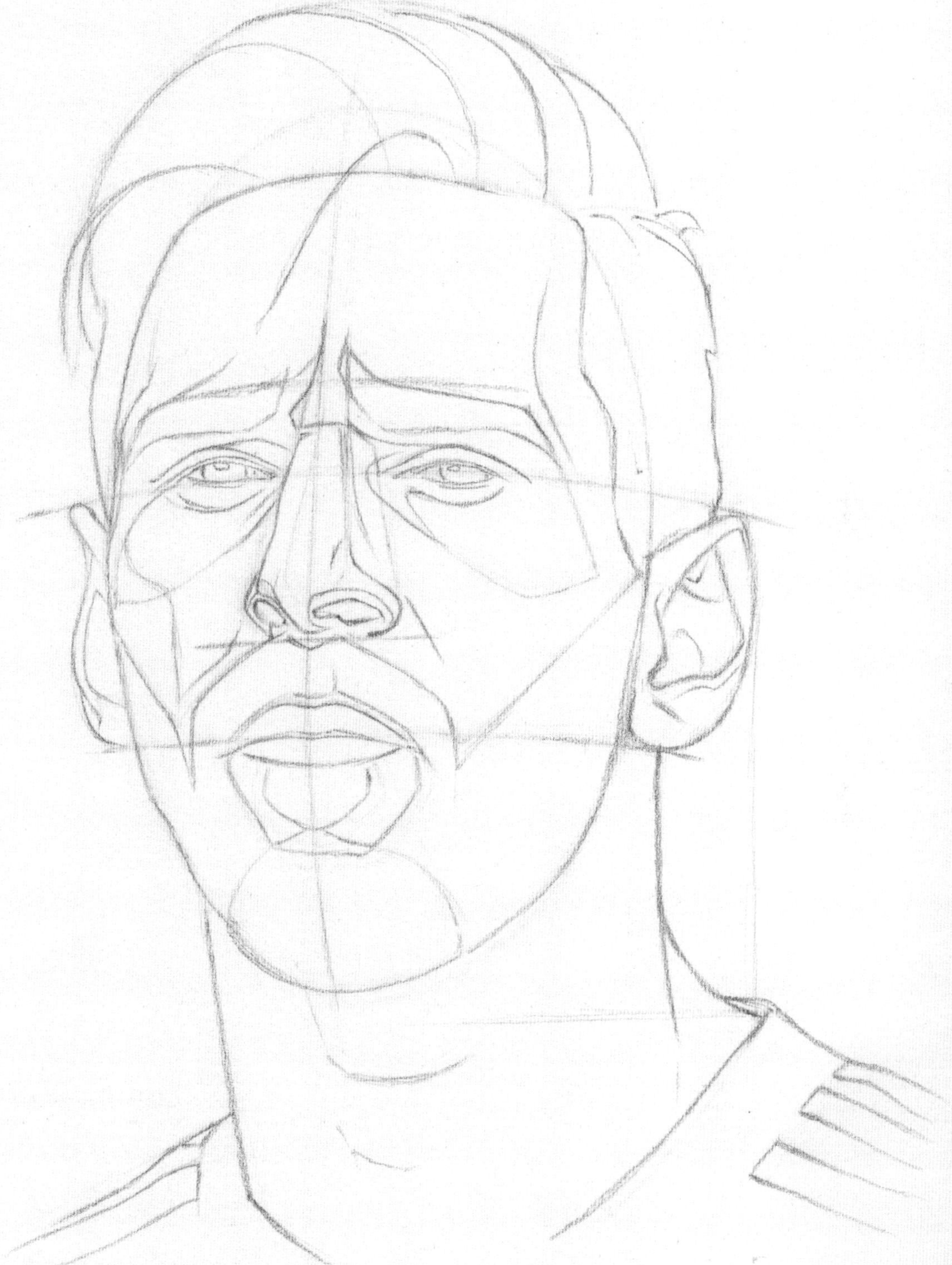

SHADING

At this point, you have completed the portrait construction and outline (either by following the previous Steps 1–12, or by simply tracing the image for Step 12). We will use basic hatching along with gradient shading. Use the longer nibbed sharpened pencil for blunt hatches. To cover maximum ground with each stroke, work with blunt pencils while shading.

1 Use the 6B pencil to shade darker shadows on the eyes, nostrils, lips and ears.

2 Use the 4B pencil to shade the shadows on the eyes, forehead and cheeks. Also hatch the ears and lips.

3 Use the 6B pencil and a hard grip to shade the hair. Follow long, curved strokes for the longer hair on top. Use short, straight strokes for the trimmed hair on the sides.

4 Hatch the facial hair using small short strokes along the surface of the face. Follow the contours of the jaw and chin.

5 Still using the 6B pencil, hatch the neck. Shade the shirt, leaving the bands unshaded. To give a "sketch" feel to the portrait, keep the pencil strokes intact instead of shading them to a smooth gradient. This is an optional style choice, but gives a great effect.

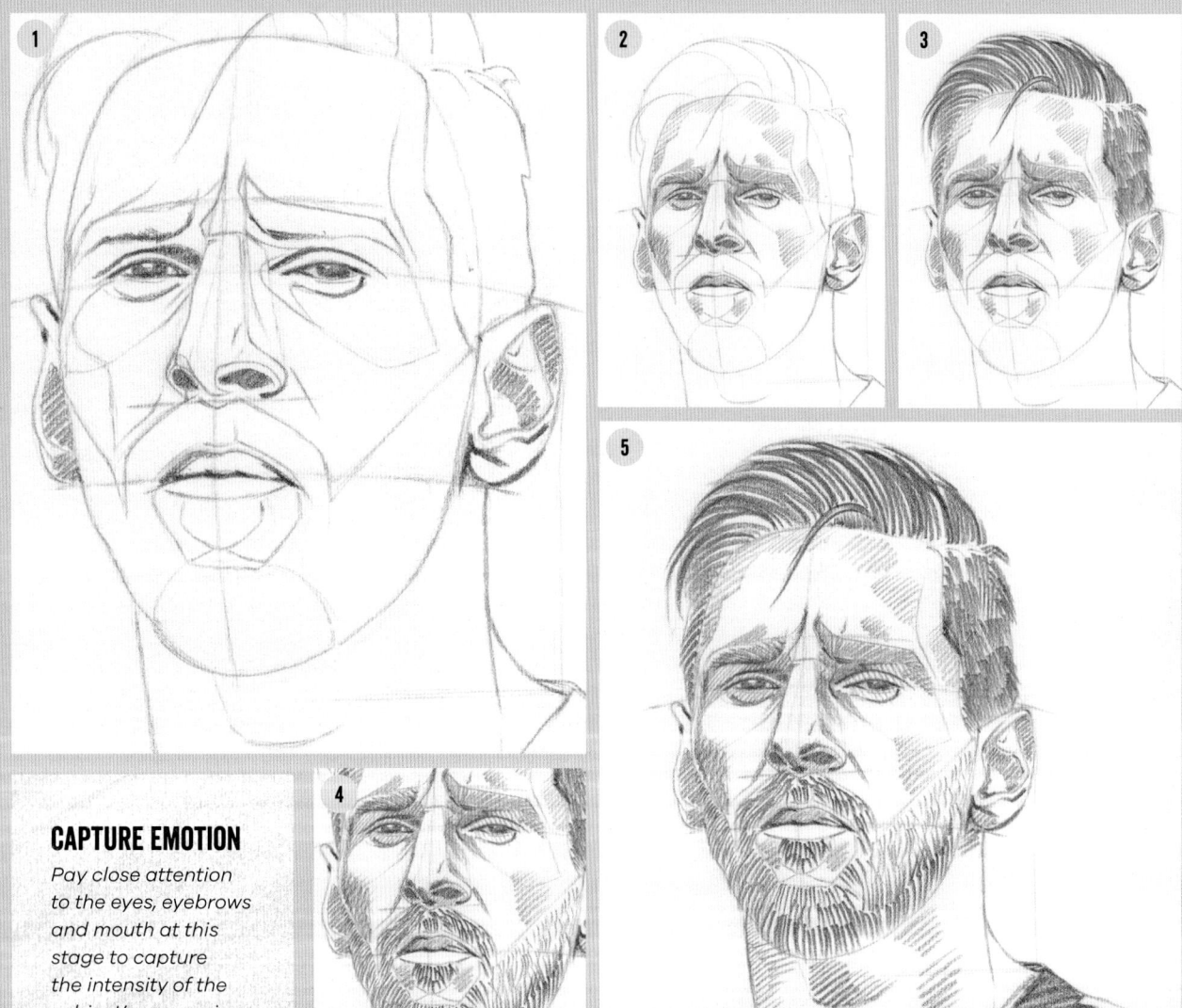

CAPTURE EMOTION

Pay close attention to the eyes, eyebrows and mouth at this stage to capture the intensity of the subject's expression.

6 Start detailing with an 8B pencil, shading the eyes, nostrils, lips and ears, similar to the shading in Step 1.

7 With the 8B pencil, rework the hair using strokes similar to those in Step 3.

8 In the same way, add another layer to the facial hair with the darkest, 8B pencil.

9 Use the 2B pencil for the final lightest layer to fill the gaps and further sharpen the highlights. Avoid sharpening the pencils to make the shading process faster.

10 Finally, step back to identify areas that need attention. In this case, I noticed the right eye was a little "off" in the previous step, so I reworked it to make it look into the camera. I also used the 8B pencil to bring the hairline slightly lower and darken the bottom of the beard to create focus on the face. The lips were also slightly reshaped to get close to the focused emotion we are trying to capture.

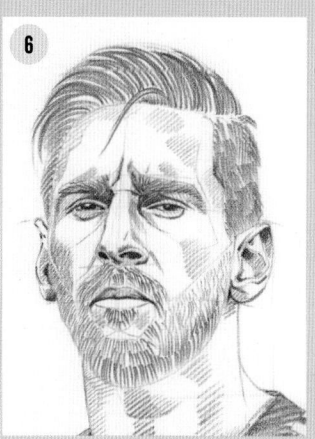

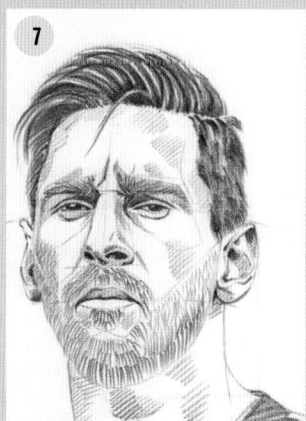

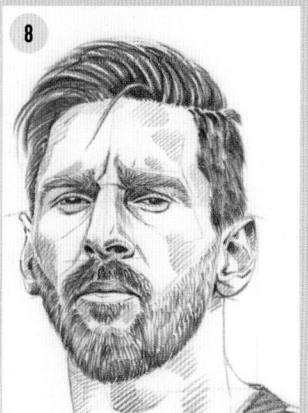

MIXING GRADES

Use various grades of pencil to layer the hair for more depth and complexity. A single grade can look dull and monotonous. Always try to work in layers!

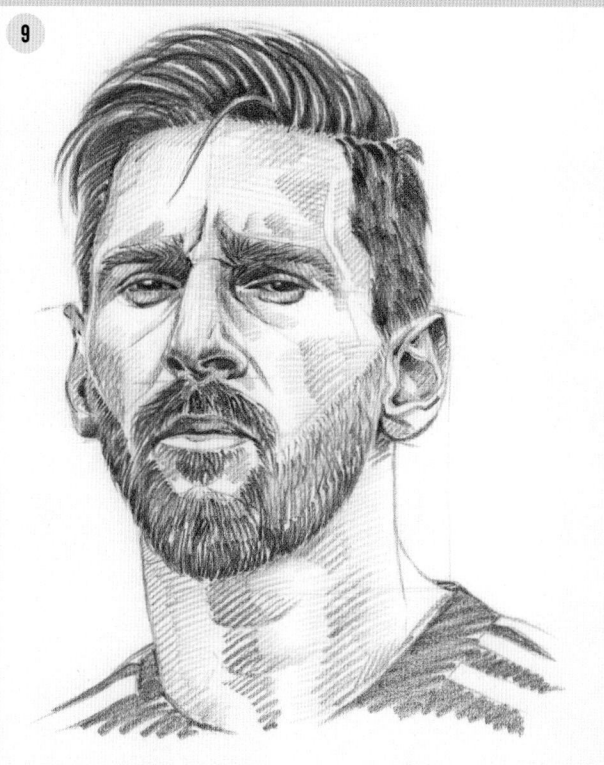

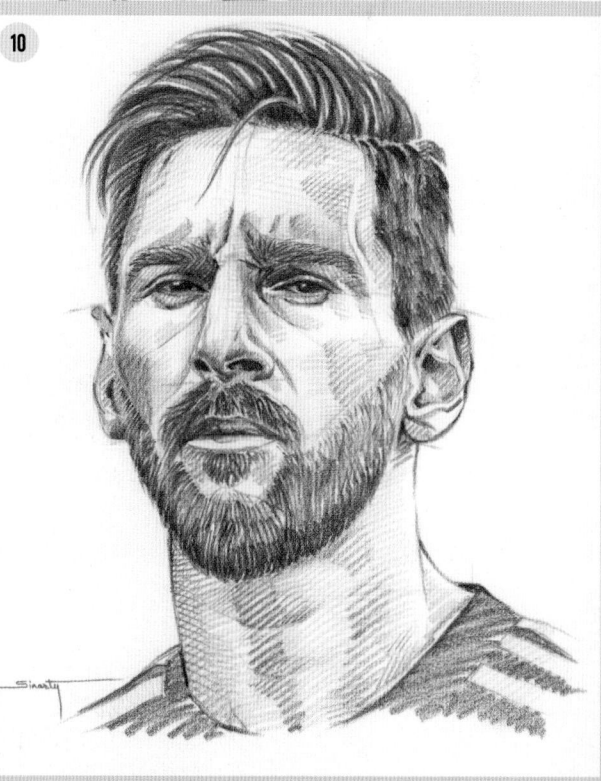

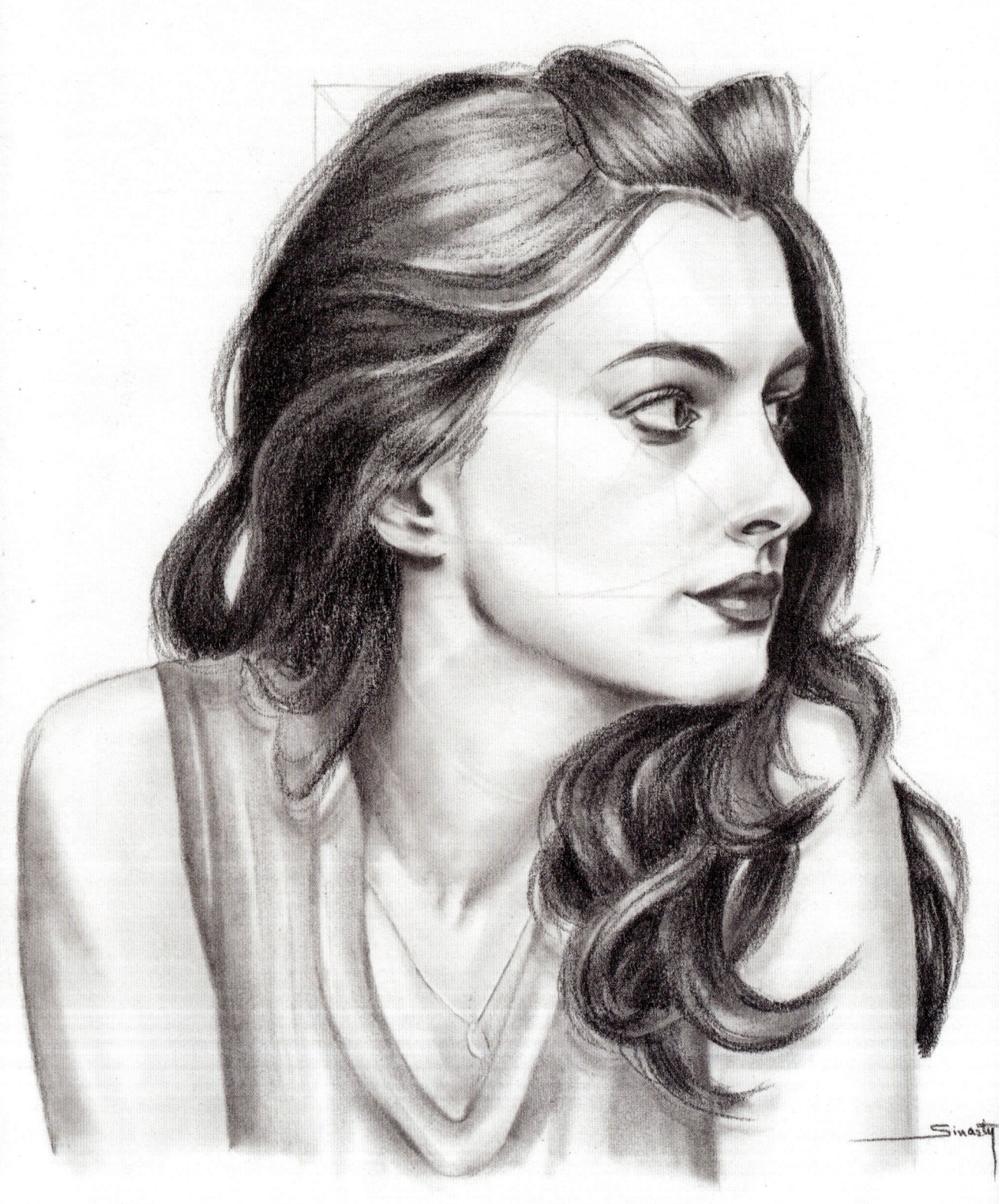

ANNE HATHAWAY

Anne Hathaway is a great subject for portrait drawing because of her perfect features. I liked this reference because of the angle of her pose. It captures Anne's minimalistic beauty perfectly, and makes the hair interesting to draw and shade.

Materials

- White sketching paper, 22.9 x 30.5cm (9 x 12in)
- Graphite pencils: 2B, 4B, 4B, 6B, 8B
- Graphite powder
- Paper stumps, cotton buds, sponge brush
- Kneaded eraser, pencil eraser
- One-sided sharpening blade

Techniques

- Proportion: Loomis head
- Shading: Gradient blending

BASIC OUTLINING

1 Begin by drawing the Loomis head. Draw a square slightly above the middle of the page and divide it into quadrants, then into eighths, to encompass the cranium (*see* the inset thumbnail for guidance). The horizontal centreline is the browline, and the bottom edge of the square is the nose line. Then, draw a circle enclosed in this square for the cranium, and a smaller ellipse for the side plane of the head.

2 Complete the basic Loomis head with the front plane and jawline (*see* Proportion Techniques: The Loomis Method).

3 Create basic outlines first to prepare for the outline detailing. First, draw simple outlines for the eye sockets and nose. Then draw the nostril and a basic outline for the lips, using the bottom edge of the cranium square as a guideline.

4 Add the basic outlines of the eyebrows, eyes, hairline and ear. Note that the eyes sit in line with the top of the ear.

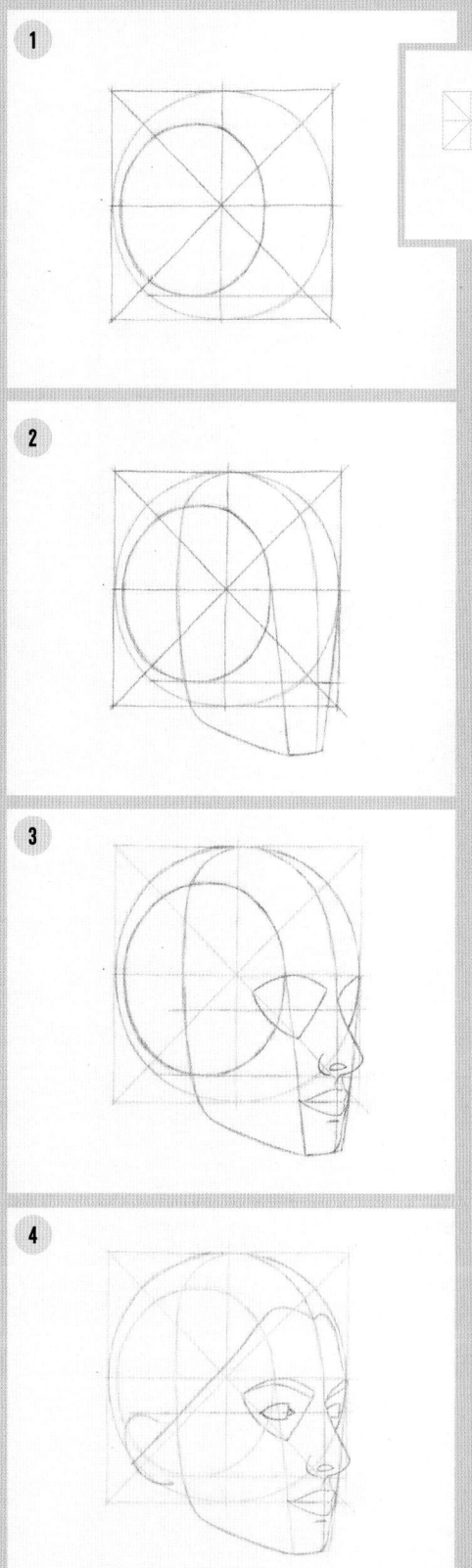

5 Draw a very basic outline of the neck, hair and arm on the right side of the portrait.

6 Complete the basic outlines of the hair and arm on the left side of the portrait. Then go back and correct any proportions if required.

7 Once the proportions are correct, move on to the final detailing phase. First, draw the details of the eyes and nose.

8 Detail the ears and hair – the details of the hair are very basic and follow the flow of the style. Draw the outline for the necklace.

9 Complete the left side of the portrait by detailing the hair and top.

GO STRAIGHT TO SHADING

Simply tracing the final outline drawing – Step 9 – provides an opportunity to jump ahead to practise shading (see Proportion Techniques: Freehand & Tracing).

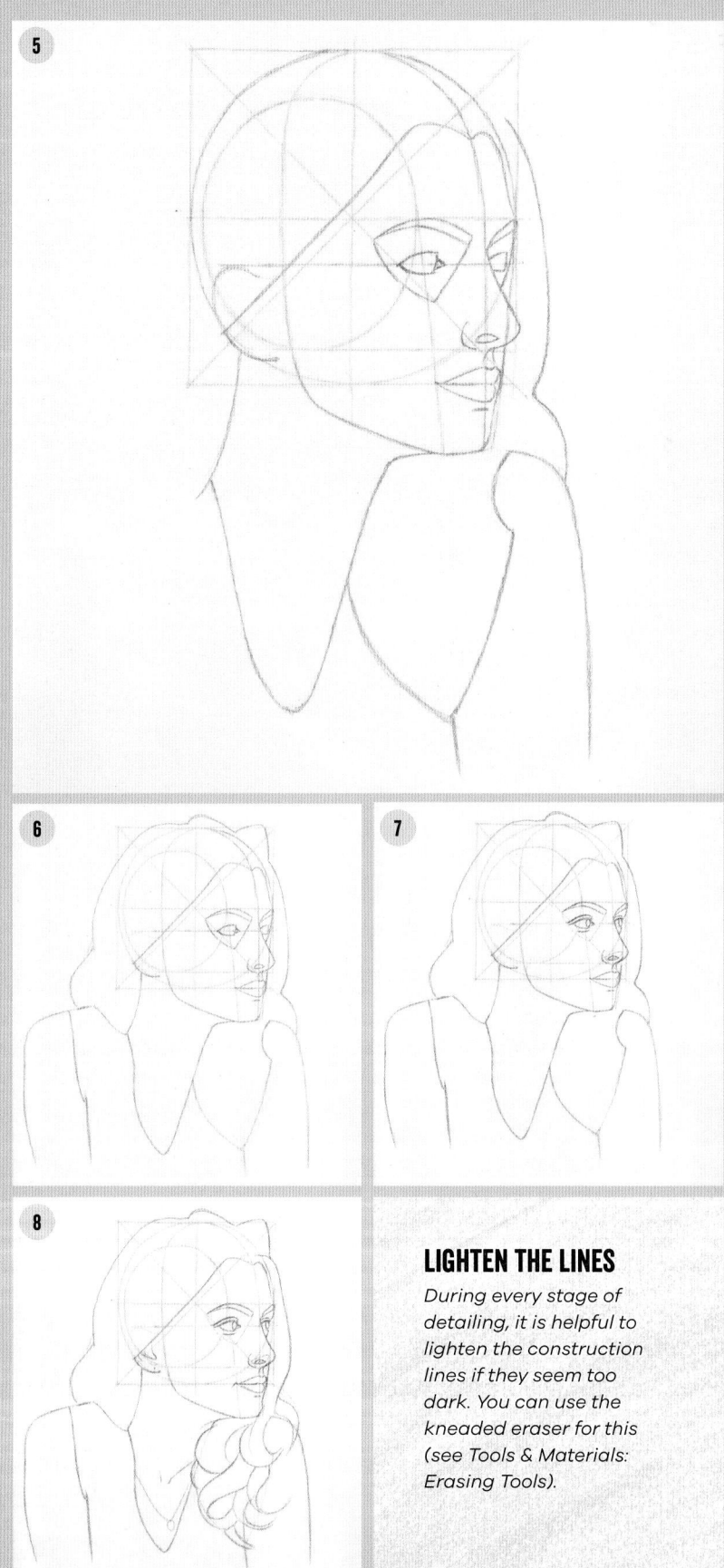

LIGHTEN THE LINES

During every stage of detailing, it is helpful to lighten the construction lines if they seem too dark. You can use the kneaded eraser for this (see Tools & Materials: Erasing Tools).

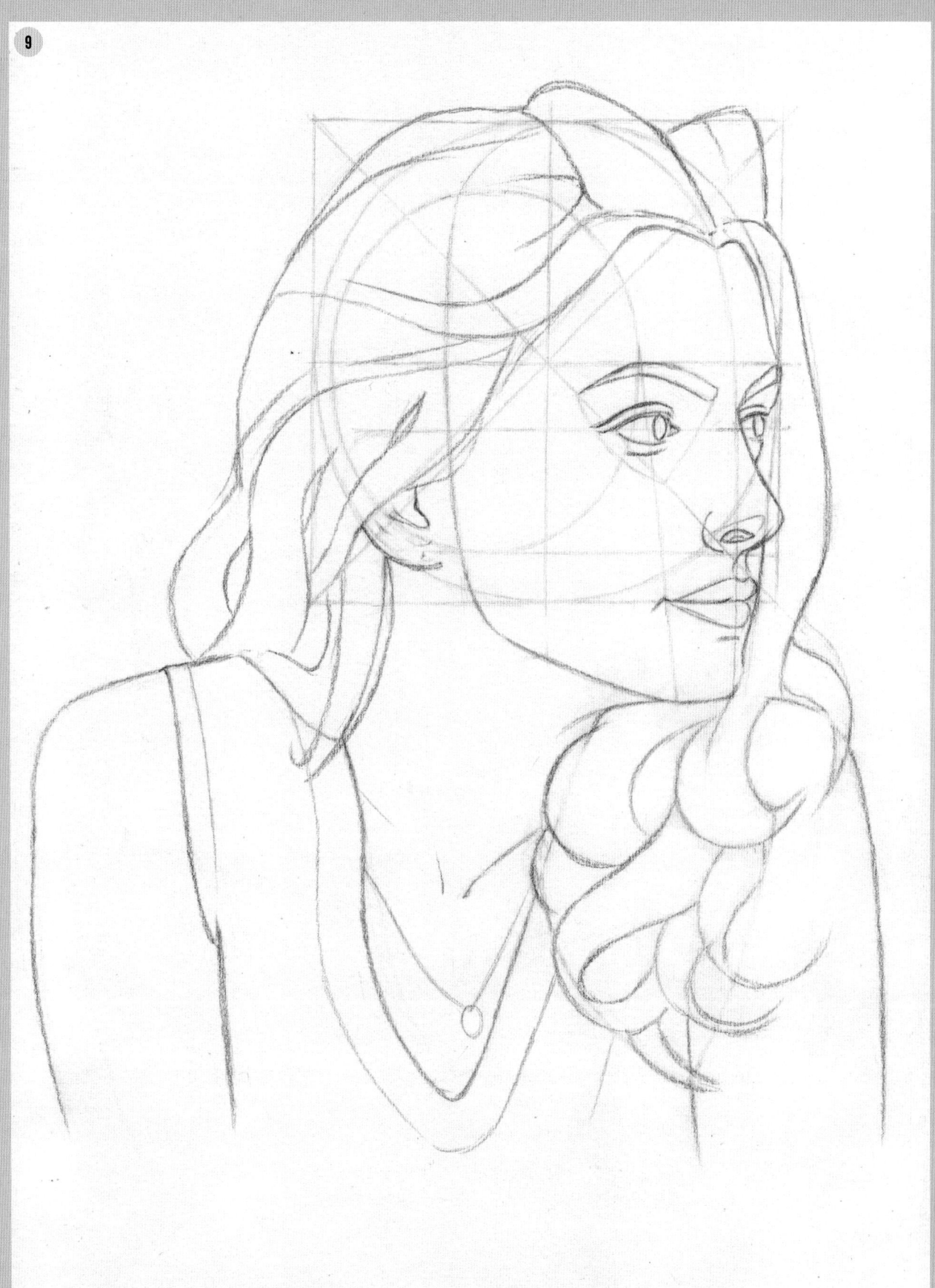

SHADING

At this point, you have completed the portrait construction and outline (either by following the previous Steps 1–9, or by simply tracing the image for Step 9).

1 Use a 4B pencil with medium grip to shade the eyebrows, eyes, lips, nostrils and the ear.

2 Use a large blending tool to blend the shaded areas (I used a sponge brush). Use the small amount of graphite on your blending tool to subtly shade the contours of the face. Use a light hand to brush over these areas.

3 Use a 6B pencil to darken the eyes, eyebrows and nose, including the nostril. Darken the lips and the shadow beneath. Next, use an 8B pencil to shade the dark region of the hair behind, and next to, the profile of the face to define a value extreme (*see* Sketching Fundamentals: Shading Techniques). This allows you to establish the base value strength when reworking the face.

4 Blend the graphite using a blending tool, and use the value extreme defined in the previous step to adjust the values of the facial features. Blend the graphite near the eyes using the blending tool. Add and rework shadows near the eyes and blend the shadows under the eyelids. Use a pencil eraser to add shine to the lips.

5 With a 6B pencil, shade the neck, chest and arms with a light-to-medium grip. Pay attention to the collar bone as you shade.

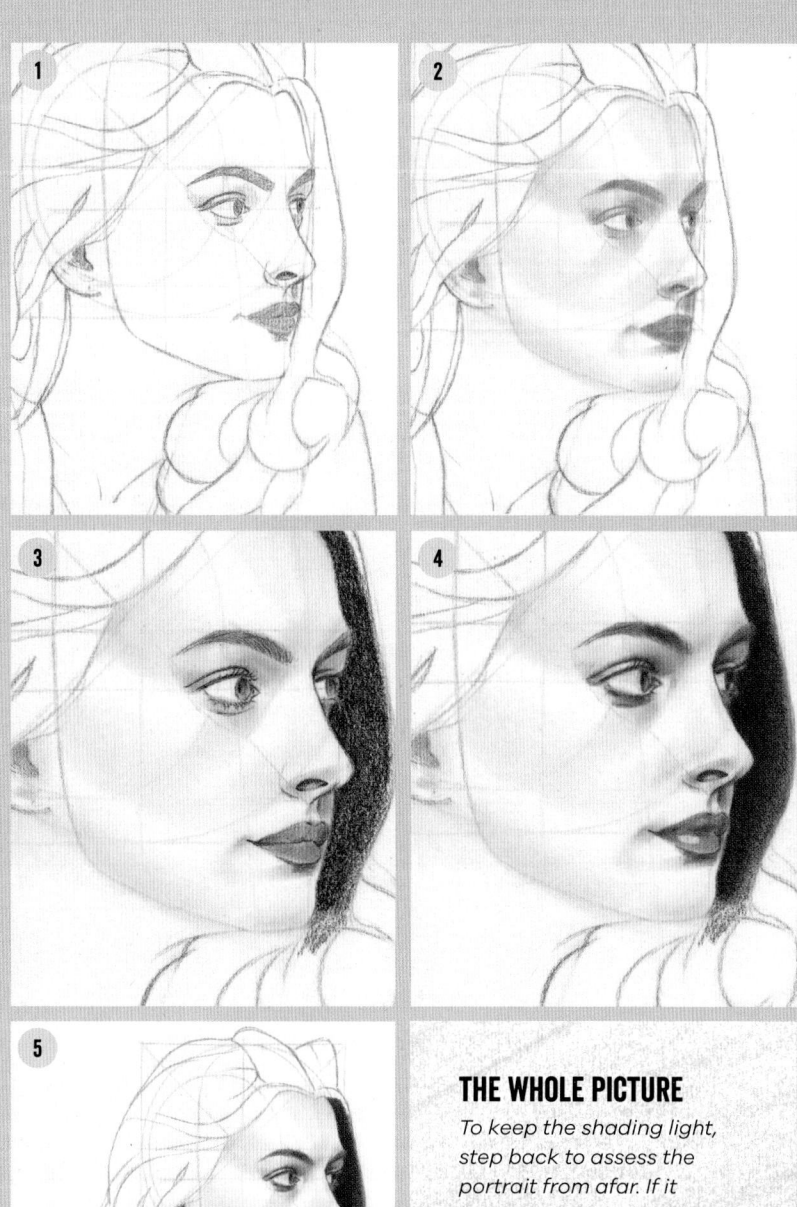

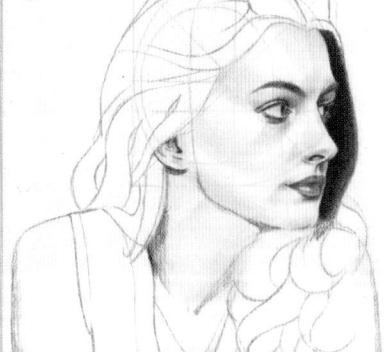

THE WHOLE PICTURE

To keep the shading light, step back to assess the portrait from afar. If it becomes too dark, use a kneaded eraser to dab away excess graphite and rework the area. Use scrap paper to remove excess graphite from the blender.

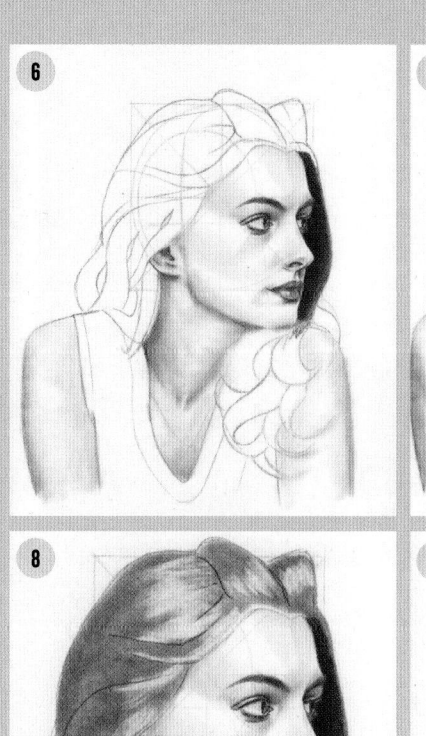

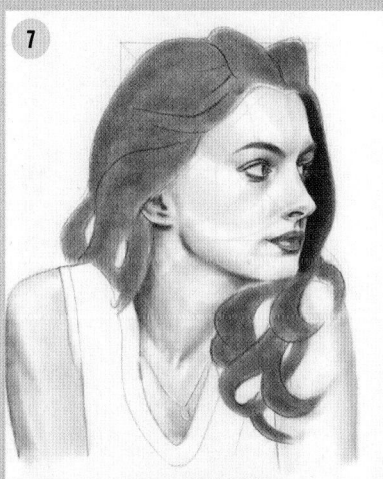

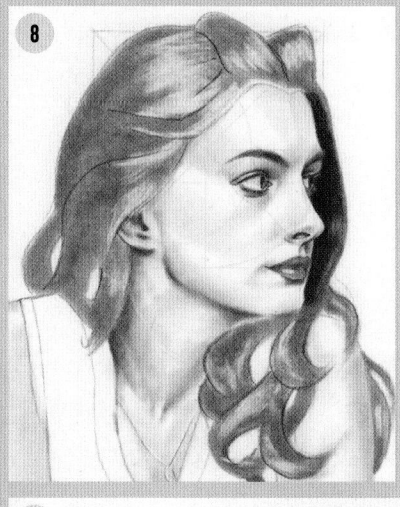

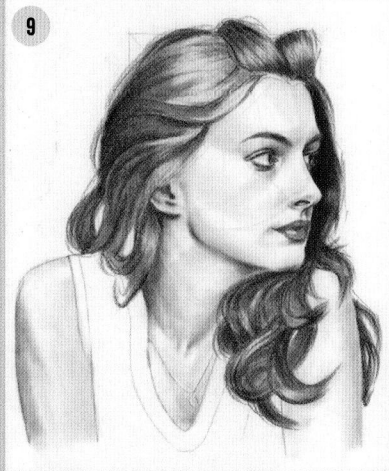

6 Blend the rest of the neck and the arms in the same way you blended the face in Step 2.

7 Use graphite powder and a large blending tool such as a sponge brush (*see* Tools & Materials: Blending Tools) to shade the hair. Use a 6B pencil to darken the details so that they are still visible. This is the first layer of hair.

8 With a kneaded eraser, create highlights on the hair, sweeping the eraser along the direction of the flow of hair. Use a 6B pencil to add hair behind the left arm.

9 Darken the hair using a 6B pencil, following the direction of hair and adding shadows. Start on the right side of the head, then move to the left.

10 Use an 8B pencil to darken the hair, but to retain the texture of the paper, do not blend – this is a style choice. Finally, use the paper stump with a little graphite powder to shade the clothes. We can go back with our pencil eraser and work on areas which need highlights and maybe sharpen any edges if necessary.

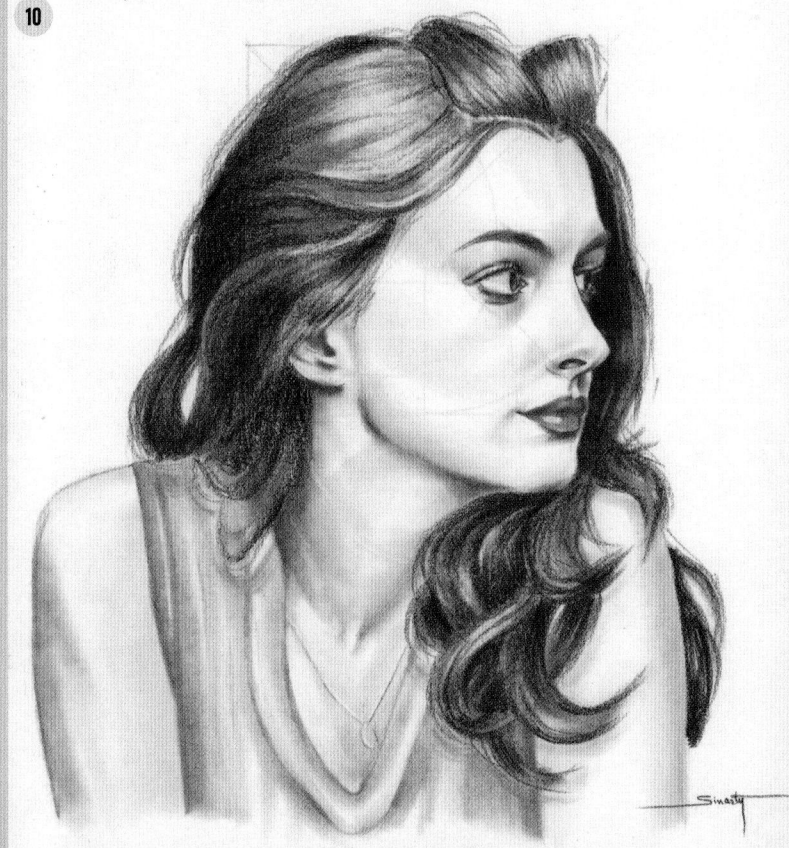

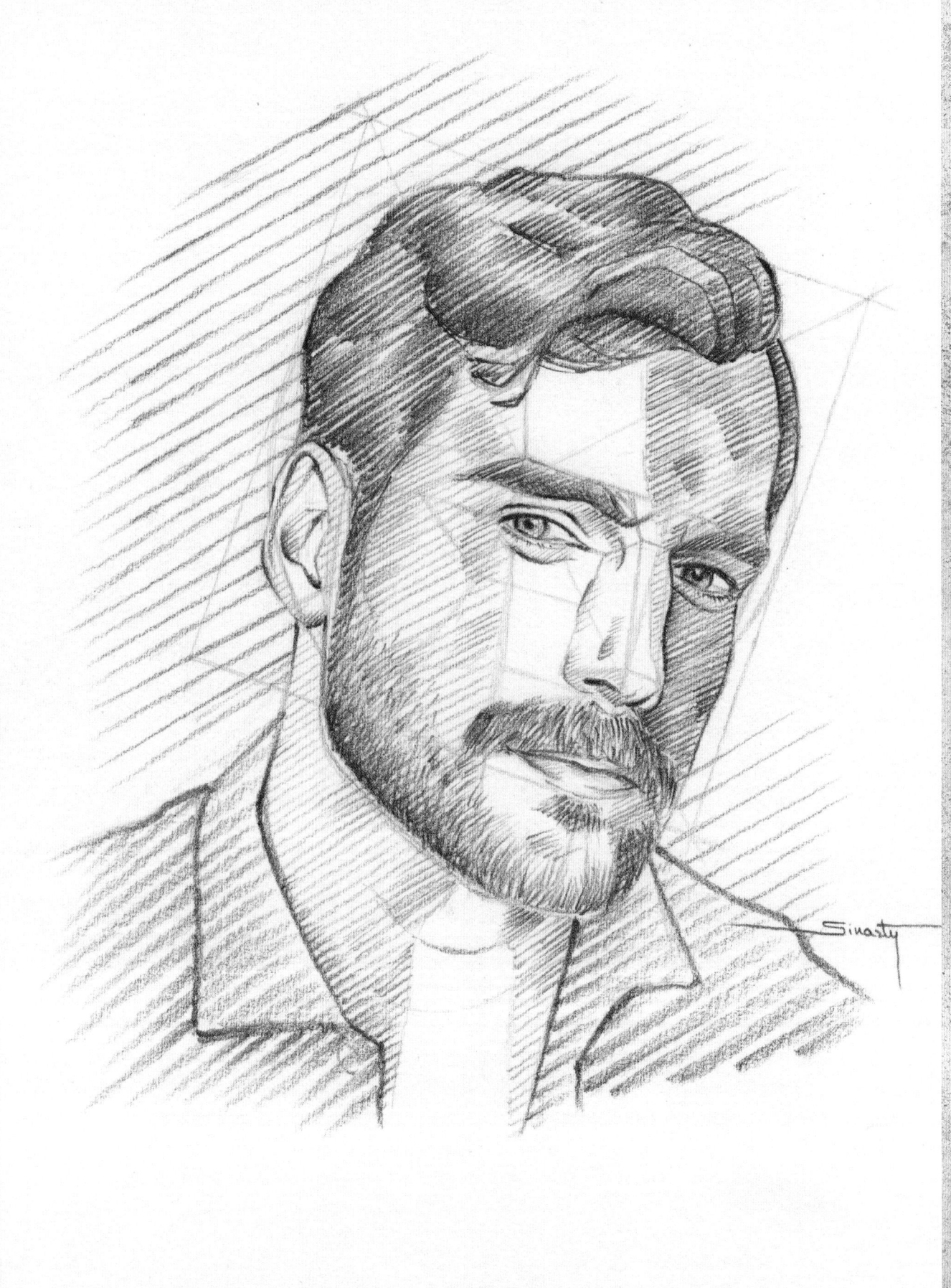

HENRY CAVILL

Chiselled features make Henry Cavill such a good subject for a portrait. This reference in particular had an interesting lighting element, with a band of light falling vertically down Henry's face and neck, while the rest of him is in shadow. We will explore the simple, yet effective unidirectional hatching technique to draw this portrait.

Materials

- White sketching paper, 22.9 x 30.5cm (9 x 12in)
- Graphite pencils: 2B, 4B, 6B, 8B
- Kneaded eraser (if required)
- Good-quality pencil sharpener

Techniques

- Proportion: Loomis head
- Shading: Unidirectional hatching

BASIC OUTLINING

1 Begin by drawing the Loomis head. Draw a square to fit the cranium in the centre of the page (see the inset thumbnail for guidance), tilted slightly clockwise. Divide it diagonally into quadrants. Then draw a circle enclosed in the square.

2 Draw a smaller circle as the side plane of the Loomis head.

3 Draw the front plane and the jawline. Mark the chin line using the square as a guide.

4 Along the front plane, draw the vertical centreline of the face. Draw the browline and nose line and extend them along the side plane of the face. Finally, extend the jaw line upwards along the side plane. We now have our completed Loomis head!

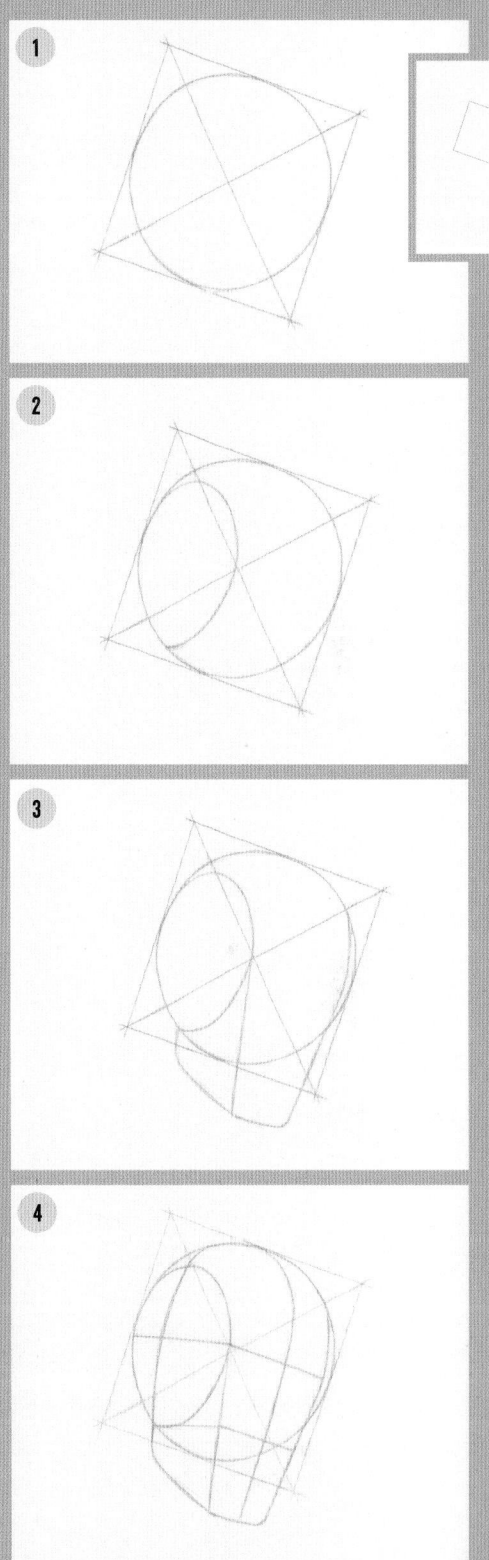

OUTLINE DETAILING

While drawing the following steps, use a 2B graphite pencil and a light-medium hand (*see* Sketching Fundamentals: Pencil Exercises).

5 Draw the nose planes, the plane groove for the eye sockets and an outline of the ear. Refer to Proportion Techniques: The Loomis Method, if required.

6 Draw the basic outline of the hair and the lips. Add the outline of the neck and shirt.

7 Draw the basic outlines for the eyes and eyebrows.

8 Detail the nose and mark the plane of the beard line.

9 Mark the lips and the iris of the eyes, then the hair and facial hair outlines. Further refine the outline of the forehead.

10 Detail the ears, the folds on the neck and the shirt button to complete our detailed outline of our portrait.

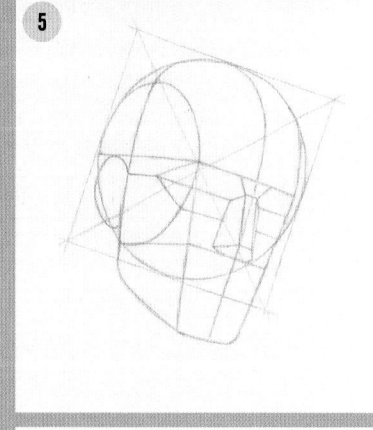
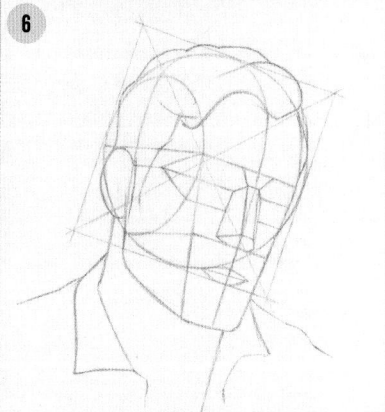
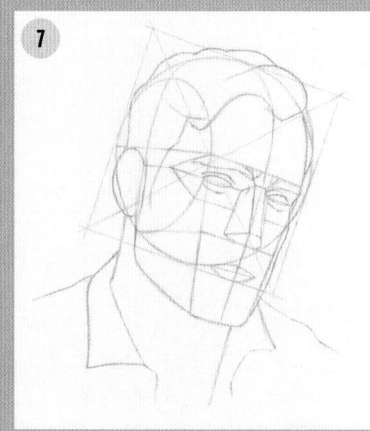
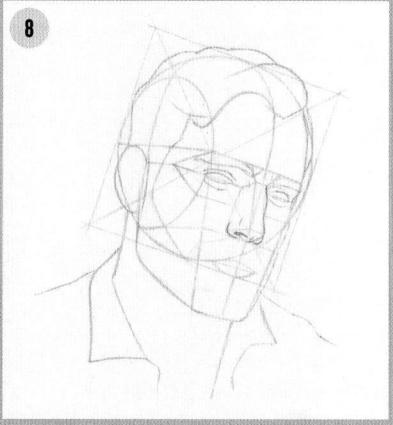
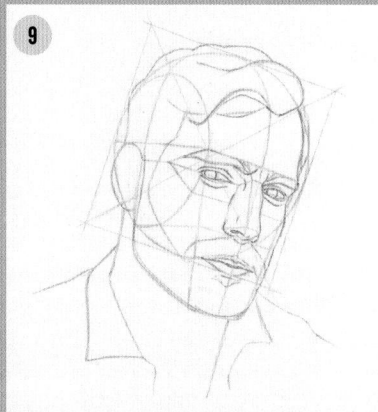

CORRECTING PROPORTIONS

Keep in mind that these are still simplistic outlines without too many details, allowing you to change the proportions at this stage if needed.

GO STRAIGHT TO SHADING

Simply tracing the final outline drawing – Step 10 – provides an opportunity to jump ahead to practise shading (see Proportion Techniques: Freehand & Tracing).

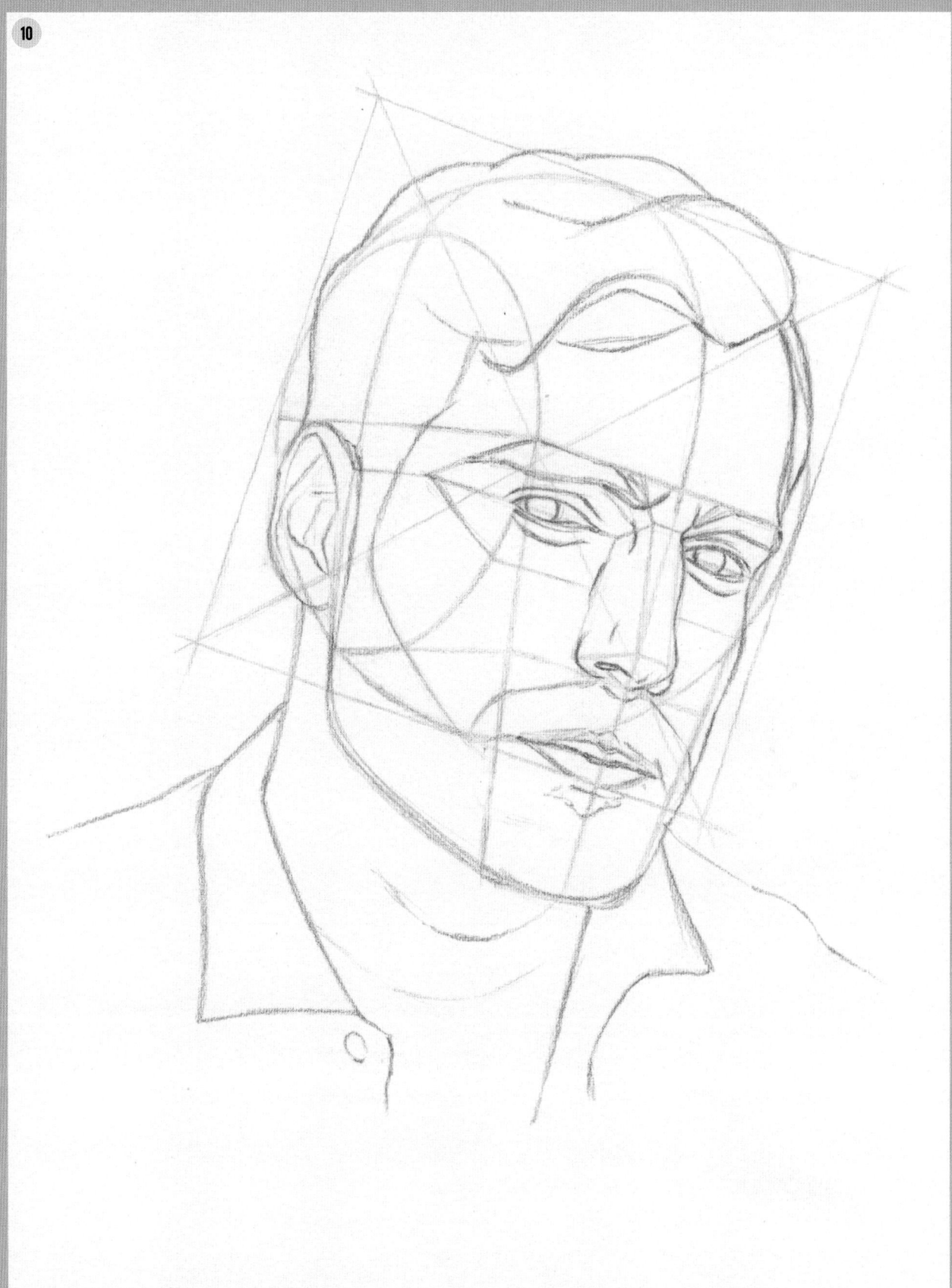

SHADING

At this point, you have completed the portrait construction and outline (either by following the previous Steps 1–10, or by simply tracing the image for Step 10)

1 For this portrait, shade using the same unidirectional hatching technique as I have (*see* Sketching Fundamentals: Shading Techniques). Shade the first layer using a 2B pencil. Note the unshaded vertical band going all the way down the centre of the face – this is where the light falls.

2 Use a 4B pencil to shade the first layer of the eyebrows, eyes and nose.

3 Still using a 4B pencil, draw facial hair following the direction of the growth, *not* the direction of the hatching. This will achieve the desired effect of stubble or a messy beard. Keep your pencil well sharpened or use a mechanical pencil (*see* Tools & Materials: Drawing Mediums).

4 Use a 4B pencil to shade the first layer of head hair, maintaining the direction of the hatching.

5 Darken the eyes and eyebrows using a 6B pencil.

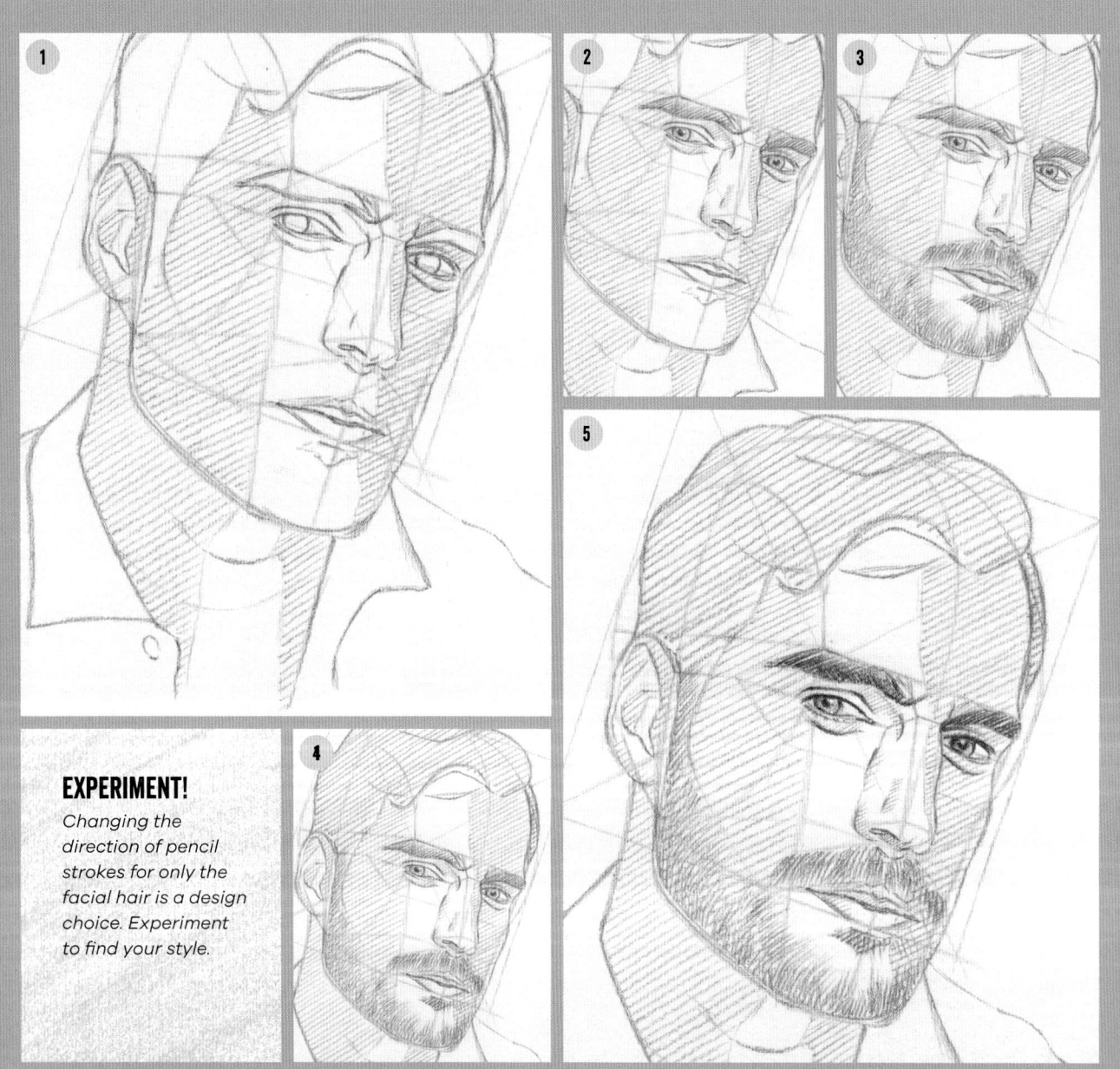

EXPERIMENT!

Changing the direction of pencil strokes for only the facial hair is a design choice. Experiment to find your style.

6 Using a 6B pencil, darken the shadows on the left side of the face, maintaining the direction of the hatch. You can decrease the distance between each line of the hatch and/or increase the pencil pressure or grade to give an effect of the shadow (see Sketching Fundamentals: Shading Techniques).

7 Darken the facial hair using the 6B pencil. Remember to maintain the direction of the hair instead of the hatch.

8 Define the edges of the hair on the head, and darken it using a 6B pencil. Note: We are not drawing the individual strands of the hair in this case, but are instead drawing the general flow of the locks.

9 Finally, go over the portrait with an 8B pencil. Sharpen the edges, darken the hair, add more shadows to the eyebrows and the eyes, and shade the clothes using the basic unidirectional hatch.

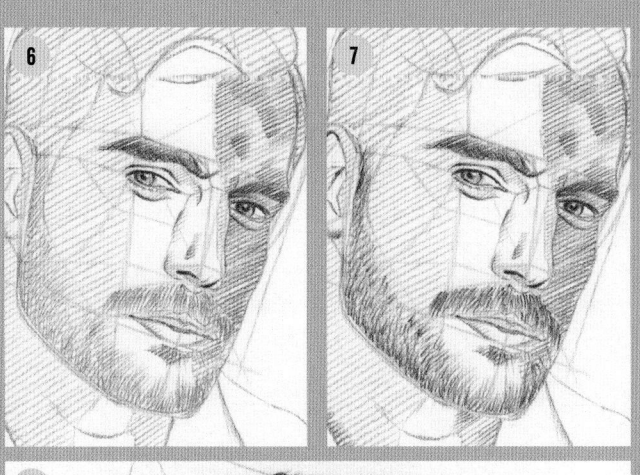

BACKGROUND DEPTH

The hatching in the background gives the portrait a sense of depth. Notice that we have kept the direction of the background hatch lines the same as the portrait hatch lines. Maintaining a single direction across the portrait gives a sense of uniformity.

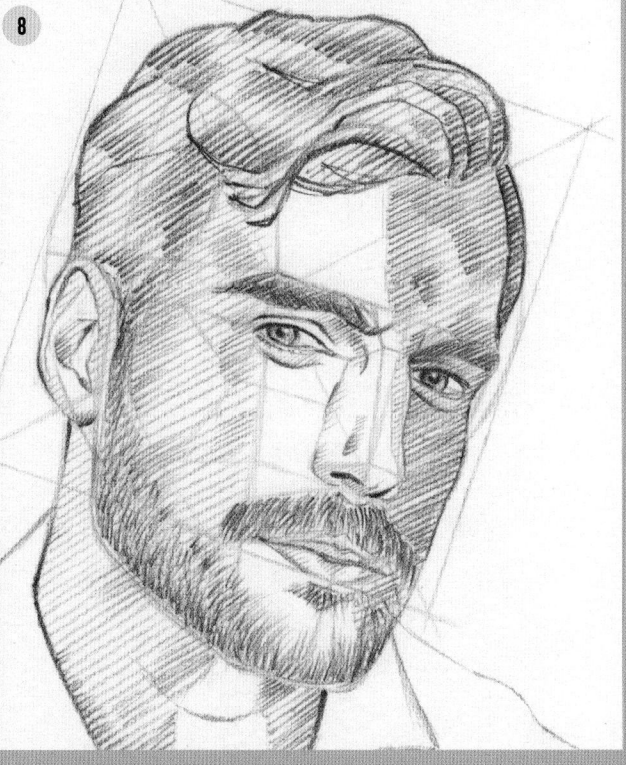

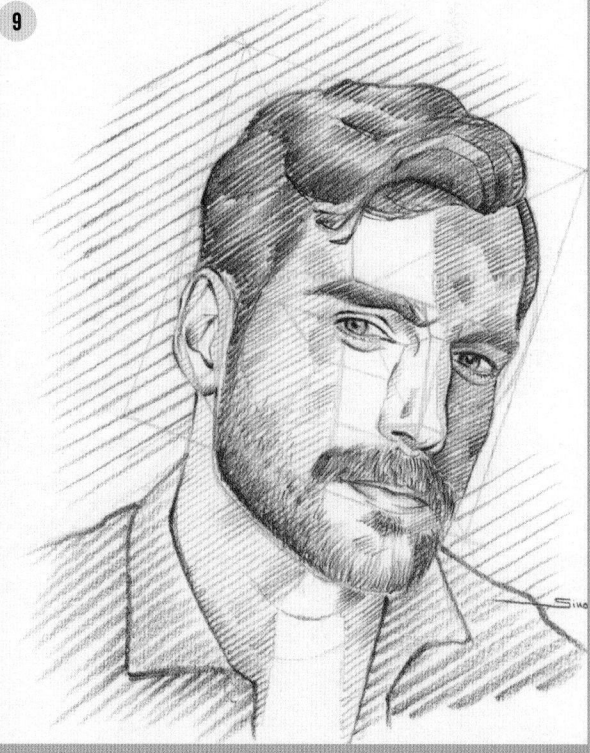

HENRY CAVILL

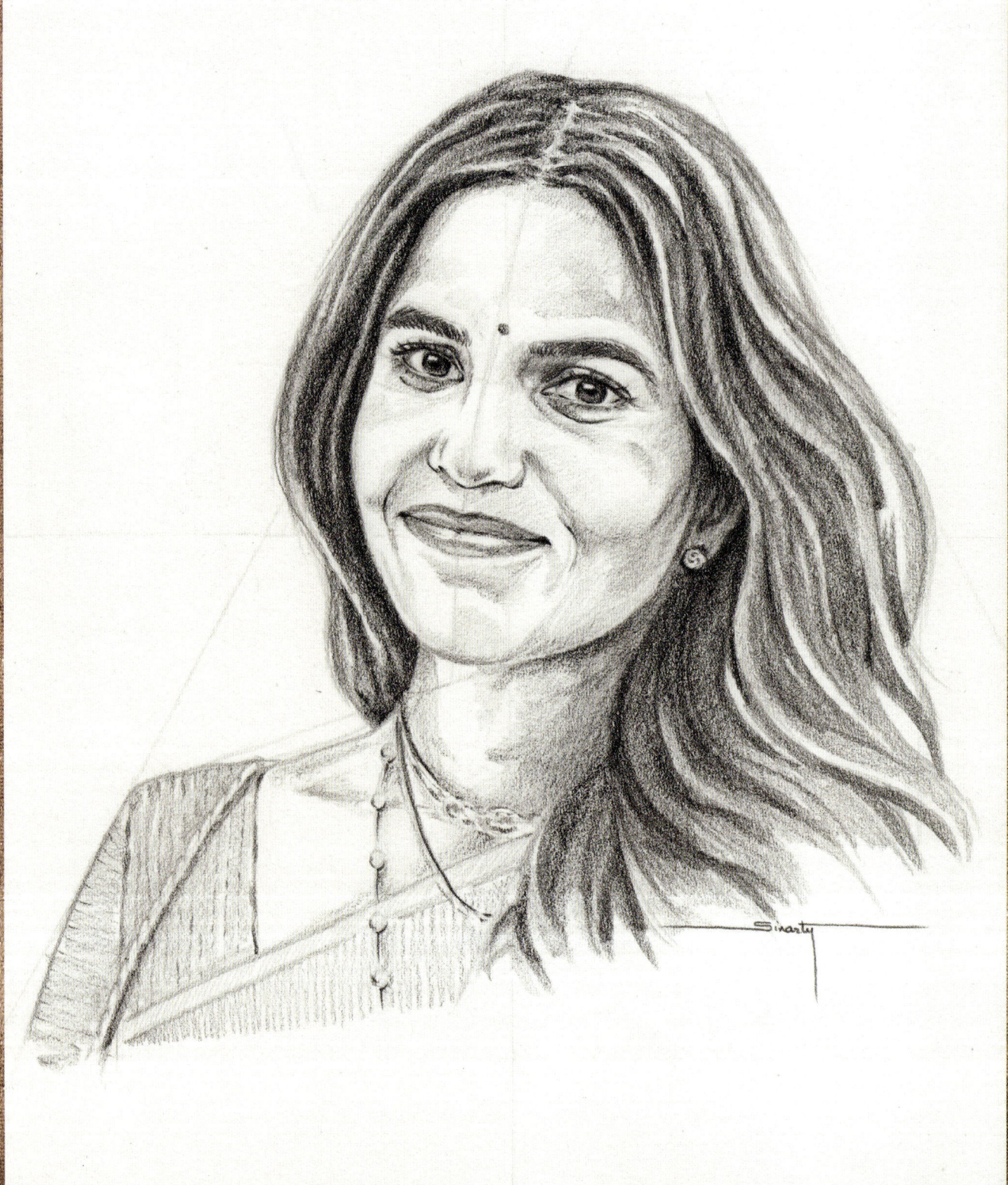

THE SMILE

This is a portrait of my beautiful mom. I would like this to be a small tribute to all the times she has been there for me and supported me throughout the years. She continues to be my pillar through life. Through this portrait, we will learn to use the block-in technique to accurately position our portrait on the paper. The shading will use layers of the gradient technique. We will avoid using the paper stumps to smudge and keep the pencil strokes intact. This will help bring out the texture of the paper to give character to our portrait. Let's begin!

Materials

- White sketching paper, 22.9 x 30.5cm (9 x 12in)

Note: The ratio of the paper used is important if mapping the placement of this particular subject. The ratio here is 3:4.

- Graphite pencils: 2B, 6B, 2H
- Ruler (if required)
- Kneaded eraser, pencil eraser
- Good-quality pencil sharpener

Techniques

- Proportion: Geometric block-in and basic grid
- Shading: Gradient blending

BASIC OUTLINING

1 To help position the portrait correctly on the page, first divide the page into quadrants to create a grid (see the inset thumbnail for guidance). Draw the first four lines to mark the approximate position of the portrait, using the grid as a guide. Note the shapes of the negative spaces to help you replicate the lines accurately.

2 Draw lines within that initial shape to position the face and hair.

3 Draw the hair, the outline of the face and the shoulder. At this point you can see the structure of the portrait taking shape.

4 Add a centreline to the face as shown, and add a few details to the hair and clothing.

5 Add more refined outline details to the hair and clothing. Draw the eyeline slightly above the middle of the face, and a curved line across the neck to position the shortest of the three necklaces.

6 Place the features, starting with the eye sockets, nose line and lip line. Also draw the ear with a circle for the earring.

7 Before focusing on details, this is a good time to check the proportions and fix anything if needed. Then draw details of the eyebrows, eyes, nose and lips.

8 Once the proportions are correct, add more details to the eyes and lips.

9 Finish the outline by adding some final details to the hair, ear and jewellery.

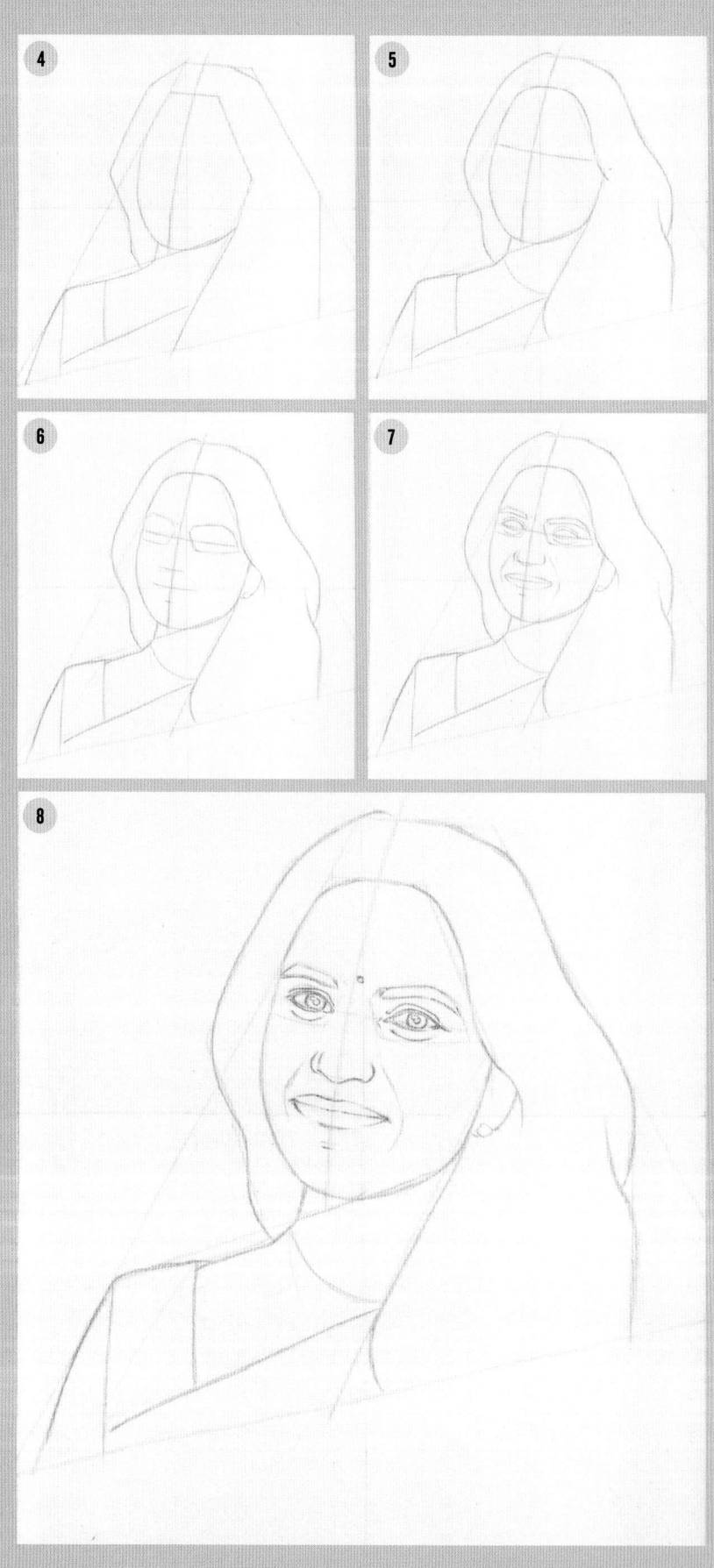

GO STRAIGHT TO SHADING

Simply tracing the final outline drawing – Step 9 – provides an opportunity to jump ahead to practise shading (see Proportion Techniques: Freehand & Tracing).

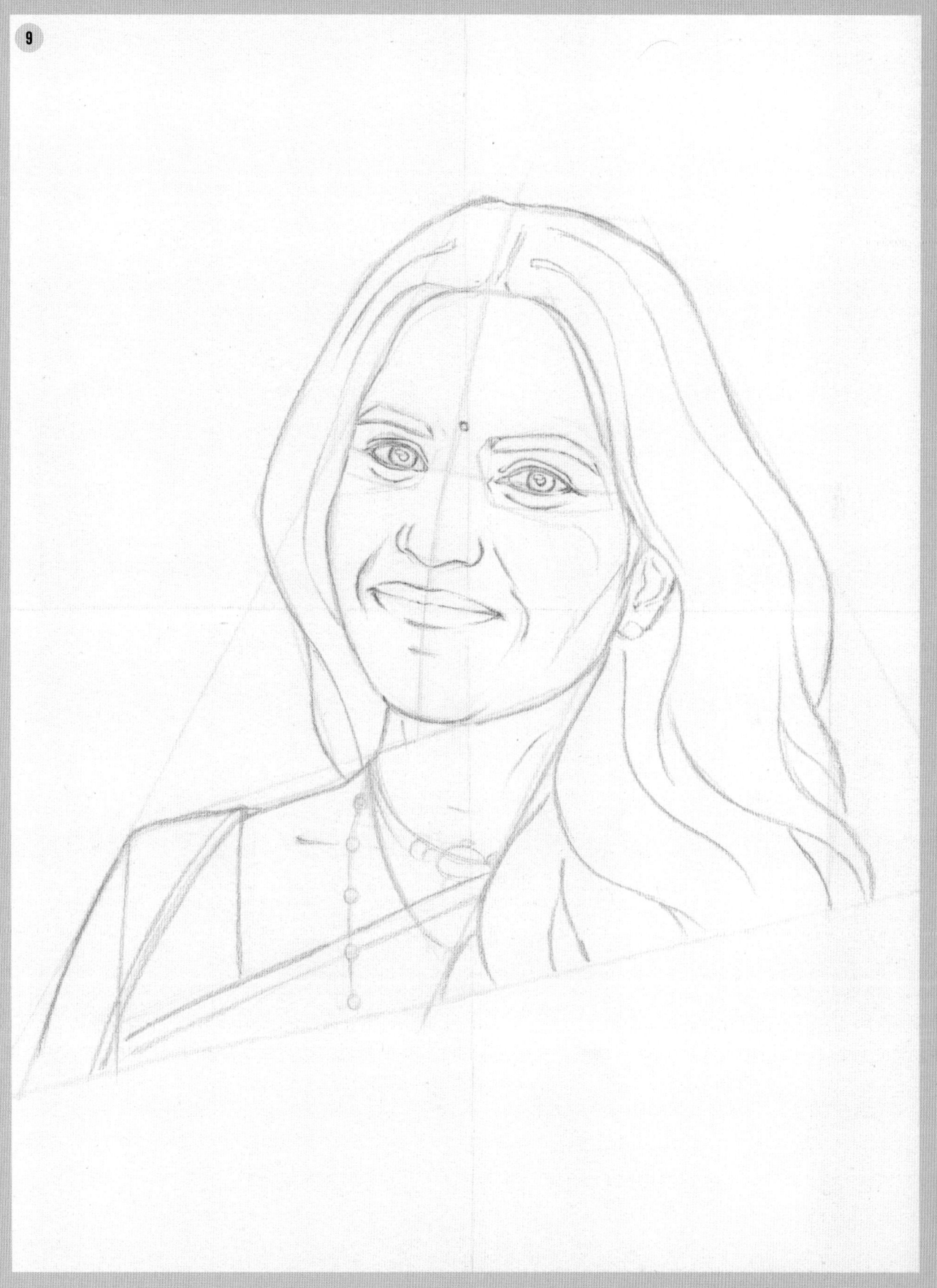

SHADING

At this point, you have completed the portrait construction and outline (either by following the previous Steps 1–9, or by simply tracing the image for Step 9).

1 Use a 6B pencil to draw the darker areas of the face and ear.

2 Use the same pencil with a medium-to-hard grip to draw the details of the hair and necklaces.

3 Now use a 2B pencil with a light-to-medium grip to draw the medium values on the face (*see* Sketching Fundamentals: Shading Techniques).

4 Still using the 2B pencil, fill in the midtone details of the hair and the clothes. Use a 2H pencil to shade the lighter values on the left side of the face.

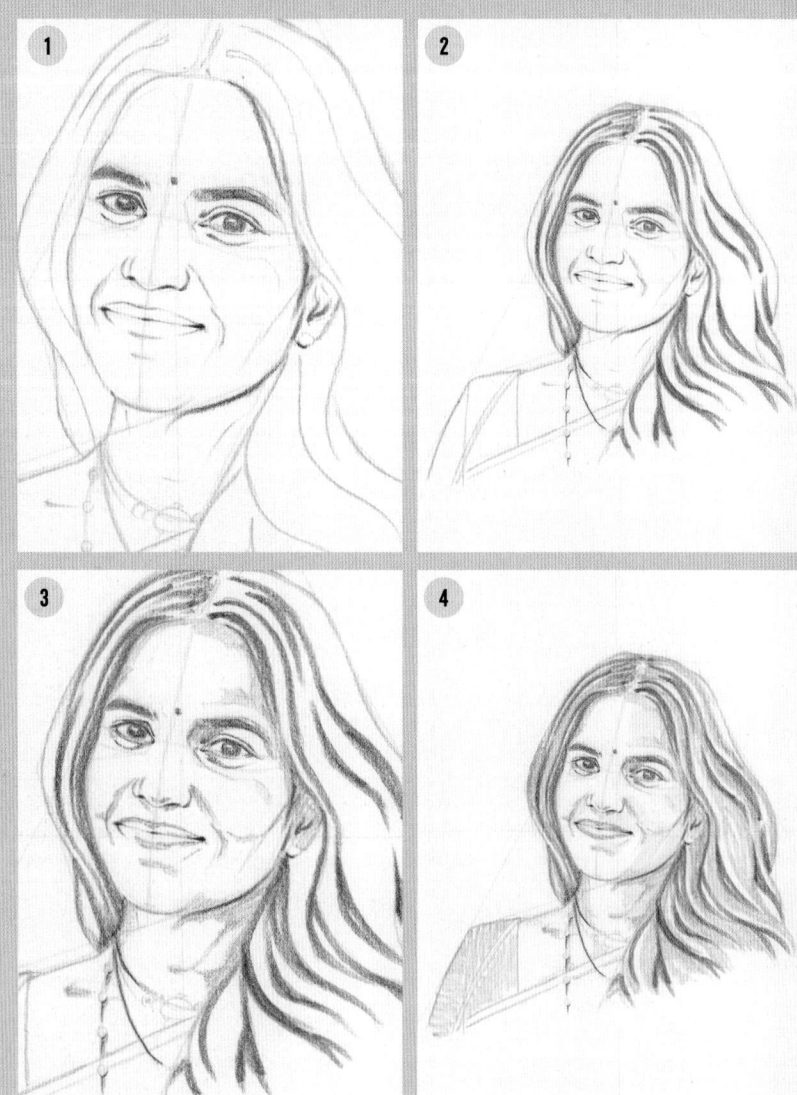

EXTRA DETAILING

Taking time to detail other aspects of the portrait apart from the face, such as jewellery, clothes and other accessories, adds character to your portraits.

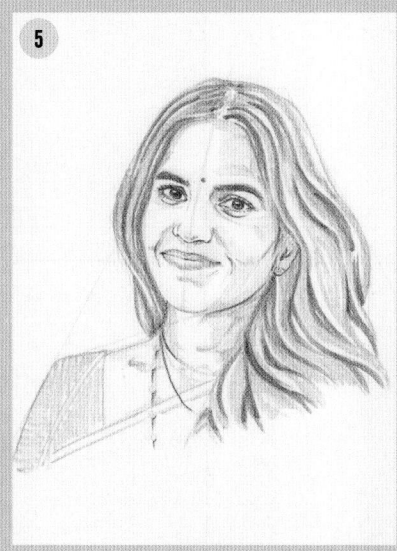

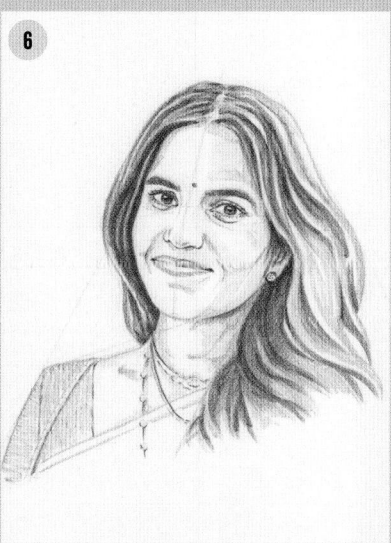

5 With the 8B pencil, build a dark top layer to give the portrait some depth. Start with the eyes and ear.

6 Detail the hair, clothes and jewellery using the same 8B pencil.

7 Finally, transition the values from dark to light to create smooth, soft edges. Use a 2H pencil to go over the lighter areas and rework them. Blend the graphite near the eyes to create some depth, using a narrow blending tool like a tortillon. Also blend the shadows under the eyelids and compare the values across your portrait to match it to the reference (*see* Proportion Techniques: The Block-in Method).

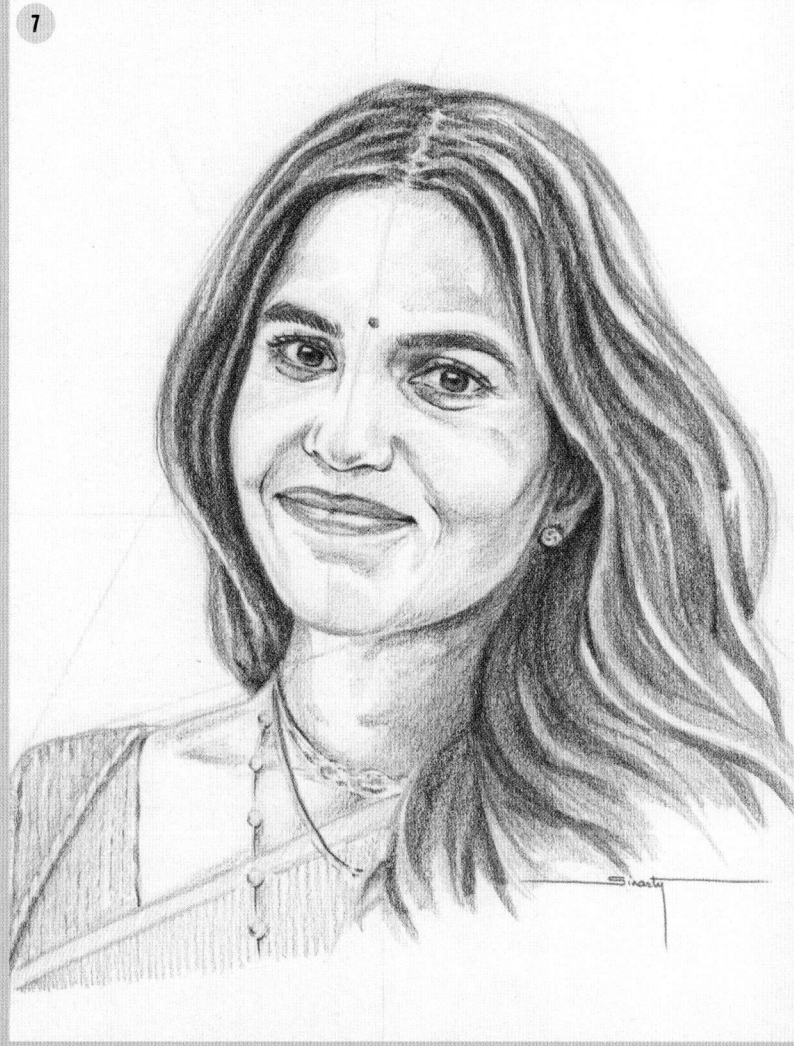

TIME TO STOP?

It is important to work on your details to keep improving the portrait, but it is easy to get carried away and overwork it. With time and experience, you will learn when to keep detailing and when to stop – another reason to practise regularly and become familiar with your workflow.

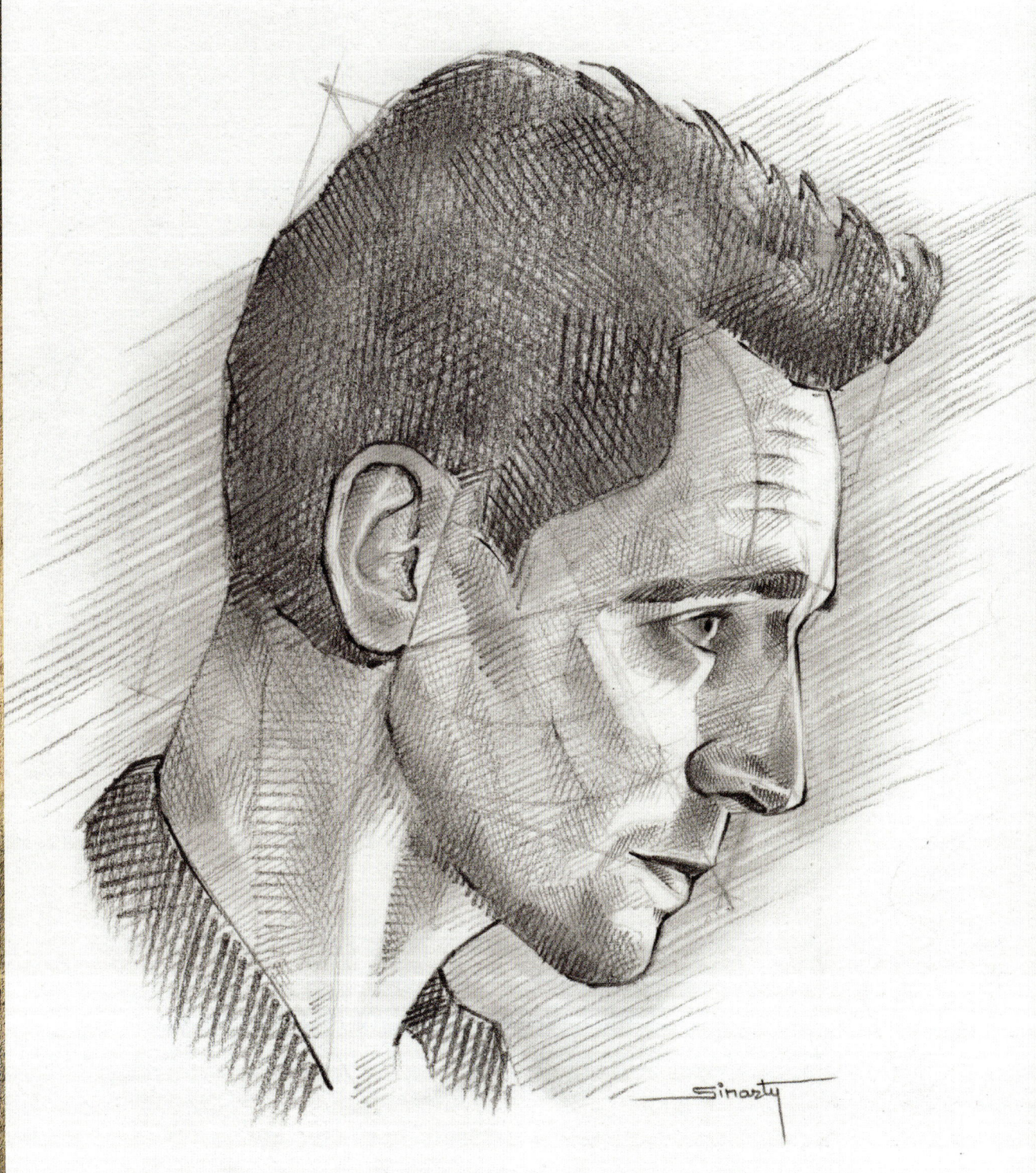

TOM HIDDLESTON

Tom Hiddleston, the acclaimed British actor, has captured hearts worldwide with his dynamic performances. This profile portrait allows artists to portray Tom's distinctive piercing eyes and sharp jawline, adding a touch of his captivating presence to your artwork. Let's start!

Materials

- White sketching paper, 22.9 x 30.5cm (9 x 12in)
- Graphite pencils: 2H, 2B, 4B, 6B, 8B
- Kneaded eraser
- Pencil sharpener

Techniques

- Proportion: Loomis head
- Shading: Cross hatching and gradient blending

BASIC OUTLINING

1 Begin by drawing the Loomis head. Draw a square, tilted a few degrees clockwise, slightly above the middle of the page (see the inset thumbnail for guidance). The angle accounts for the tilt in the head of the portrait. Draw the two diagonals of the square.

2 Draw two concentric circles. The outer circle is the cranium, while the inner circle is the side plane of the head. Mark the centrelines – the centreline across the square from left to right is the browline.

3 Complete the side of the Loomis head by adding the jaw and the front plane line (*see* Proportion Techniques: The Loomis Method).

4 Draw a simple outline of the nose following the front plane of the face.

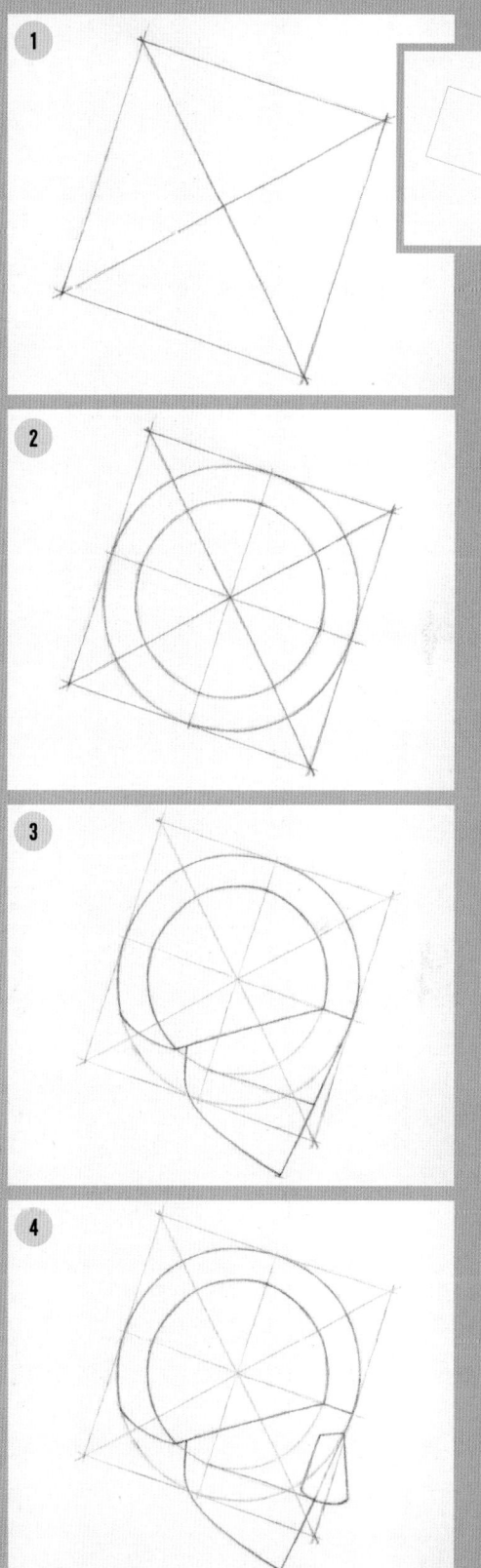

5 Draw the front and the side planes of the nose, as well as an indication of the nostril.

6 Draw a basic eye socket groove and brow using the square as a grid.

7 Add the ear and the silhouette of the lips. Draw the bottom part of the jaw.

8 We complete the basic structure of the head by adding the outline of the hair, neck, collar, and lips. The eye-socket plane was adjusted in this step to make it parallel to the browline.

OUTLINE DETAILING

While drawing the following steps, use a 2B graphite pencil and a light-medium hand (*see* Sketching Fundamentals: Pencil Exercises).

9 Using the guidelines from the Basic Outlining stage, draw a simple outline of the eyebrow and eye.

10 Add detail to the contours of the chin, lips and nose. On the forehead, add faint lines to represent creases.

11 Add detail to the outline of the hair, including the hairline. Also detail the ear.

12 Refine the proportions, thinning out the eyebrows. Add the pupil and highlight details near the eye. Outline the value transitions on the forehead and near the bridge of the nose with a light hand.

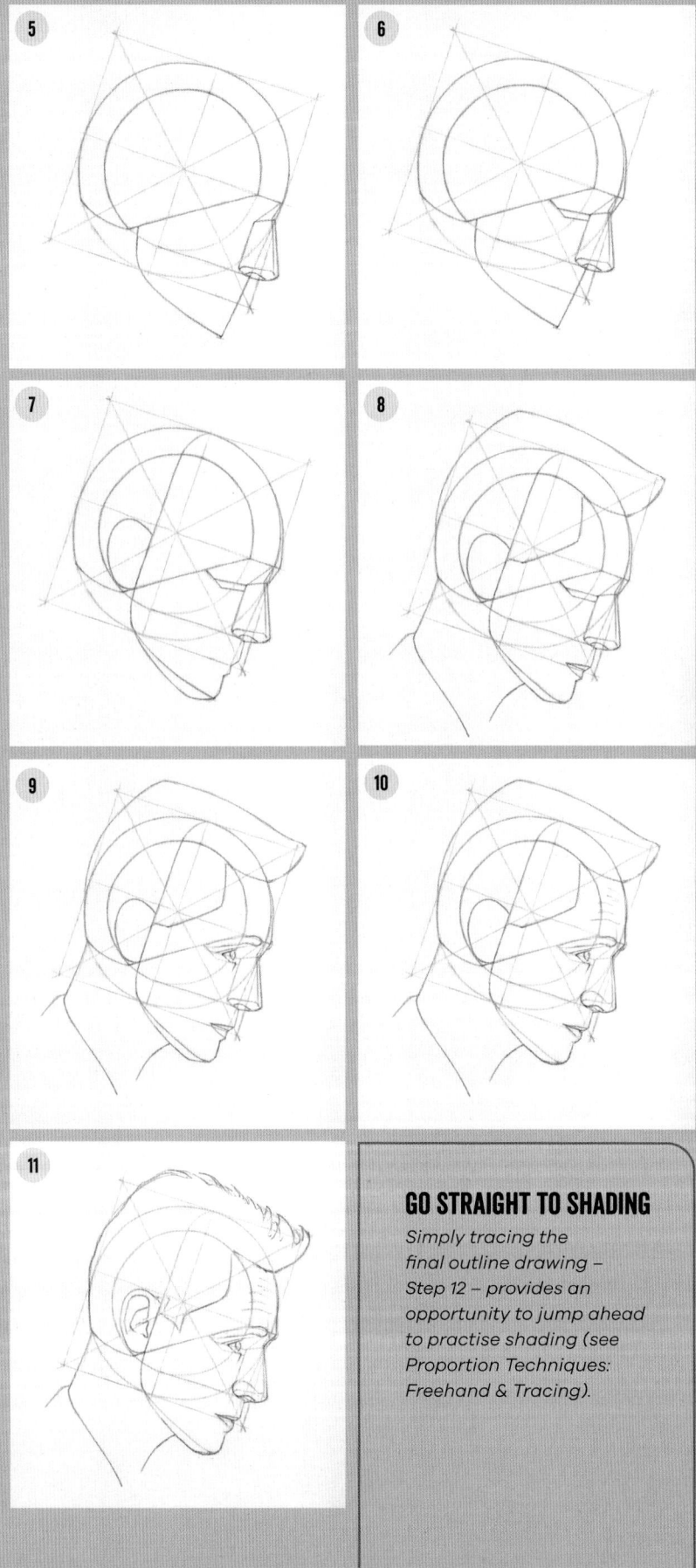

GO STRAIGHT TO SHADING

Simply tracing the final outline drawing – Step 12 – provides an opportunity to jump ahead to practise shading (see Proportion Techniques: Freehand & Tracing).

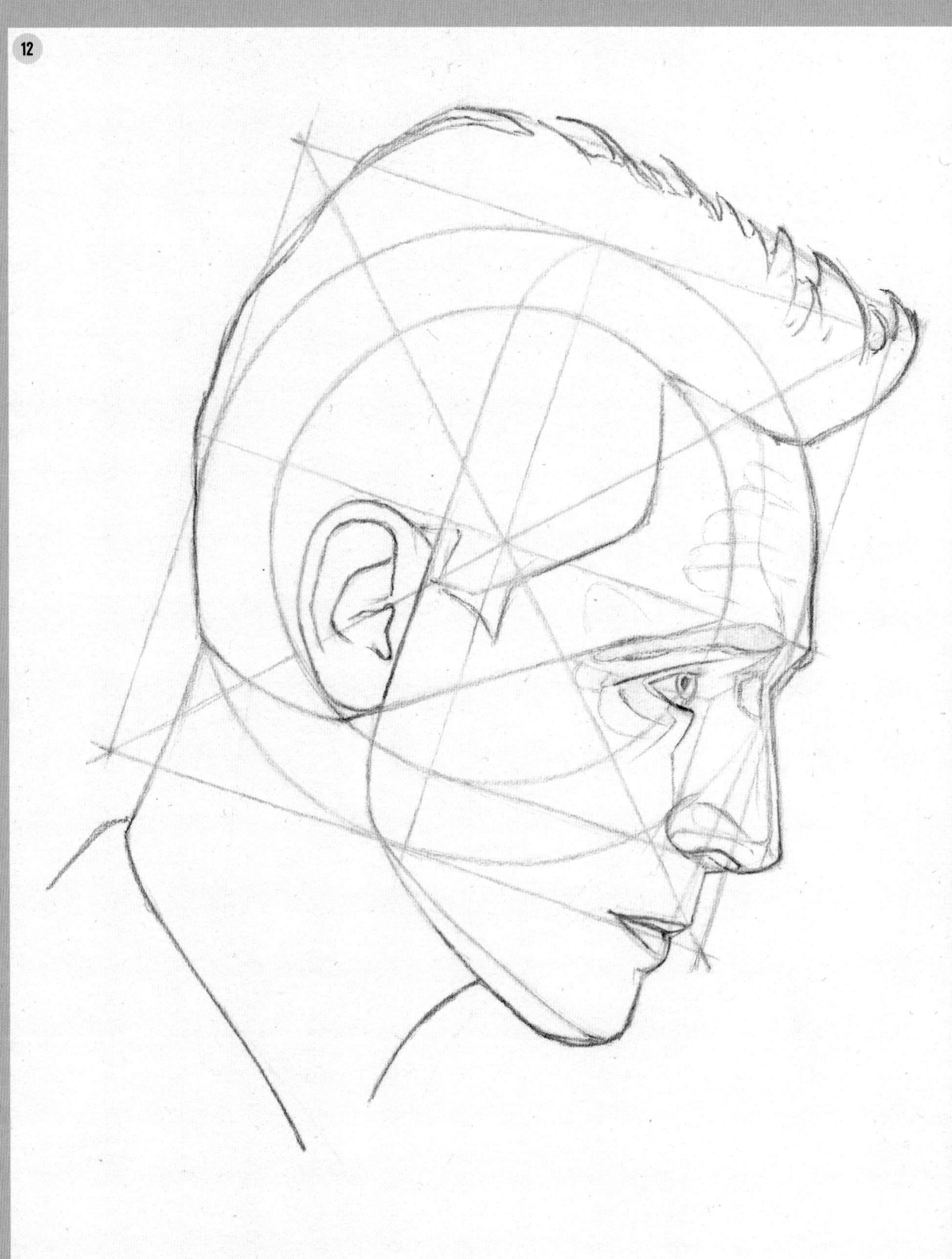

SHADING

At this point, you have completed the portrait construction and outline (either by following the previous Steps 1–12, or by simply tracing the image for Step 12).

1 To begin shading the face, use a 2B pencil with a medium pressure grip and hatch the upper part including the side of the forehead, eyes and nose. This creates a base for the cross hatch.

2 Use a 4B pencil with a medium grip to cross hatch in areas where there is shadow, like the eyebrows and the bridge of the nose.

3 To finish these shaded areas, use a 6B pencil for the darker shadows of the face including the nostrils, pupil, eyelashes and the eyebrows.

4 Map out the highlights and shadows as you did before (refer back to Outline Detailing, Step 12).

5 Follow the three-step technique used in Steps 1–3 to shade the rest of the face. Start by creating the base for cross hatching with a 2B pencil and medium pressure grip.

6 As before, use a 4B and 6B pencil for the darker areas where the features cast the deepest shadows, including beneath the nose and along the jawline.

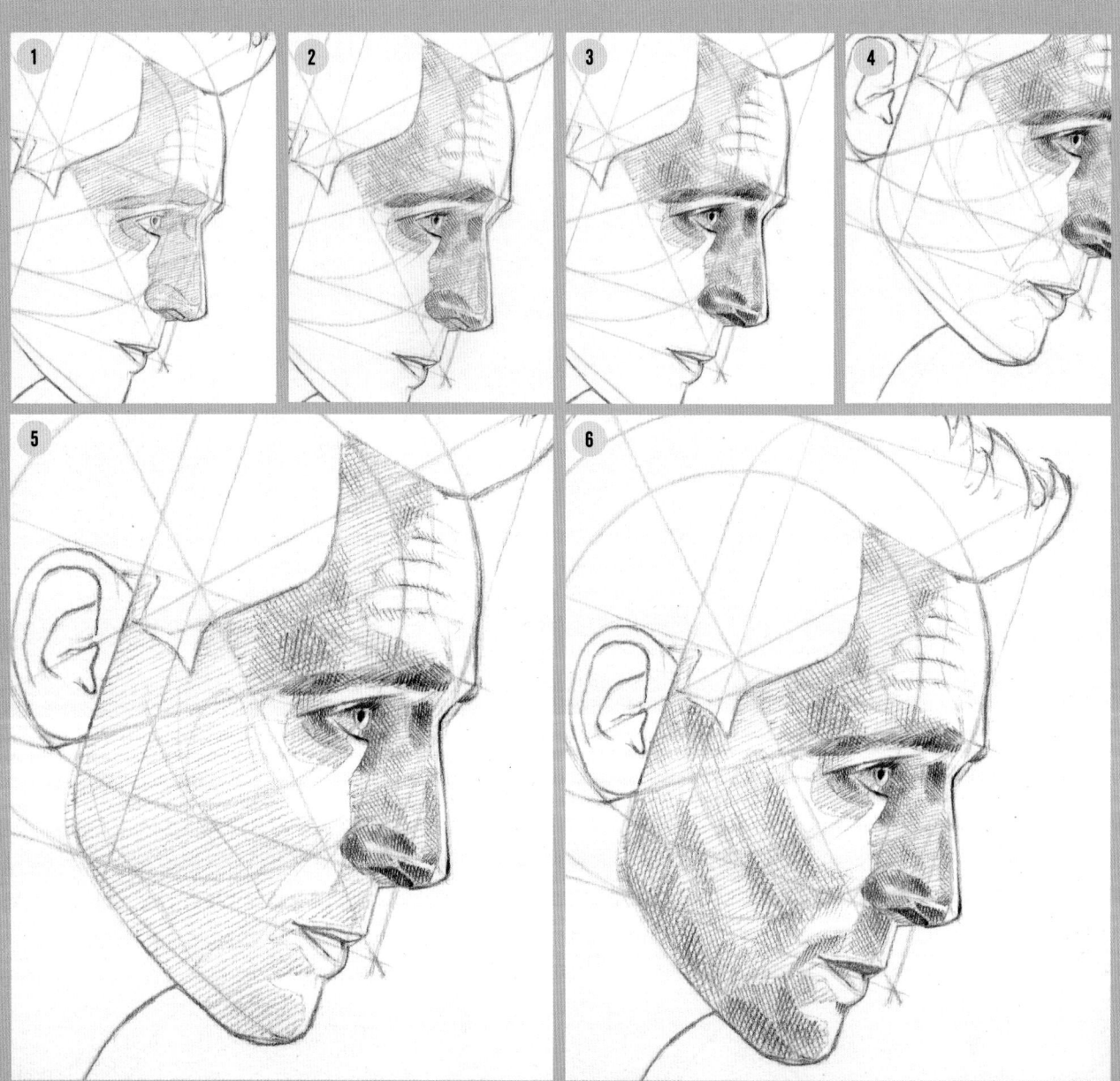

7 Shade the hair, ear, neck and shirt collar. The neck needs a few vertical lines to map out the shadow and light of the clavicle before the base hatching is added. For the hair and shirt, use a 4B pencil to draw bolder lines that are spaced slightly wider apart than the hatch lines on the face. This will emphasize the difference in texture between the skin and the other areas.

8 Cross hatch the neck and hair. Again, create a wider-spaced and darker cross hatch on the hair.

9 Build cross hatching layers on top of Step 8 using 6B and 8B pencils. Also notice the darkened outlines of the profile.

10 Use a blending tool such as a sponge brush to shade the shadow areas of the face and hair. Make sure you don't lose the cross-hatch strokes underneath the blending. These add depth to your portrait. Fill the background as shown with a hatch pattern, blending it to make the profile pop out. Use a pencil eraser to create highlights which might have been lost during the blending process.

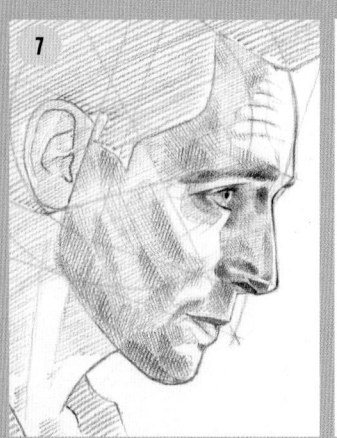

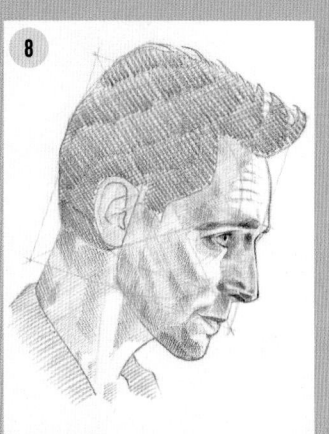

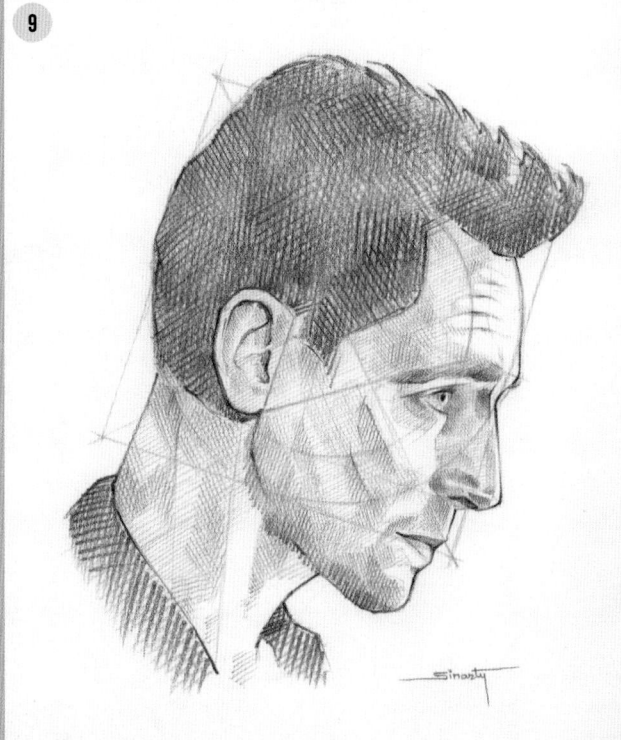

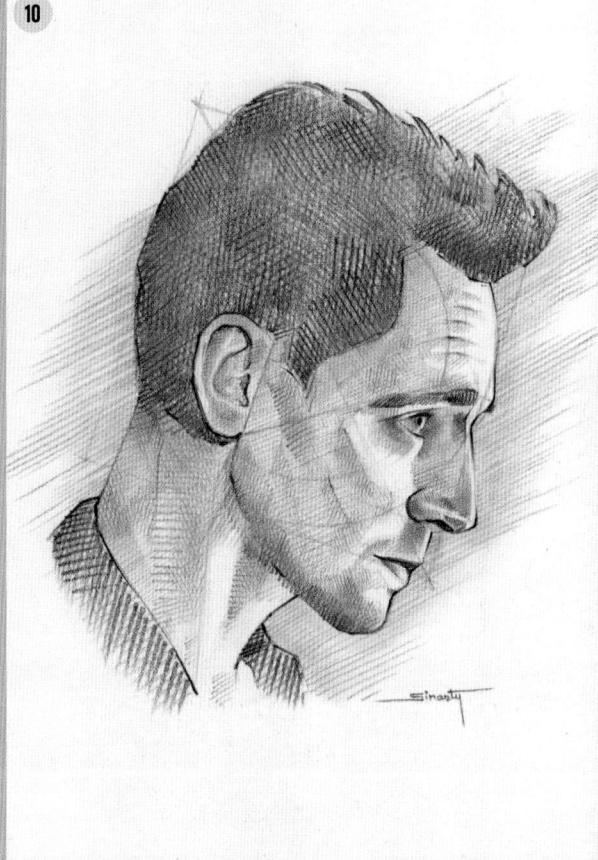

TIRED OF SHARPENING?

We need a sharp pencil tip to get consistent hatching patterns, so try using a mechanical pencil to keep the point sharp.

TOM HIDDLESTON

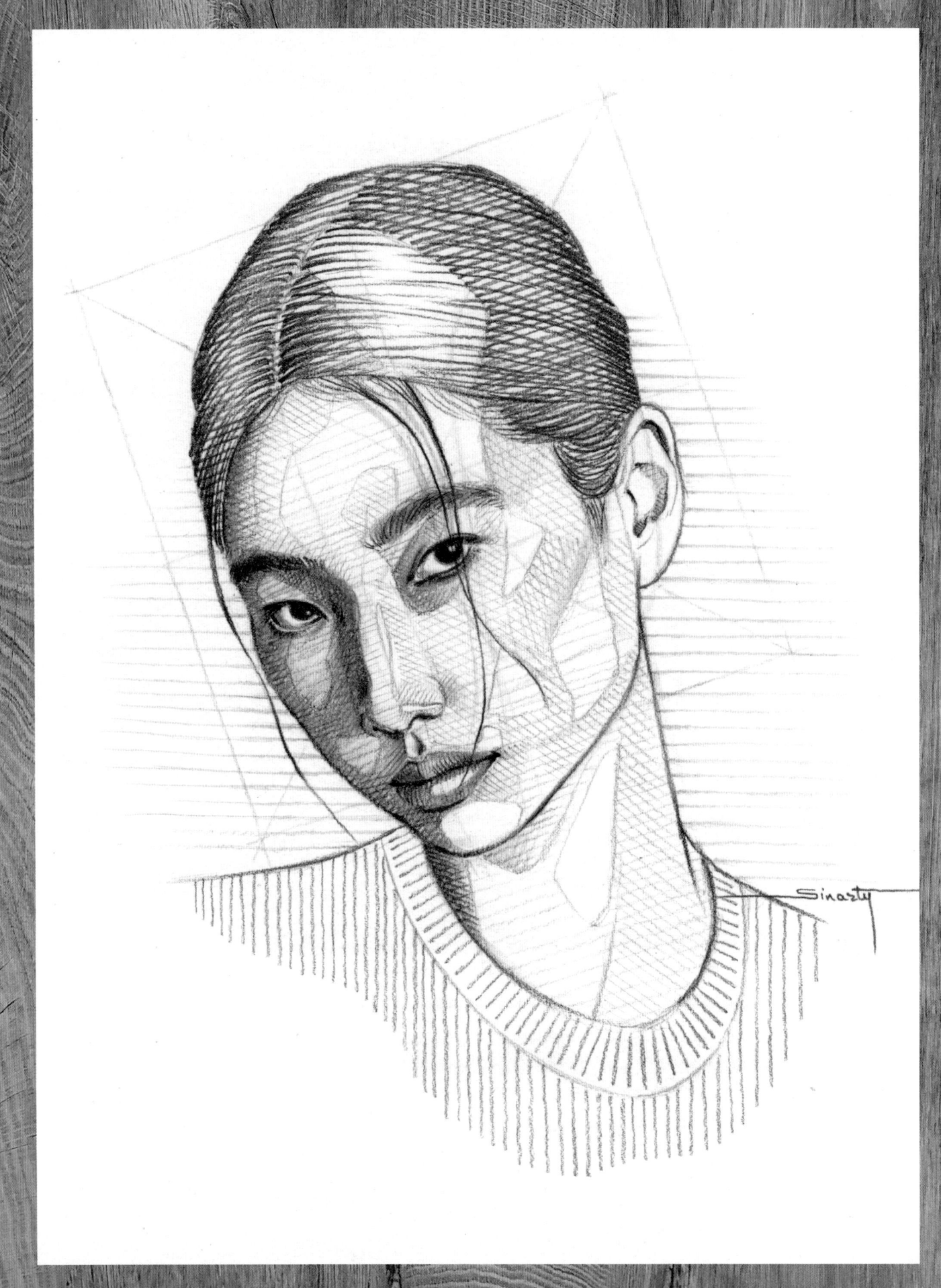

HOYEON JUNG

This portrait of HoYeon Jung, a South Korean actress and model, explores contour cross hatching. The subject has a symmetrical face with defined angles – the cross hatches will run in the direction of the shaded surfaces. Loose strands of hair falling over the face will be an interesting finishing touch to this quick and fun portrait.

Materials

- White sketching paper, 22.9 x 30.5cm (9 x 12in)
- Graphite pencils: 2B, 4B, 6B, 8B
- Mechanical pencil: 0.5mm
- Kneaded eraser
- Good-quality pencil sharpener

Techniques

- Proportion: Loomis head
- Shading: Contour cross hatching and blending

BASIC OUTLINING

1 Begin by drawing the Loomis head positioned towards the top of the canvas, tilted slightly anti-clockwise (see the inset thumbnail for guidance). Divide the square into quadrants, then into eighths, as a grid for more accurate proportions. Hoyeon has a slightly elongated face, so instead of a circle for the cranium, draw a vertically oblong ellipse.

2 Draw the side plane of the face, then draw a facial centreline that runs all the way down and beyond the ellipse as shown.

3 Complete the basic Loomis head by drawing the front plane and the jawline.

4 Draw the browline, nose line and a basic outline of the ear. Notice the outline of the right side of the face, which gives the cheek area some added volume.

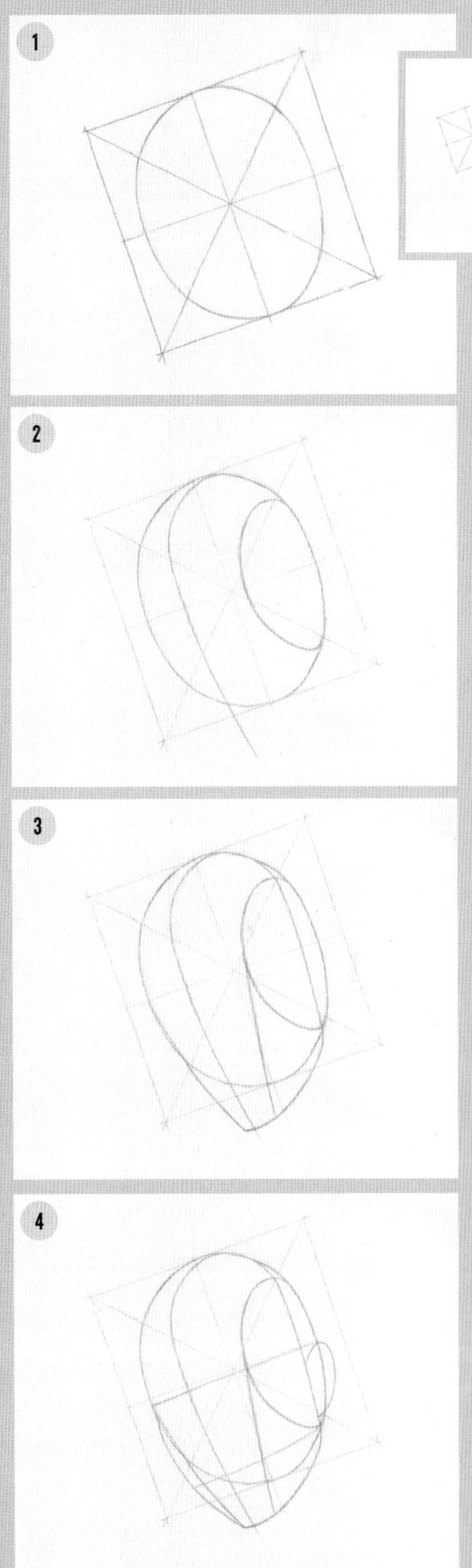

5 Draw the planes of the nose and eyes (*see* Proportion Techniques: The Loomis Method).

6 Draw the lips and the hairline. Keep the front of the hairline slightly lower than the top edge of the side plane.

7 Complete the construction by drawing a basic placement for the eyes and the neck.

OUTLINE DETAILING

While drawing the following steps, use a 2B graphite pencil and a light-medium hand (*see* Sketching Fundamentals: Pencil Exercises).

8 Begin the outline by detailing the nose.

9 Draw the eyebrow outlines and the details of the eyes.

10 Next, draw the basic outlines of the lips, hair and ears. Before proceeding further, check that the proportions are correct.

11 Finish the detailing by blocking in the value transition lines (shadows and highlights) on the face, hair and neck. Let's move on to the shading.

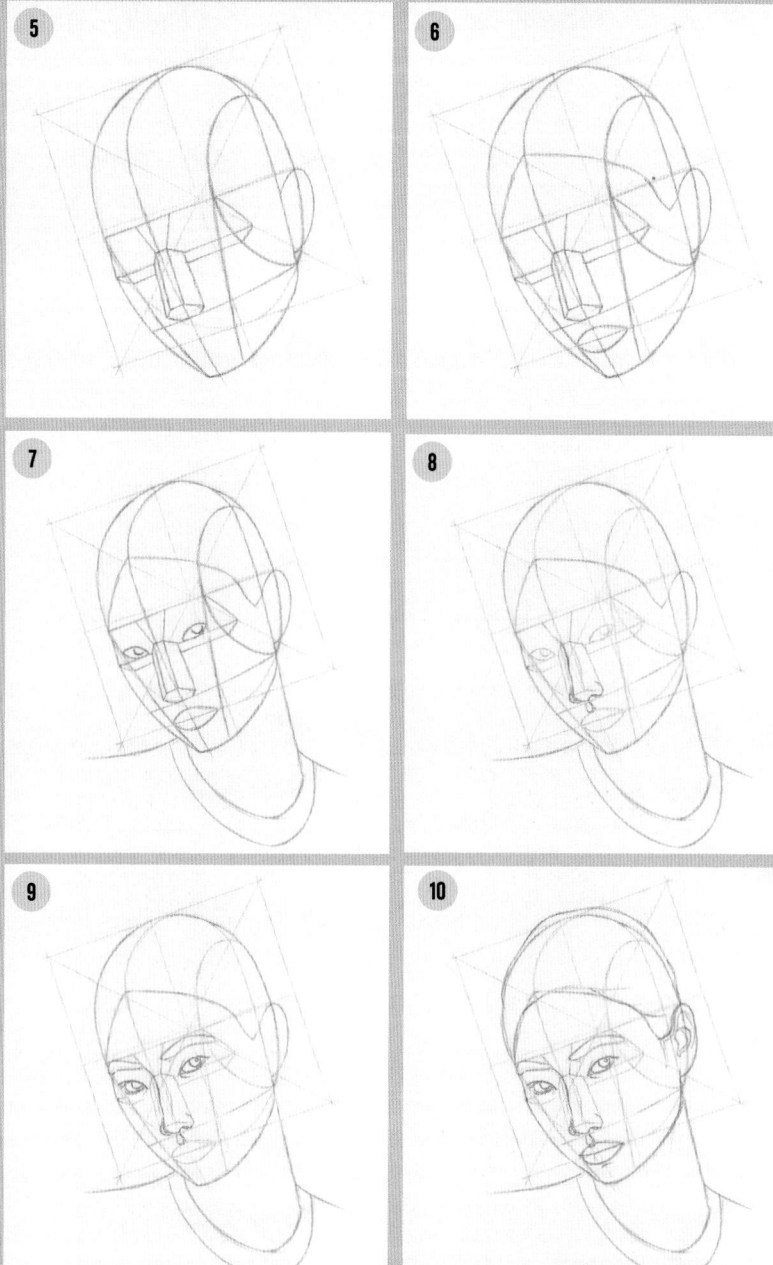

LIGHTEN LINES

Before shading, lighten the outlines by dabbing away excess graphite with a kneaded eraser. This allows the outlines to show up in our final portrait (see Tools & Materials: Erasing Tools).

GO STRAIGHT TO SHADING

Simply tracing the final outline drawing – Step 11 – provides an opportunity to jump ahead to practise shading (see Proportion Techniques: Freehand & Tracing).

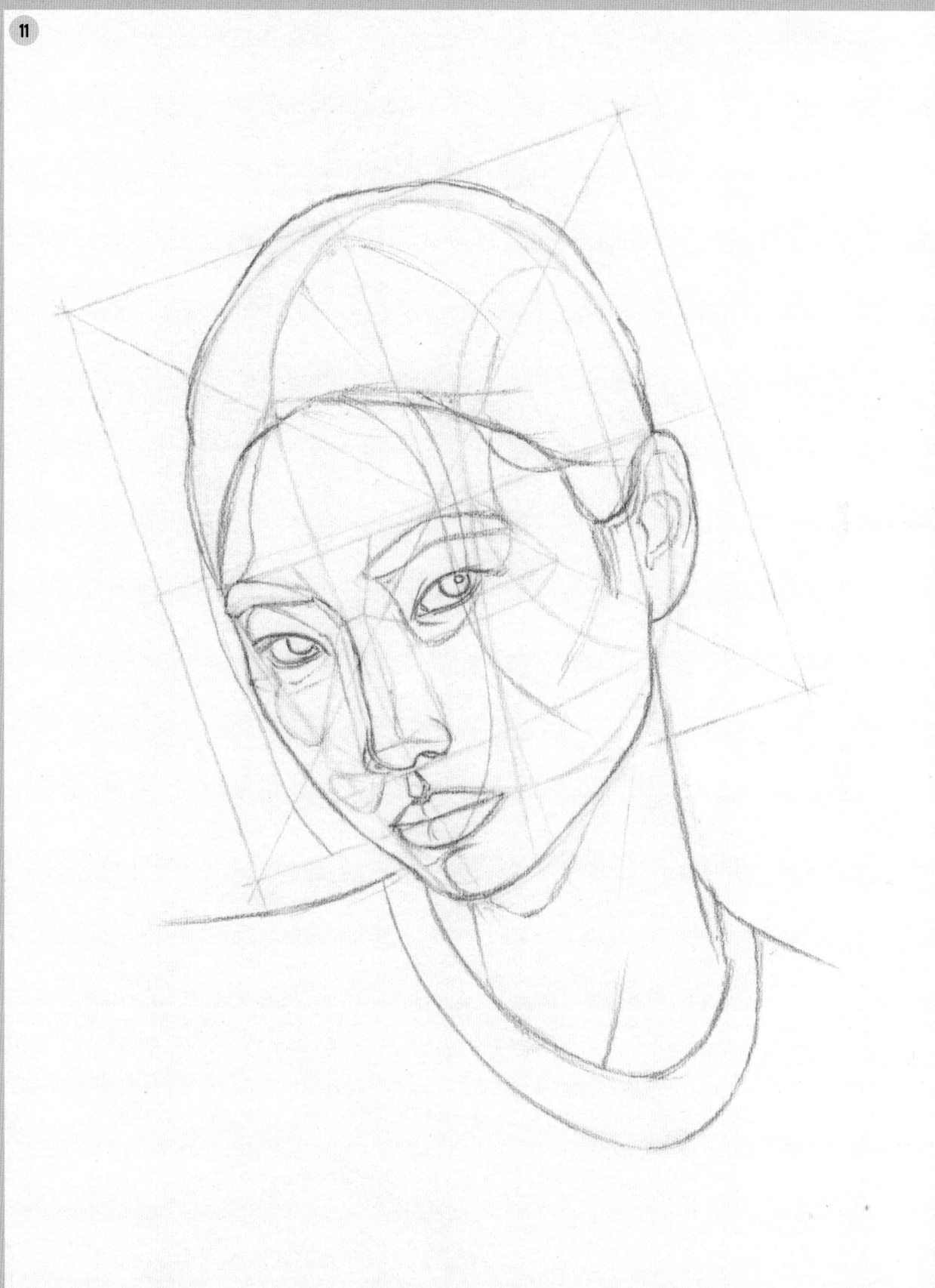

SHADING

At this point, you have completed the portrait construction and outline (either by following the previous Steps 1–11, or by simply tracing the image for Step 11).

1 Using a 2B pencil, shade the first layer of the right side of her face, including the neck. Choose a hatching direction for this first layer then keep this direction consistent throughout the shading process for all the first layers.

2 Use a 4B pencil for the second layer of cross hatching. Note the different directions of the cross hatch, which change according to the surface/contours of the face.

3 Shade the third layer with a 6B pencil. Shade the eyebrows and eye details in this step.

4 Repeat Steps 1–3 for the left side of the face. To begin, draw the first layer using a light-to-medium grip. Shade the second layer using a 2B pencil and the same grip.

This is because the right side of the face is in shadow, and the left side in the light. Leave the small highlighted areas unshaded.

5 Using a medium grip, add the cross hatching, following the contours. Make sure the value of this cross hatch is not darker than the right side of her face. Draw the left eye and eyebrow details.

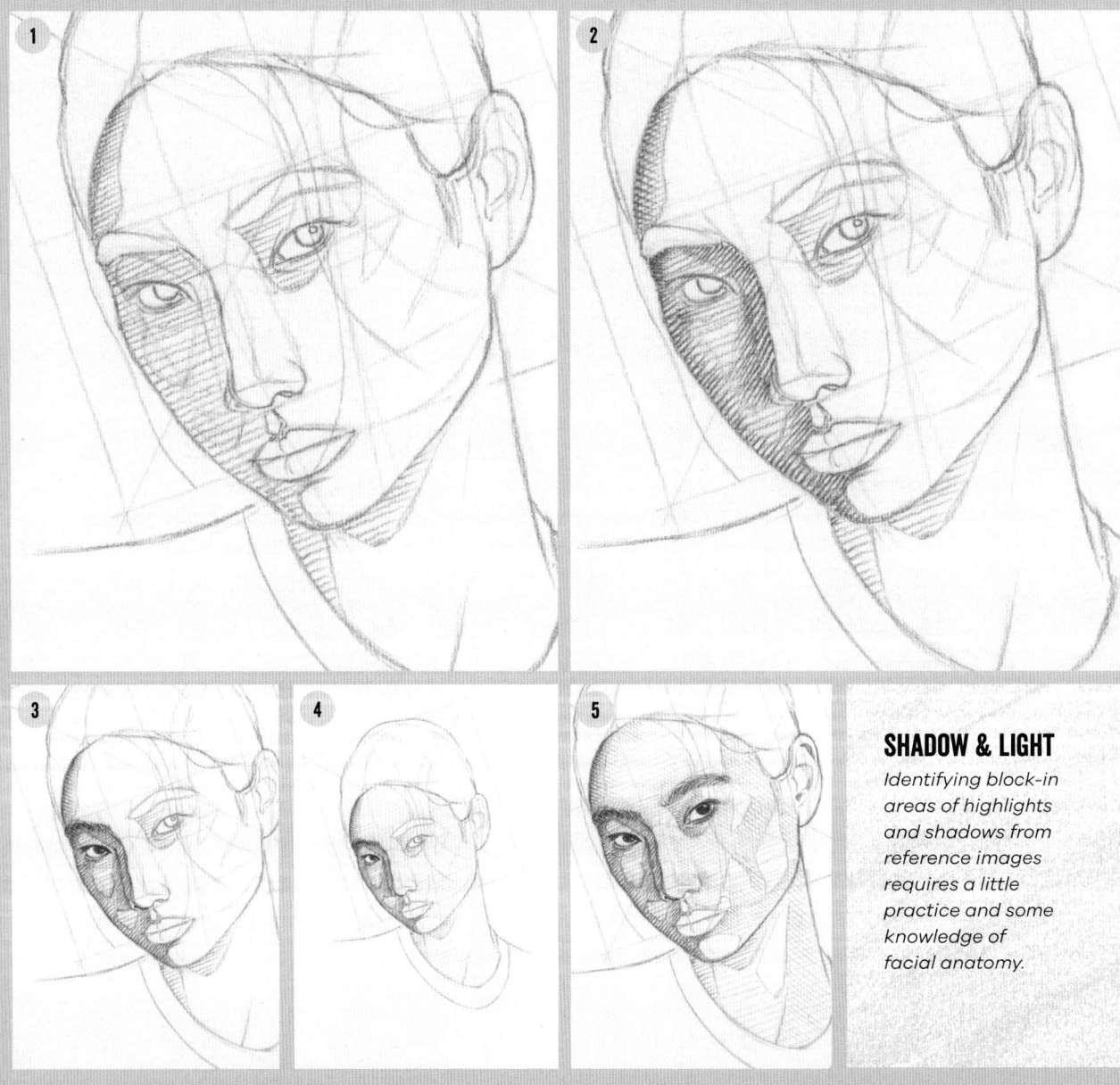

SHADOW & LIGHT

Identifying block-in areas of highlights and shadows from reference images requires a little practice and some knowledge of facial anatomy.

6 Draw the lips in the same way. The first layer uses vertical strokes instead of the horizontal strokes used for the rest of the face. This style choice separates the different surfaces of the face.

7 Use a 6B pencil for the darker cross hatches on the lips, the shadows of the neck and the right side of the face.

8 Move on to the hair. Keeping the highlighted region unshaded, use a medium-to-firm grip to draw the first layer of hatches.

9 Draw the second layer of hatches, following the direction of the hair. Draw stray hair strands falling around the face. Shade the clothes using the basic unidirectional hatching technique to keep things simple (*see* Sketching Fundamentals: Shading Techniques).

10 Refine the edges of the portrait and enhance the contrast. You can use a blending tool to shade the darker shadows of the portrait to add depth, but do not overdo this to preserve the contour cross hatching underneath. Finally, add the shadows of the strands of stray hair on her face – use a 2H pencil for a subtle effect. Horizontal background lines add a certain dynamic to the portrait.

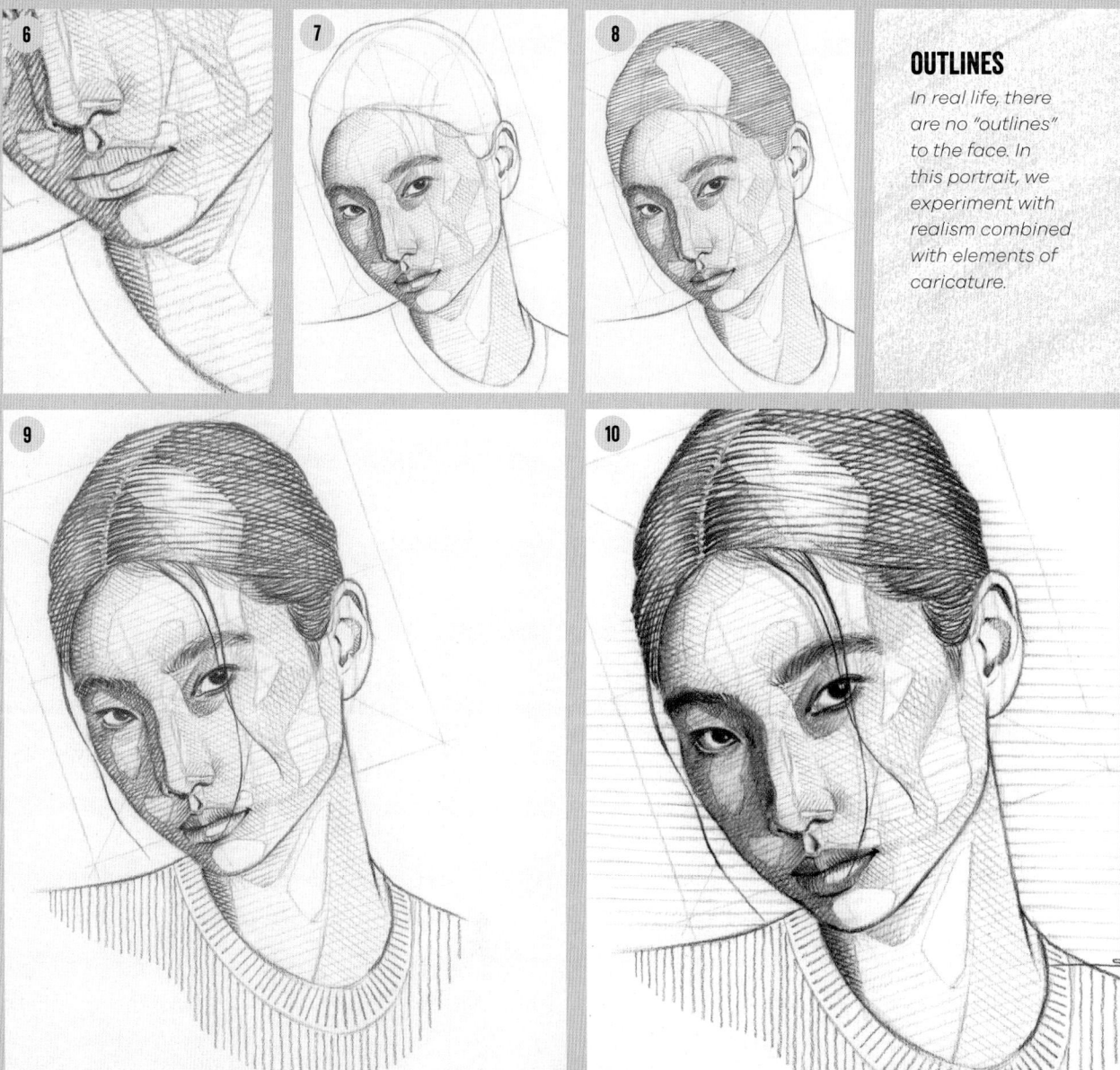

OUTLINES

In real life, there are no "outlines" to the face. In this portrait, we experiment with realism combined with elements of caricature.

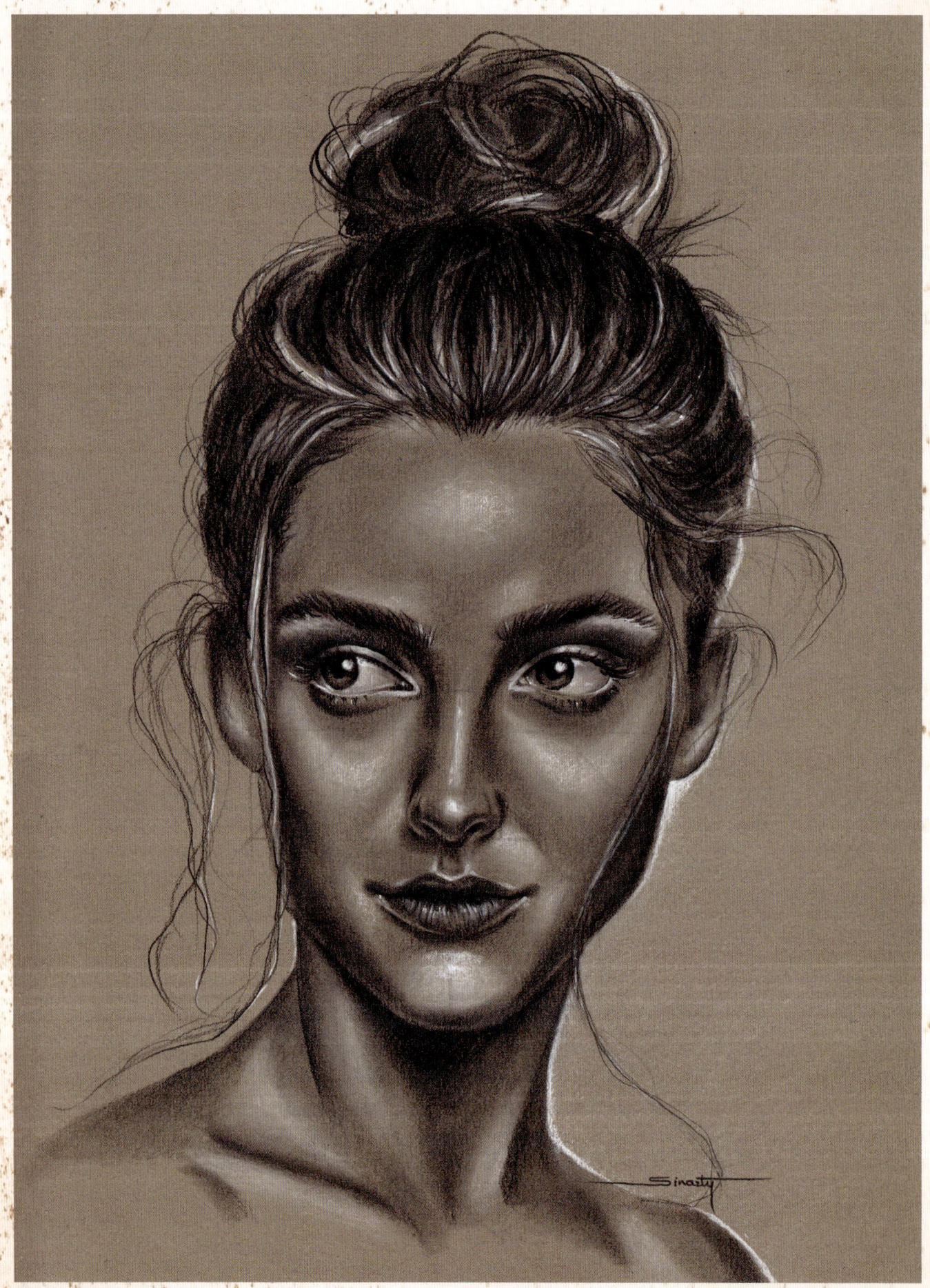

THE LOOK

This portrait is particularly interesting due to the subject's expression – there Is a mischievous curiosity in her look which will be a lot of fun to draw. The eyes, nose, lips and hair in this portrait are covered in more detail as part of the Facial Features section, which we will refer to while drawing.

Materials

- Toned tan sketching paper, 18.2 x 25.7cm (7¼ x 10in)
- Graphite pencils: 2B, 4B, 6B, 8B
- White charcoal pencil
- Paper stumps, cotton buds
- Kneaded eraser, pencil eraser
- Good-quality pencil sharpener, one-sided sharpening blade

Techniques

- Proportion: Geometric block-in
- Shading: Gradient blending

BASIC OUTLINING

1 Draw a square slightly above the middle of the page (see the inset thumbnail for guidance) – this will encompass the cranium. Draw the two diagonals of the square, and the horizontal centreline. This is the browline, while the bottom edge of the square is the nose line.

2 Draw the vertical centreline, extending it downwards to meet the horizontal chin line. Observe that the distance between browline and nose line is slightly larger than that of the nose line and the chin line.

3 Add guidelines for the overall area of the nose and the shape of the eyebrows as shown.

4 Using these guidelines, draw the planes of the nose, then the symmetrical pentagons for the eye socket placements.

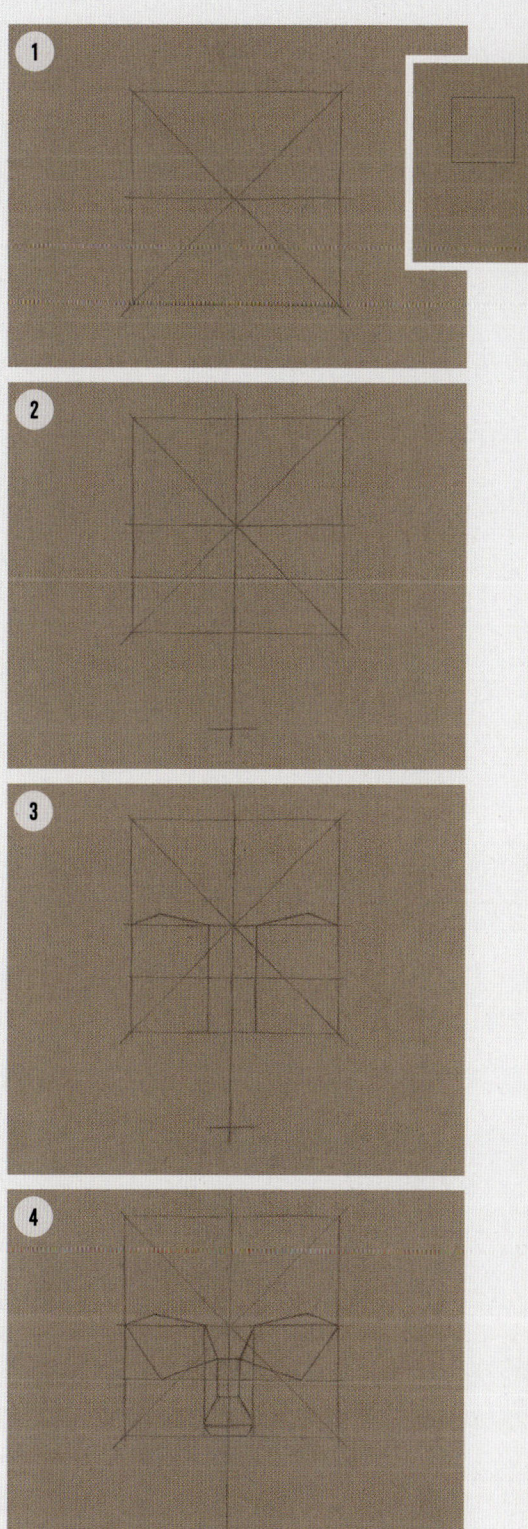

5 Draw the outline of the face. Note that it is not exactly symmetrical since the subject in the reference is looking slightly to her right.

6 Draw the basic shapes for the lips and the ears. Notice the bottom of the lip is in the centre of the nose line and the chin line.

7 Complete the basic outline by drawing the bun hairstyle, neck, and right-hand shoulder.

OUTLINE DETAILING

While drawing the following steps, use a 2B graphite pencil and a light-medium hand (*see* Sketching Fundamentals: Pencil Exercises).

8 Add the detail outlines of the eyebrows and the eyes enclosed in the eye-socket pentagons drawn in Step 4.

9 Add detail outlines of the nose and lips.

10 Detail the eyes, including the iris, pupil and the small highlight adjacent to the pupil. Don't forget the inner planes of the eyelids. Make sure the proportions of the facial features are correct at this point. For example, I corrected the outer part of the nostrils to be more tapering towards the top.

11 Add details to the ears and the hair. For the hair, ensure you capture the flow of the locks of hair tied up in a bun and the strands falling on either side of the face. Also notice that the lower lip is made slightly fainter in preparation for shading.

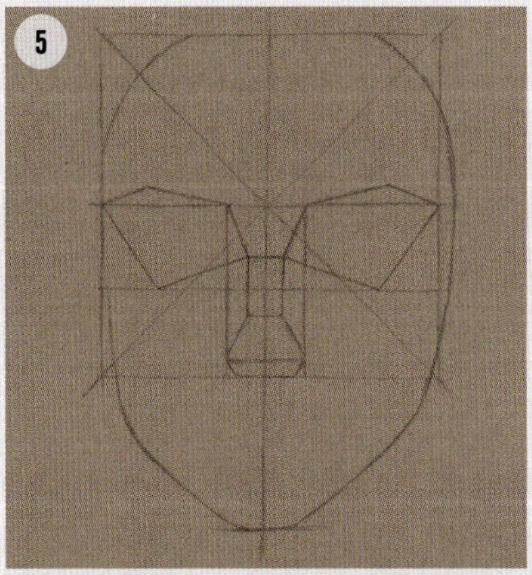

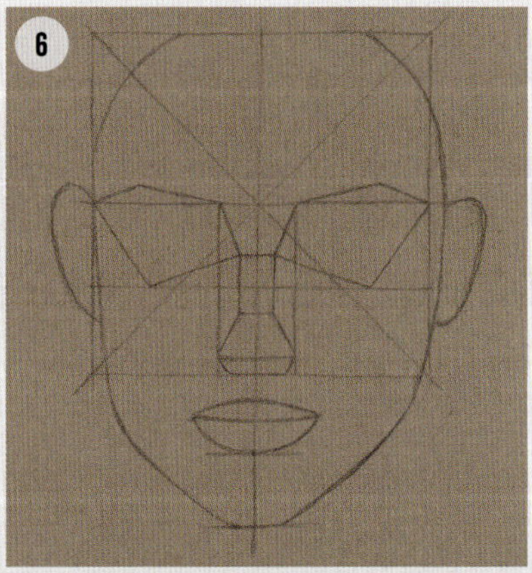

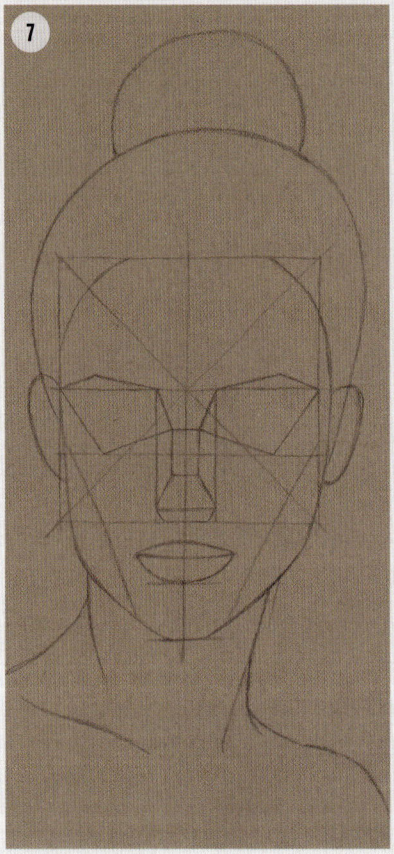

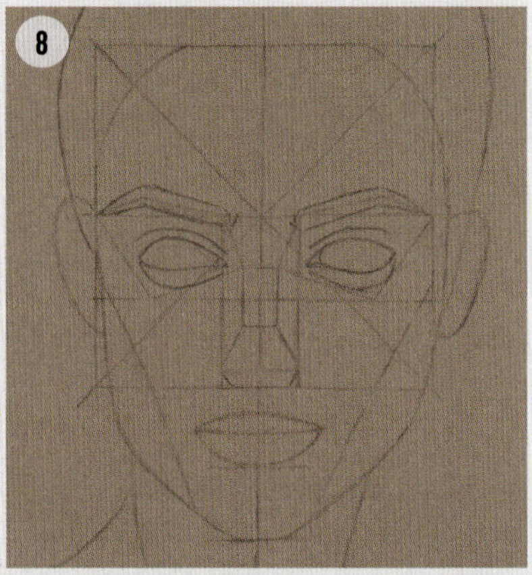

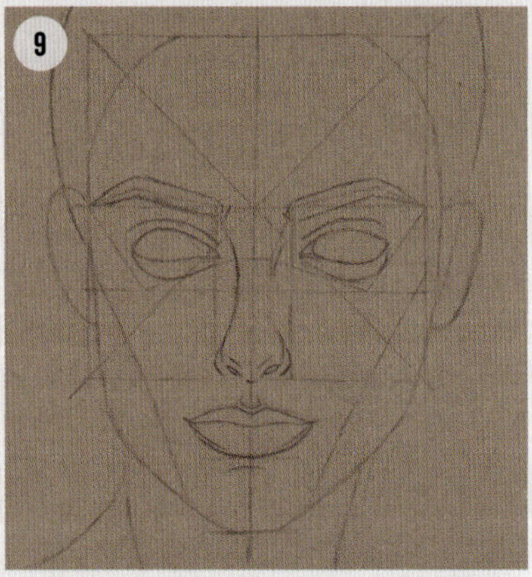

GO STRAIGHT TO SHADING

Simply tracing the final outline drawing – Step 11 – provides an opportunity to jump ahead to practise shading (see Proportion Techniques: Freehand & Tracing).

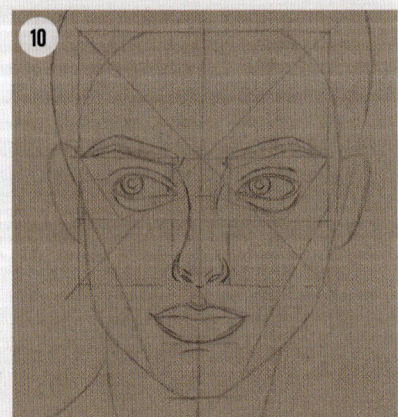

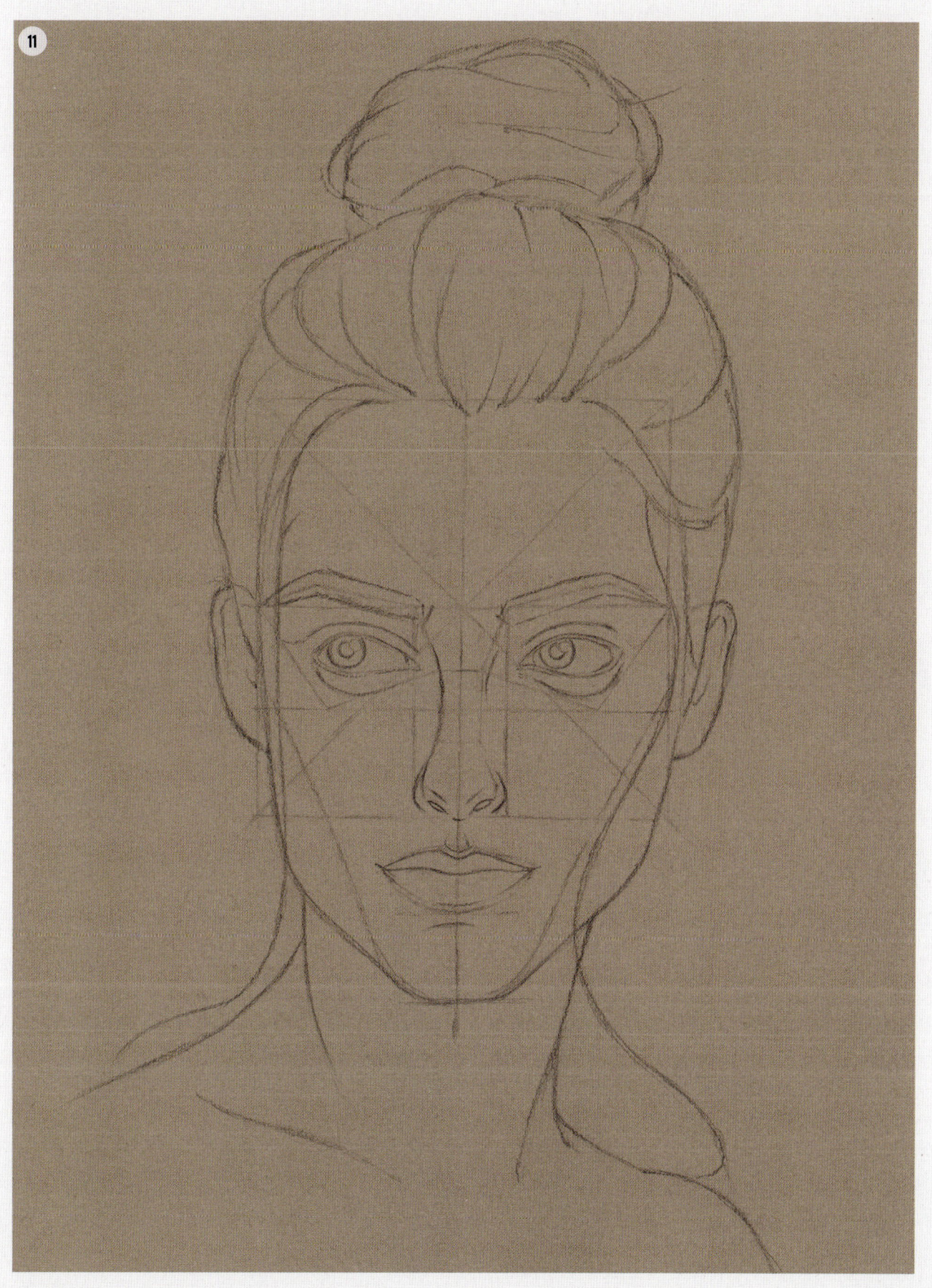

SHADING

At this point, you have completed the portrait construction and outline (either by following the previous Steps 1–11, or by simply tracing the image for Step 11).

1 Begin with the eyes (*see* Facial Features: Eyes). Use a white charcoal pencil to add highlights to the right eye.

Then use the 4B pencil with medium pressure to shade the eyebrows, iris and bottom eyelid. Blend these together using a paper stump.

2 Draw the individual hairs of the eyebrow following the movement (*see* Facial Features: Eyes). Then darken the shadow areas of the eye with a 6B pencil and blend using a paper stump.

3 Finally, use an 8B pencil to add eyelashes (*see* Facial Features: Eyes) and sharpen other details of the eye.

4 Repeat Step 1 for the left eye and blend as before.

5 Complete the left eye by repeating Steps 2 and 3.

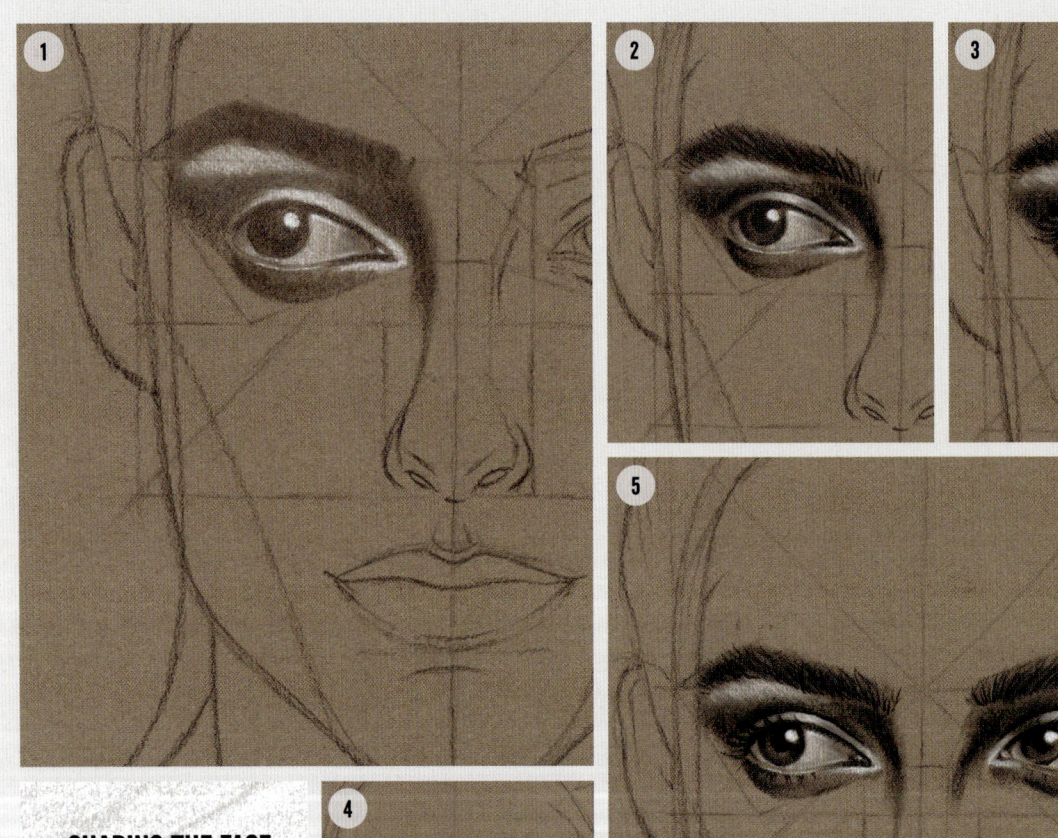

SHADING THE FACE

For additional guidance and techniques for shading the various parts of the face and hair, refer to the Facial Features section.

6 Moving to the nose, add highlights down the bridge and the tip using a white charcoal pencil (*see* Facial Features: Nose). Use a 4B pencil to evenly shade the rest of the nose, and blend the values with a paper stump.

7 Use a 6B pencil to add shadows to the nose. With a paper stump, blend these with the midtones.

8 Next, use an 8B pencil to sharpen the shape of the nose and darken the value extremes, such as the nostrils.

9 With the same shading technique, use the white charcoal and 4B pencil to shade the lips in even tones, then blend them together using a paper stump (*see* Facial Features: Lips).

10 Use a 6B pencil to add the dark tones between and under the lips. Use smaller stumps to blend these with the midtones

11 Sharpen the details of the lips further using the 8B pencil. Add lighter areas of highlights to the lips using a kneaded eraser to create a three-dimensional effect.

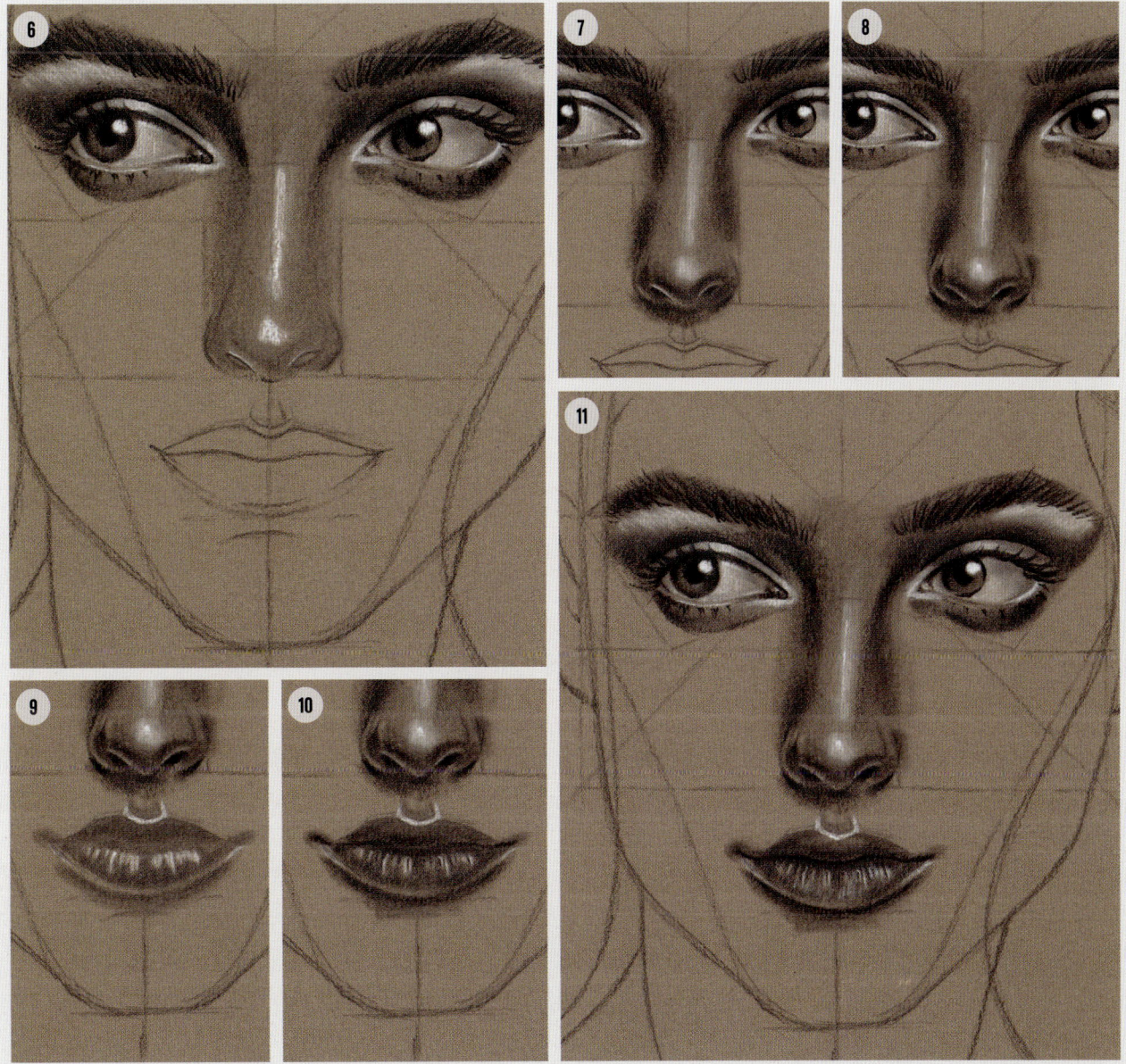

12 Use white charcoal pencil to depict the highlights on the forehead, cheeks, ears and chin. Then shade the rest of the face using a 2B pencil with light-to-medium pressure grip.

13 Use a blending tool such as a paper stump or cotton bud (*see* Sketching Fundamentals: Blending Tools) to blend the light tones with the whites.

14 Add shadows below the cheeks, chin and on the ears using a 6B pencil. Blend these darker tones with the lighter tones to create midtones.

15 Now move onto the neck, shading it with white charcoal pencil and 4B pencil. Use a medium grip.

16 Blend these midtones together using a paper stump. You can use the flat part of the stump for blending over larger areas. Don't forget to clean the stump using a sandpaper strip (*see* Sketching Fundamentals: Blending Tools) before blending into the whites.

17 Add shadows under the chin and other areas of the neck using a 6B pencil. Then use the stump to blend the darker tones with the midtones. If required, darken the shadows further with an 8B pencil and re-blend until you reach the desired values.

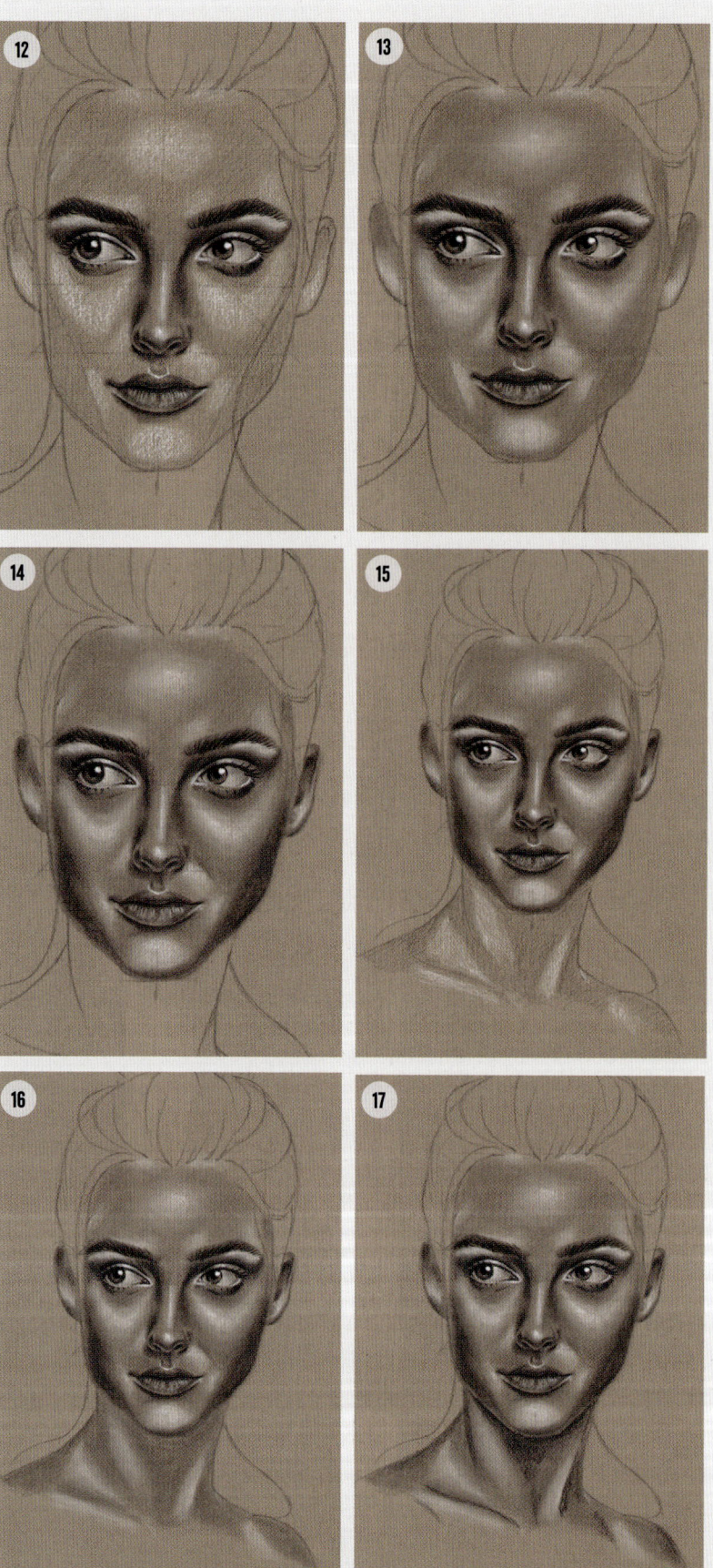

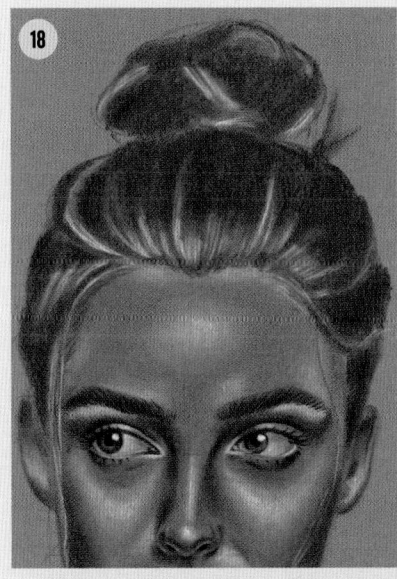

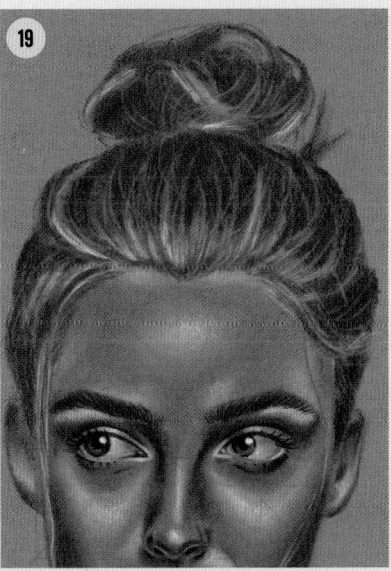

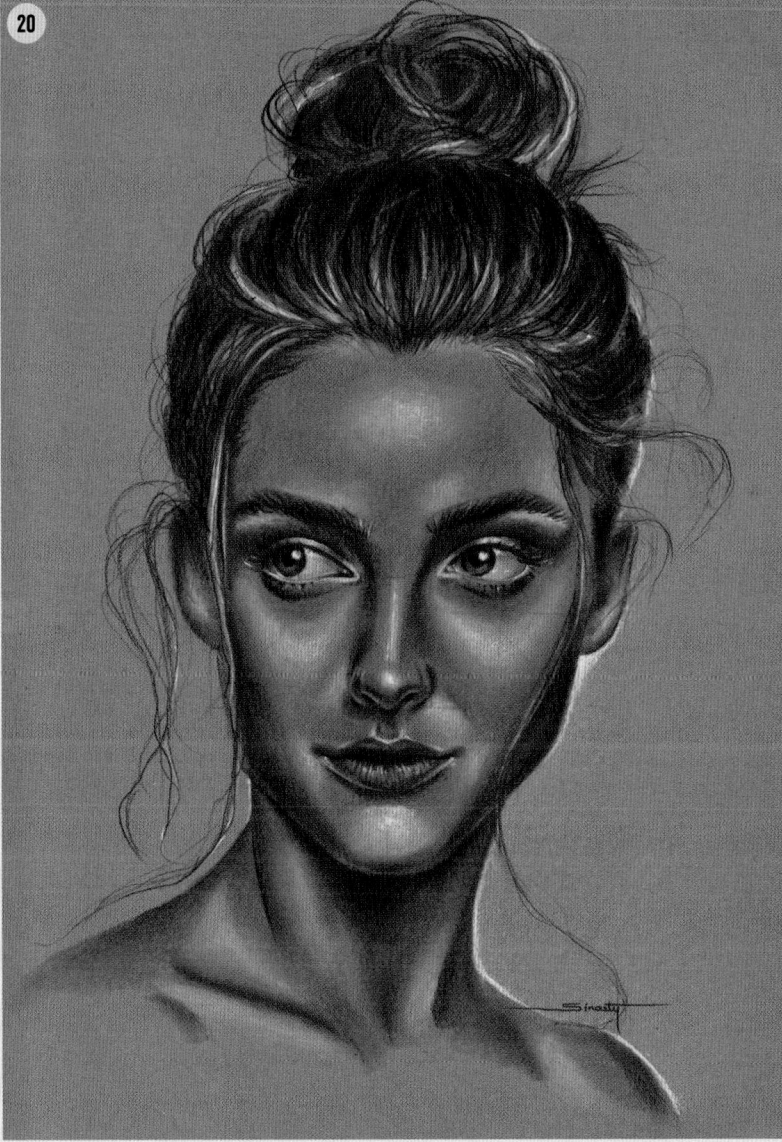

18 Use the white charcoal and a 6B pencil with medium-hard grip to shade the hair, following its movement (*see Facial Features: Hair*). Use a paper stump to blend these values together.

19 Use a pencil eraser to add individual hair-strands.

20 Finally, use an 8B pencil to add details to the hair, including the outer stray hair and the strands along the side of the face. Go over the entire sketch and correct any proportions or improve the contrast to your liking. In this final step, observe that the areas near the eyes are shaded to be slightly darker. You can also add these details using the graphite left on the paper stump from blending. In addition, darken the shadows near the ears, cheeks and lips if needed. I also added a few highlights using the white charcoal pencil near the eyebrows and eyelashes.

ILLUMINATING CONTRAST

In the finished portrait (Step 20) note the highlighted outlines near the ear, neck and shoulder. The highlights are used to provide contrast between the shadowy areas of the portrait and the background. The contrast adds depth to the drawing and pops the subject out of the frame, creating focus.

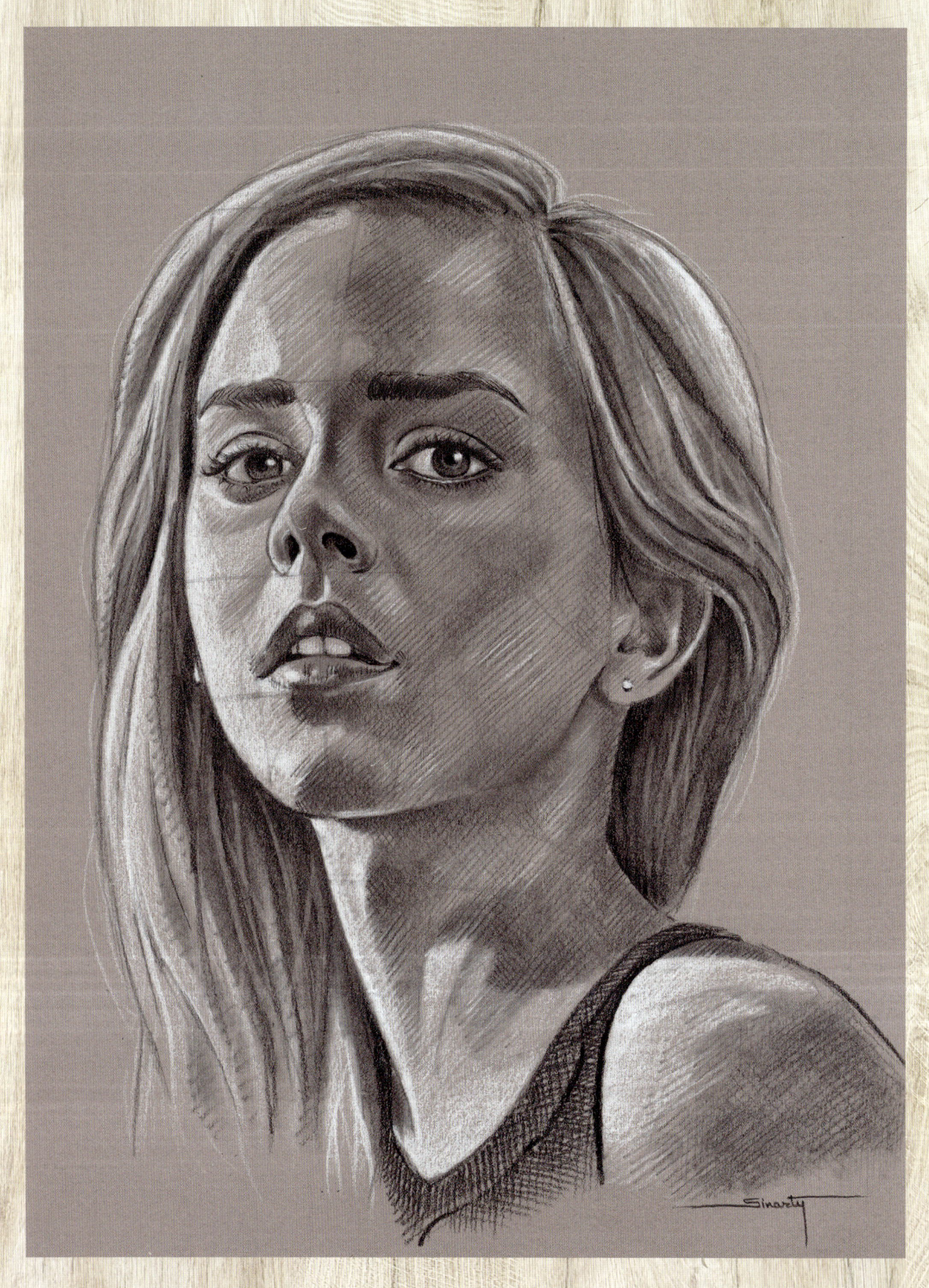

EMMA WATSON

An accomplished actress and activist, this portrait offers the opportunity to capture the grace, intelligence and strength that Emma embodies, both on and off the screen. It will also be an exciting challenge to recreate her wondrous expression. Let's begin!

Materials

- Toned grey sketching paper, 18.2 x 25.7cm (7¼ x 10in)
- Graphite pencils: 2H, 2B, 4B, 6B, 8B
- White charcoal pencil
- Paper stumps
- Kneaded eraser, pencil eraser
- Good-quality pencil sharpener, one-sided sharpening blade

Techniques

- Proportion: Loomis cuboid
- Shading: Cross hatching and blending

BASIC OUTLINING

1 Draw a curved vertical rectangle towards the left of the canvas (see the inset thumbnail for guidance) – this will be the frontal plane of the face. Divide it into six sections starting with the vertical centreline – this line is not perfectly central due to perspective. Add the browline and nose line. The forehead-to-brow, brow-to-nose and nose-to-chin distances keep increasing slightly as the chin of the subject is slightly tilted up.

2 Draw the bottom and side planes – think of this cuboid as being slightly above your eye level. Notice the lines are not parallel to each other and appear to be meeting a vanishing point in the bottom right of the paper.

3 Extend all the remaining guidelines to each plane.

4 With the cuboid complete, draw the circle for the side-plane of the head. This circle appears to go along the side surface of the cuboid making it not a perfect circle, but a vertical ellipse.

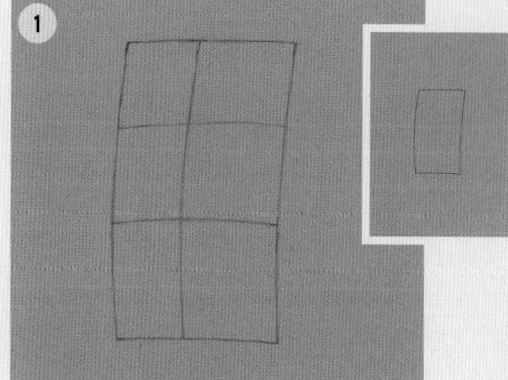

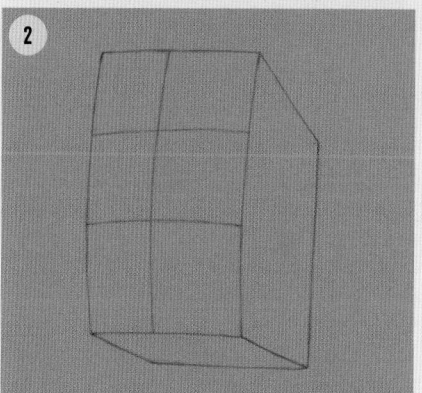

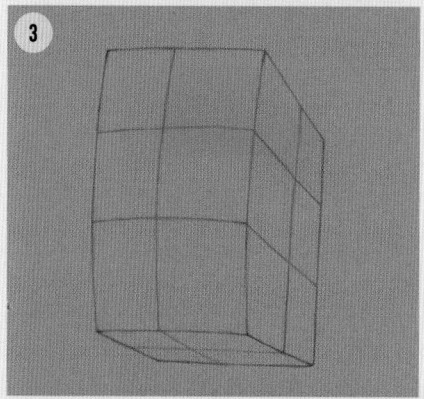

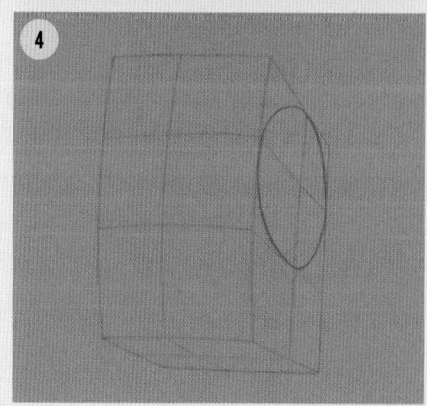

5 Draw a general outline of the face, with the chin enclosed within the front surface of the cuboid.

6 Draw a horizontal line between the browline and the nose line. This is the eyeline which extends back to give us the start of the ear (*see* Proportion Techniques: The Loomis Method). Then draw a line halfway between the nose line and the chin line. This will be the bottom lip line.

7 With the guidelines defined, draw the planes of the nose as viewed from beneath (*see* Facial Features: Nose). Then draw the basic shapes of the eyebrows and the eyes (*see* Facial Features: Eyes).

8 Draw the basic shapes of the upper and lower lips as well as a rough outline of the hair.

OUTLINE DETAILING

While drawing the following steps, use a 2B graphite pencil and a light-medium hand (*see* Sketching Fundamentals: Pencil Exercises).

9 Detailing begins with the nose. This is a three-quarter bottom view of the nose (*see* Facial Features: Nose).

10 Next, draw the outlines of the iris and the front teeth.

11 Add details to the ears and draw a small horizontal line to mark the start of the chin.

12 In the final step of this stage, detail the hair, complete the neck and the shoulders, and depict shadows and highlights of the face and the eyes.

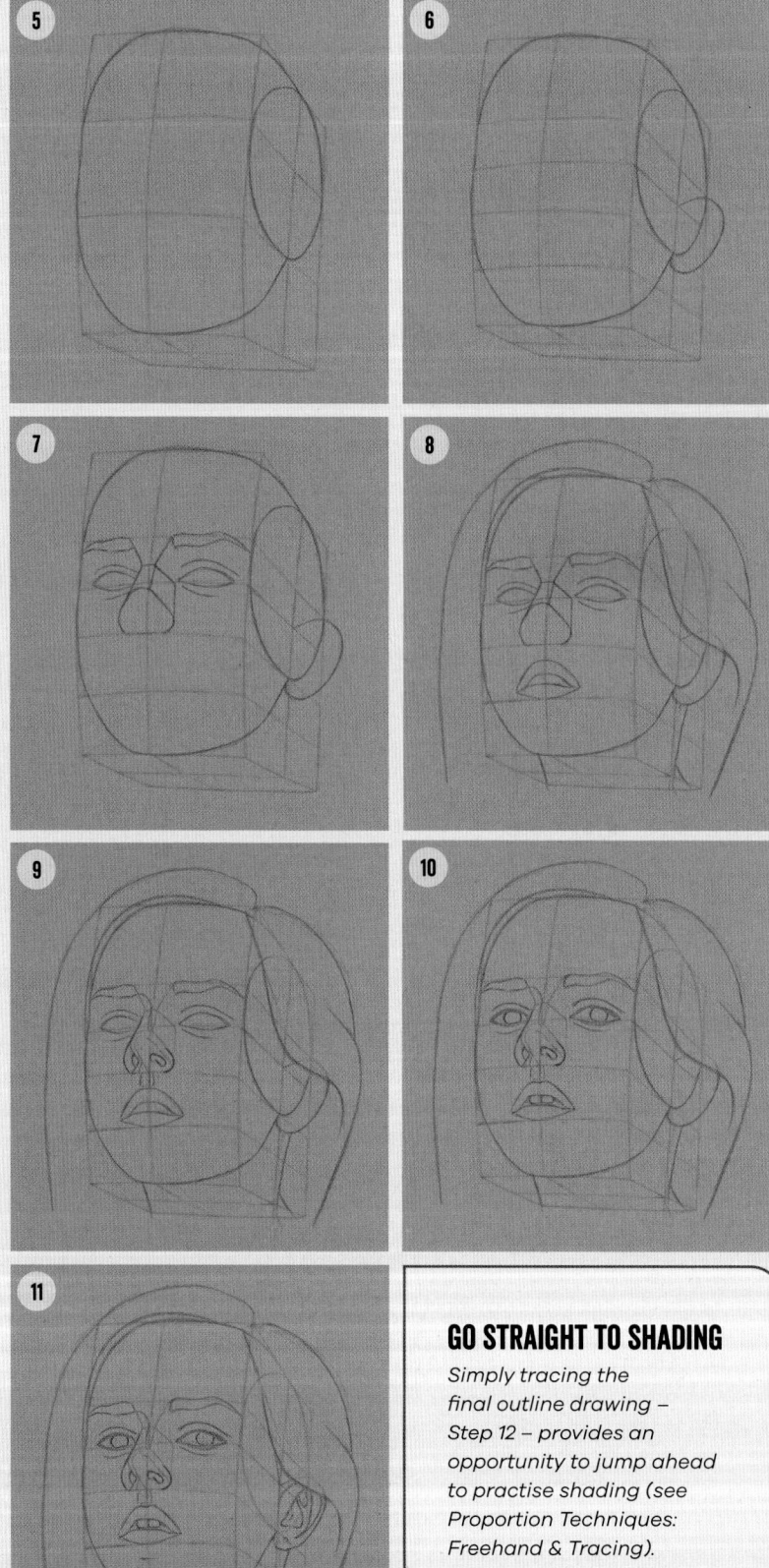

GO STRAIGHT TO SHADING

Simply tracing the final outline drawing – Step 12 – provides an opportunity to jump ahead to practise shading (see Proportion Techniques: Freehand & Tracing).

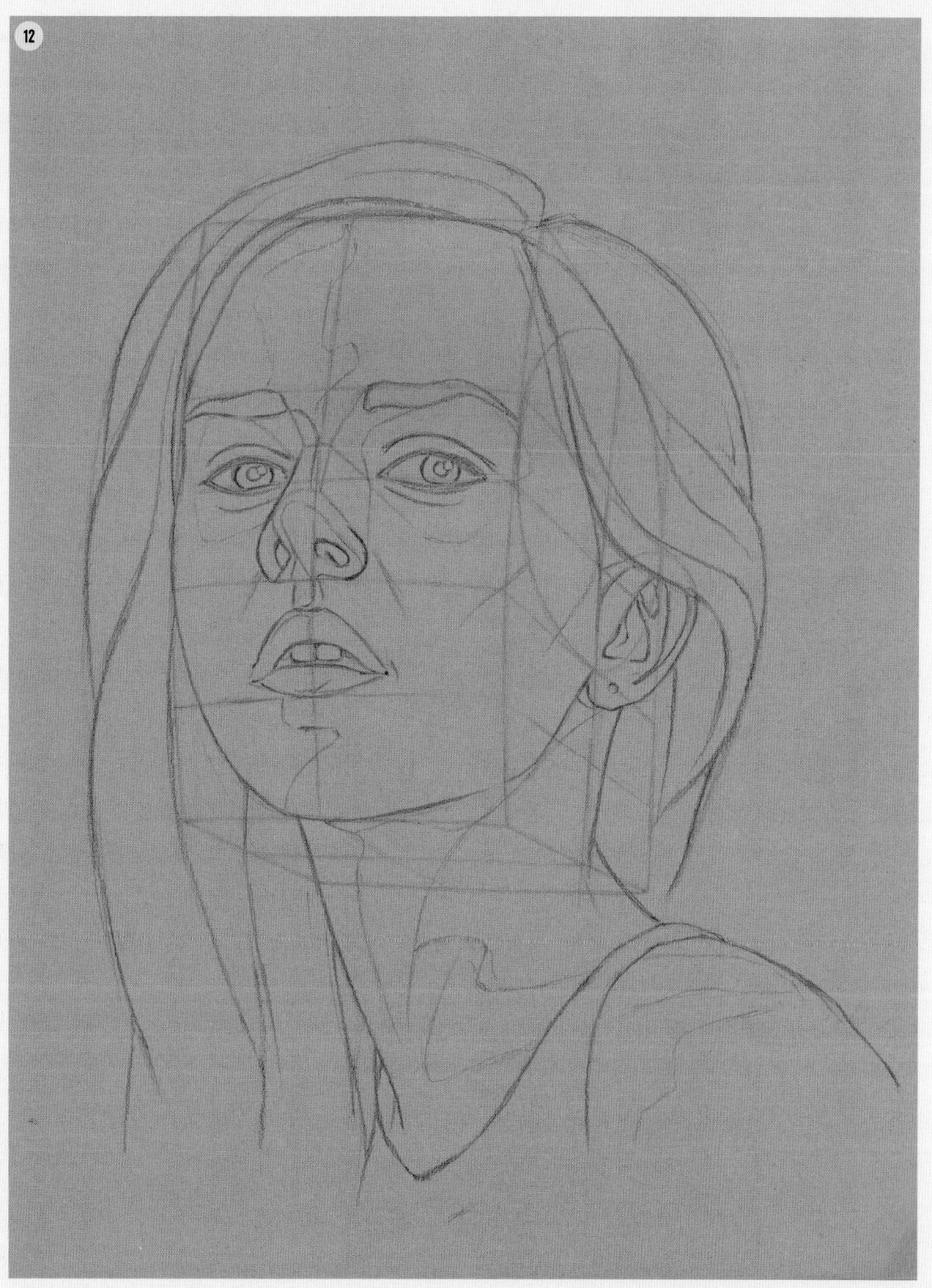

SHADING

At this point, you have completed the portrait construction and outline (either by following the previous Steps 1–12, or by simply tracing the image for Step 12).

1 Use the white charcoal pencil and a light hand to depict the highlights along the face, neck, shoulder and hair.

2 Use some pressure this time with your white pencil to make the light value extreme of your sketch pop out.

3 Use an 8B (or the darkest pencil you have) to define the dark value extreme for the sketch. These include the pupils, nostrils and the negative space of the mouth, among others. Also, shade in the darkest parts of the hair and hatch in the texture on her top.

4 Now focus on the skin. Use a 2B pencil and medium pressure to begin the first layer of shading. Take your time with this hatching.

5 Use a slightly darker 4B pencil as a second layer to depict some darker regions of the face, neck and shoulder. Make sure the hatching direction of this layer matches the first layer.

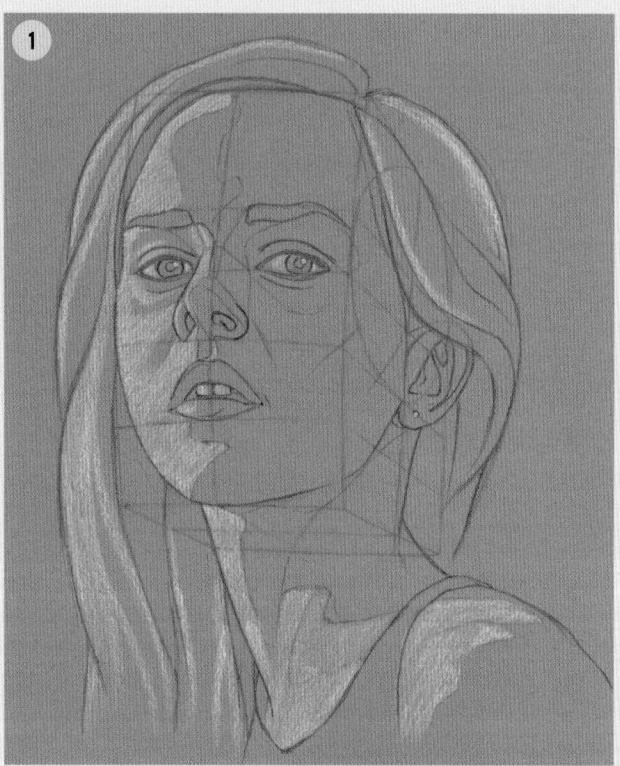

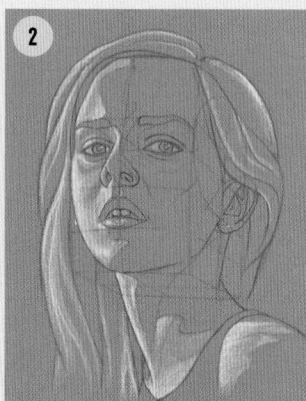

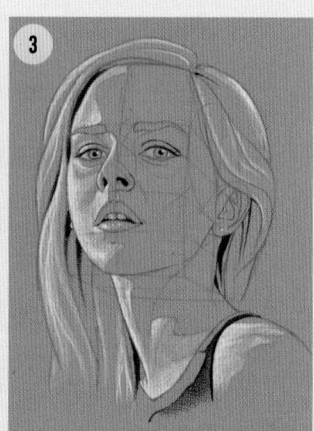

VALUE EXTREMES

To define your value extremes, start with the darkest and lightest parts of your drawing and work inwards on your value scale.

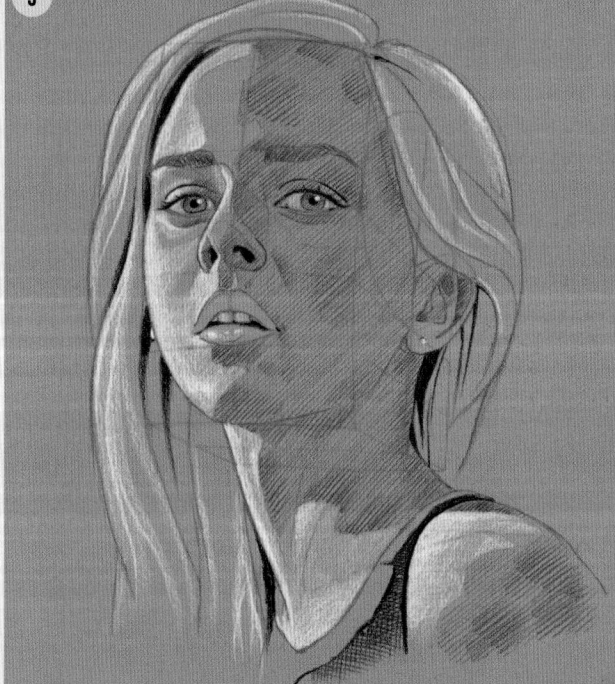

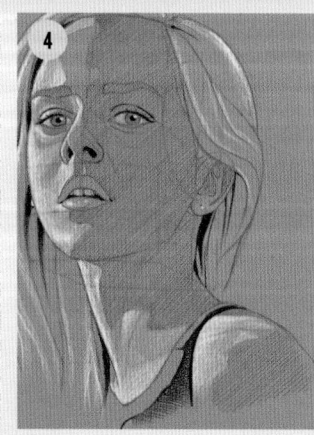

6 Use a 6B pencil and medium pressure to focus detailing around the eyes. Use cross hatching technique to provide some depth to the darker areas. Also shade in the iris (*see* Facial Features: Eyes).

7 Use similar cross hatching technique to shade darker regions under the nose, lips and the neck.

8 Shade the lips using a 4B pencil and shade the hair using the hatching technique.

9 Use the paper stumps to blend the graphite making sure to still retain the hatching underneath.

10 Finally, go over your entire sketch again to refine your proportions and sharpen your edges. Make changes to match the expression to your reference. Use the white charcoal pencil to hatch some last-minute highlights on Emma's forehead, nose, cheek and neck areas, as I have.

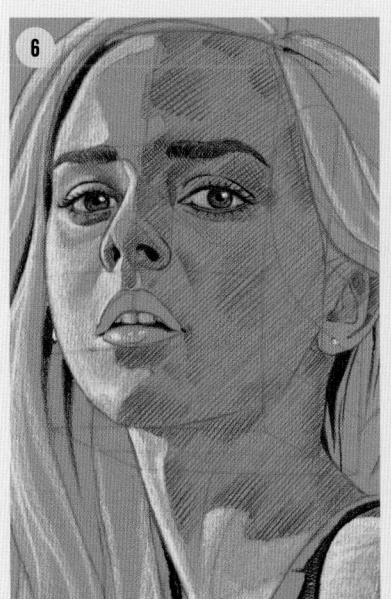

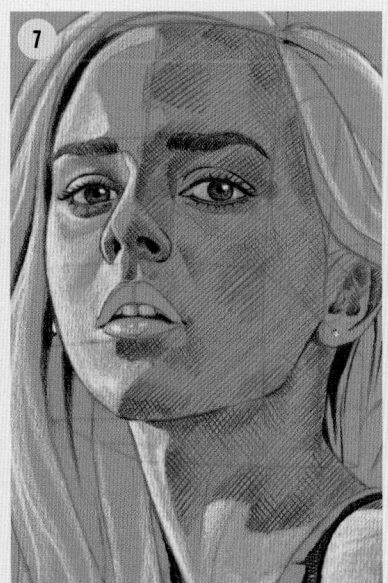

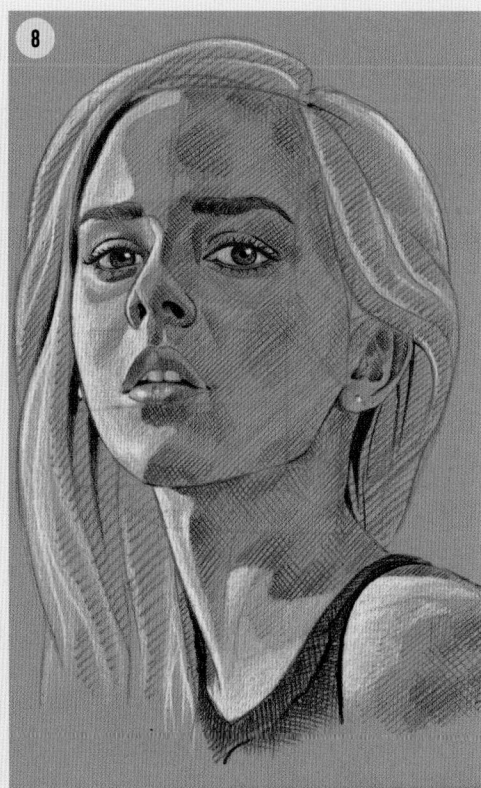

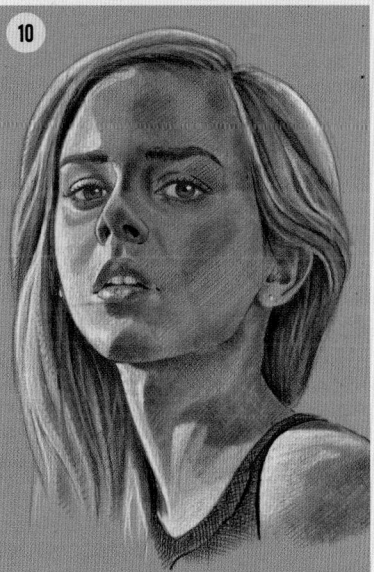

REFINING THE EXPRESSION

Slight changes to the eyes, eyebrows and lips can significantly alter the expression of a face. Keep going back to your reference to observe and match these subtle differences. Practise will make you an overall observant artist.

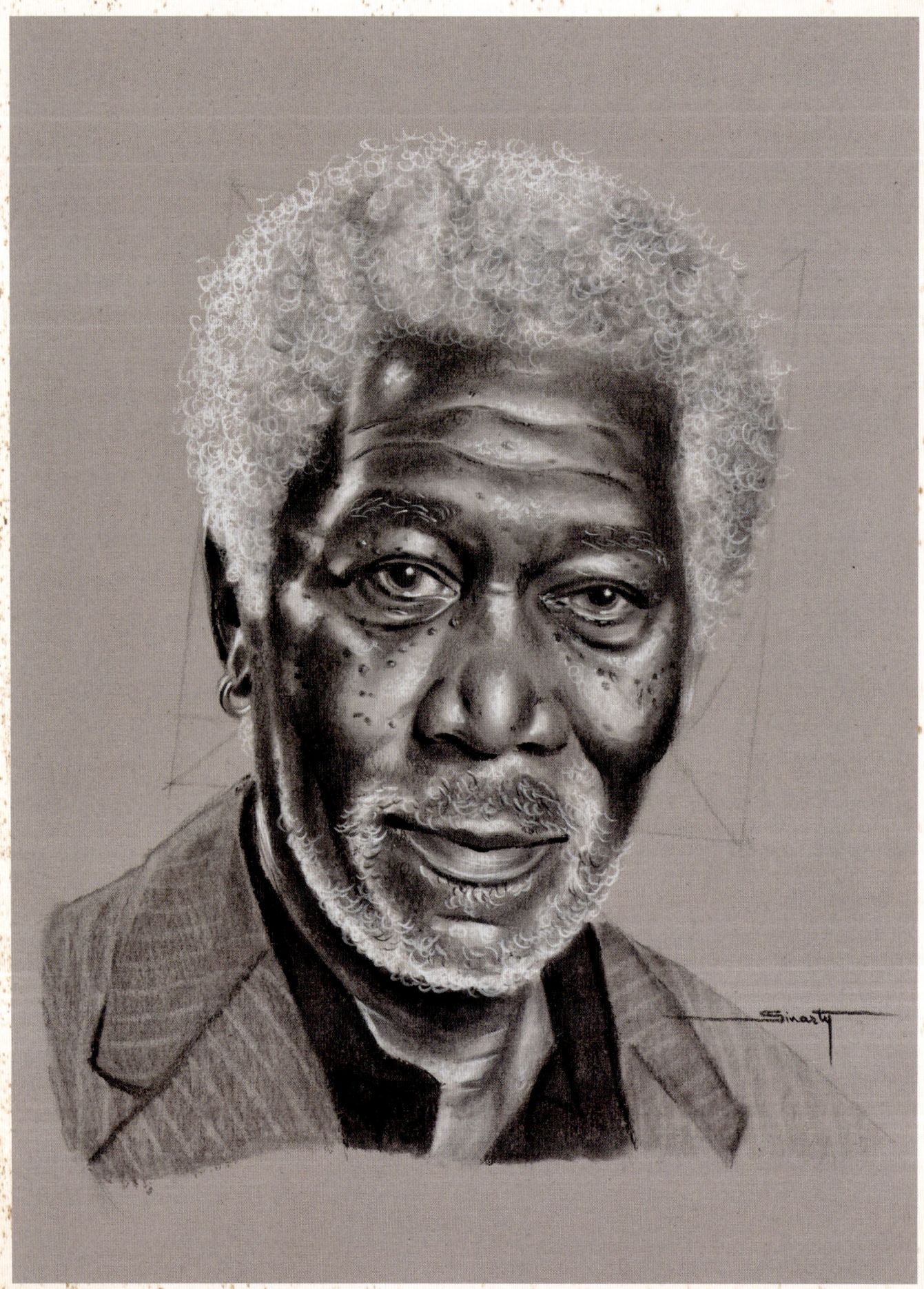

MORGAN FREEMAN

Veteran actor Morgan Freeman has many distinctive features that will make your drawing easily recognizable. The shading process requires patience, but the results will be worth it.

Materials

- Toned grey sketching paper, 18.2 x 25.7cm (7¼ x 10in)
- Graphite pencil: 2B
- Black charcoal pencils and charcoal powder
- White charcoal pencil
- Kneaded eraser, pencil eraser
- Paper stumps, cotton swabs, sponge brush
- Kneaded eraser, pencil eraser
- Good-quality pencil sharpener, one-sided sharpening blade

Techniques

- Proportion: Block-in
- Shading: Squiggles and gradient blending

BASIC OUTLINING

1 Draw a square, turned a few degrees clockwise, above the middle of the page (see the inset thumbnail for guidance). Divide the square into eighths and draw an enclosed circle.

2 The horizontal centreline is the browline. On the centre vertical line, mark the eyeline, nose line and chin line. The head is turned slightly to the left, so represent this angle with a second vertical line placed slightly to the right of the first. Extend this vertical line down to the chin line.

3 Mark the basic outline of the face as an elongated oval that tapers slightly towards the chin.

4 Draw an outline of Morgan's hair and ear. For the nose, add markings equally spaced on either side of the off-centre vertical line. Note that the background square guidelines are lighter than the face structural guidelines.

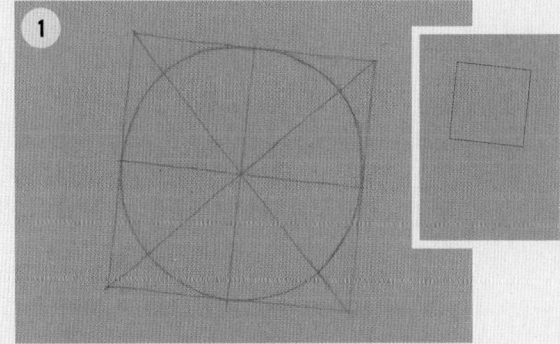

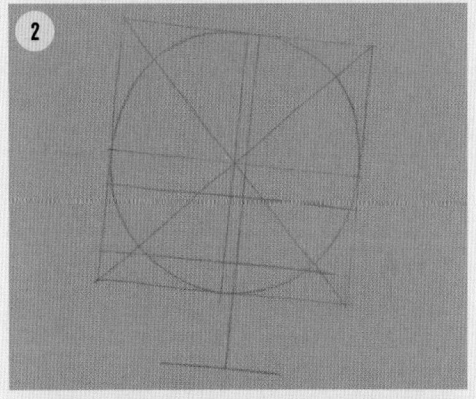

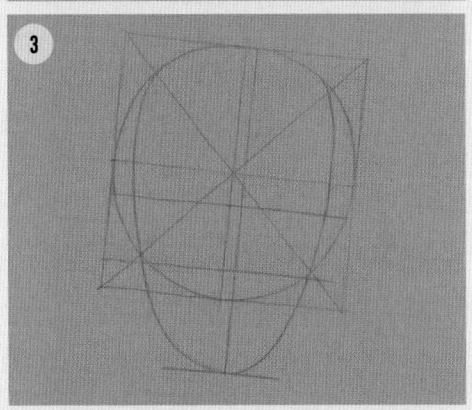

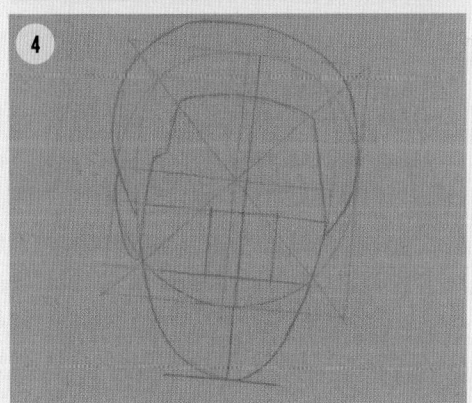

5 Within the markings made in the previous step, block in the eye sockets and a triangular shape for the nose.

6 Draw simple outlines, starting with the eyes, nose and lips. Keep these outlines basic for now – there is no need for finer details at this stage.

7 Add two lines from the eye socket block-ins to indicate the side planes of the face and mark the forehead. Add a horizontal line to indicate the start of the chin, and draw the outline of the suit.

OUTLINE DETAILING

While drawing the following steps, use a 2B graphite pencil and a light-medium hand (*see* Sketching Fundamentals: Pencil Exercises).

8 Starting with the eyes and the eyebrows, begin to outline more details.

9 At this point, make sure all the proportions of the features of the face are correct. I fixed the proportions of the nose and detailed the lips as shown.

10 Now, we draw the facial hair and some markings for the shadows and wrinkles on the face. Also, don't forget the earring.

GO STRAIGHT TO SHADING

Simply tracing the final outline drawing – Step 10 – provides an opportunity to jump ahead to practise shading (see Proportion Techniques: Freehand & Tracing).

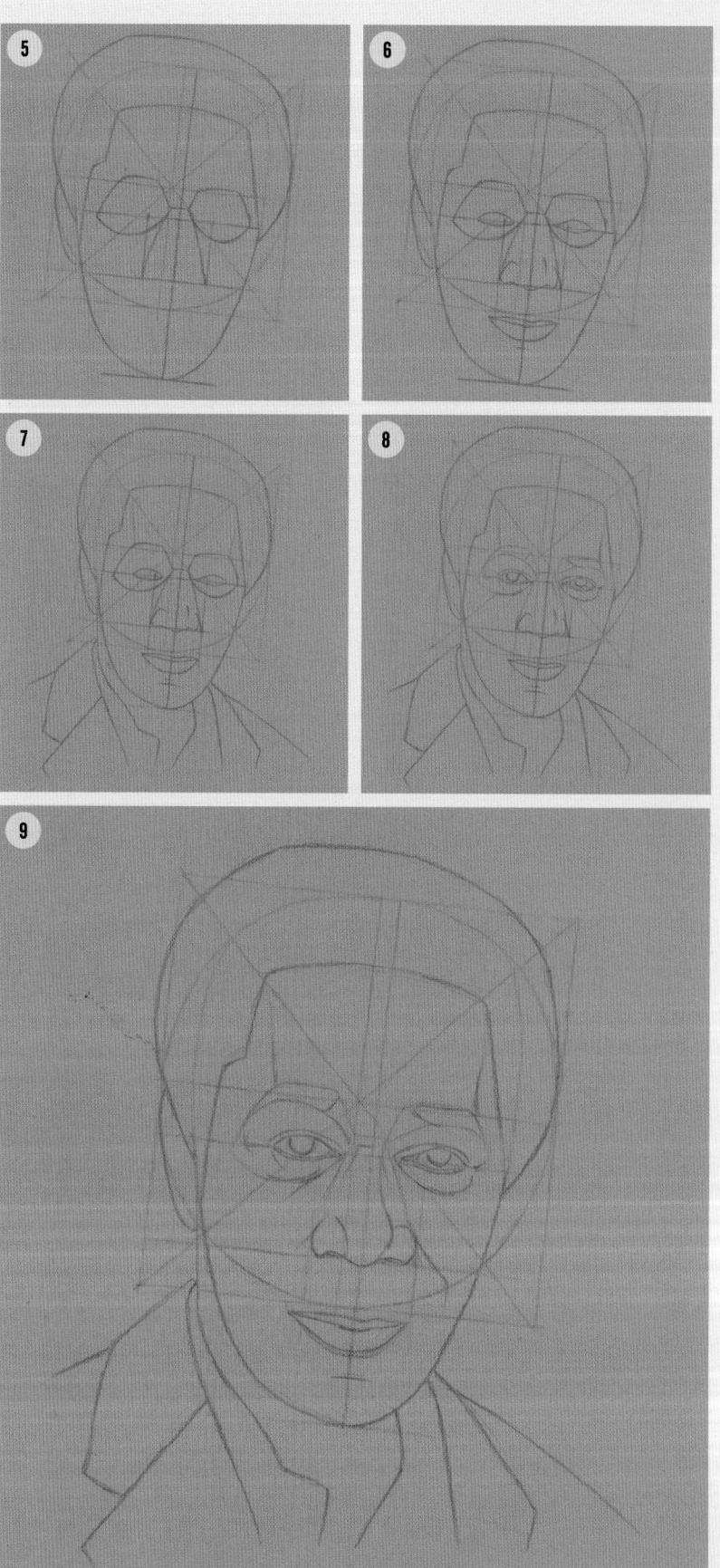

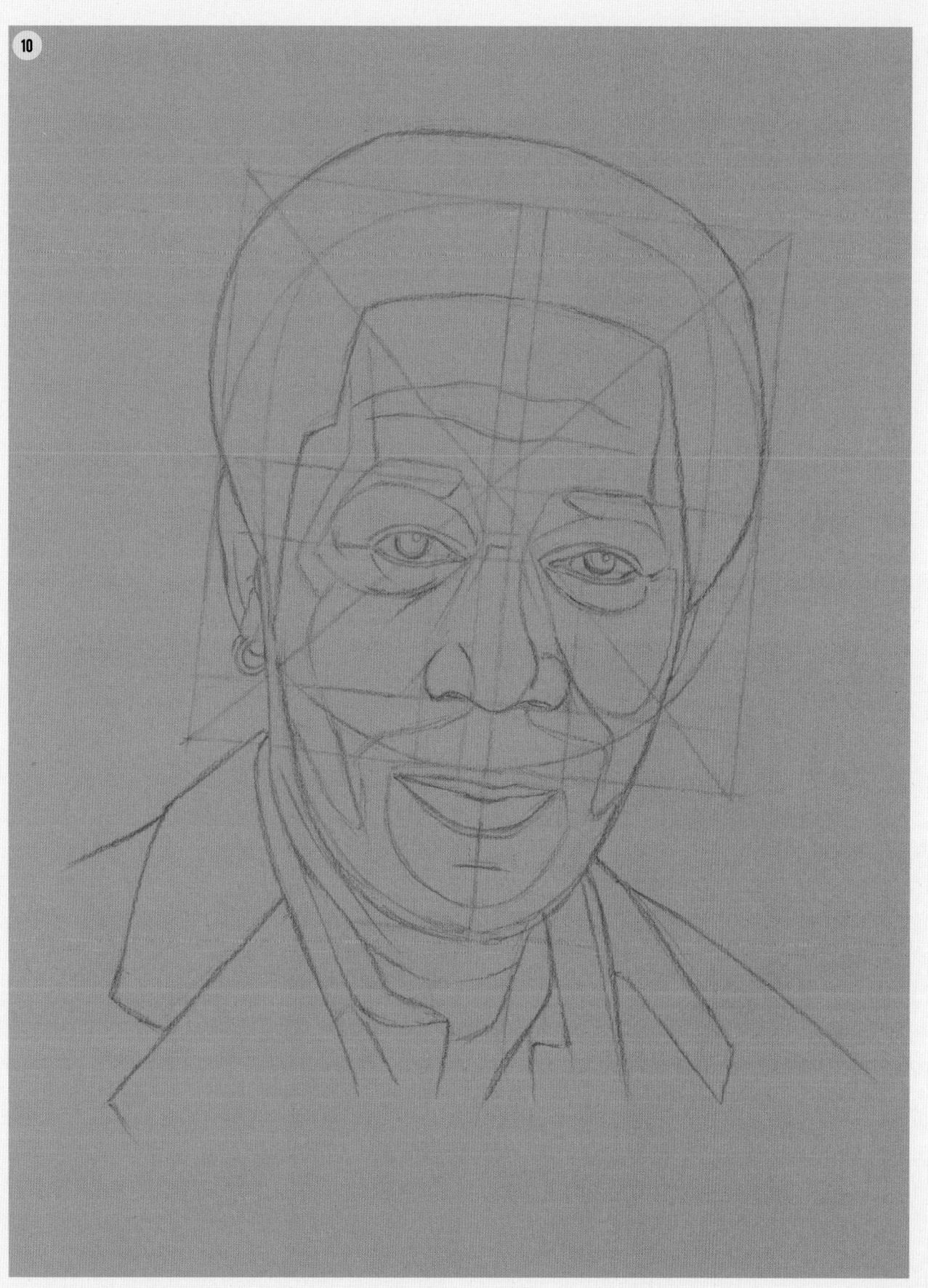

SHADING

At this point, you have completed the portrait construction and outline (either by following the previous Steps 1–10, or by simply tracing the image for Step 10).

1 Use the squiggle method (*see* Sketching Fundamentals: Shading Basics) to shade the hair. Do this with a sharpened white charcoal pencil and light-to-medium grip.

2 Go over the highlighted sections of the hair again, building the texture and density. This time use a medium-to-hard grip.

3 Using white charcoal pencil, start to shade the highlights on the right side of Morgan's face, including the eye, cheek, forehead and ear.

4 In the same way, shade the highlights on the left side of his face. Also shade the nose and lips with the white charcoal pencil, using a medium grip.

5 Use some squiggles and white charcoal pencil to fill in the facial hair (I have also added a little hair that's visible from the back of the head, just below the ear). Add highlights to the neck.

6 Using black charcoal pencil, start adding darker extremes. First, outline the dark shadows and edges around the eyes, ears, nose, cheeks, lips and neck with 2B charcoal and a medium-to-firm grip.

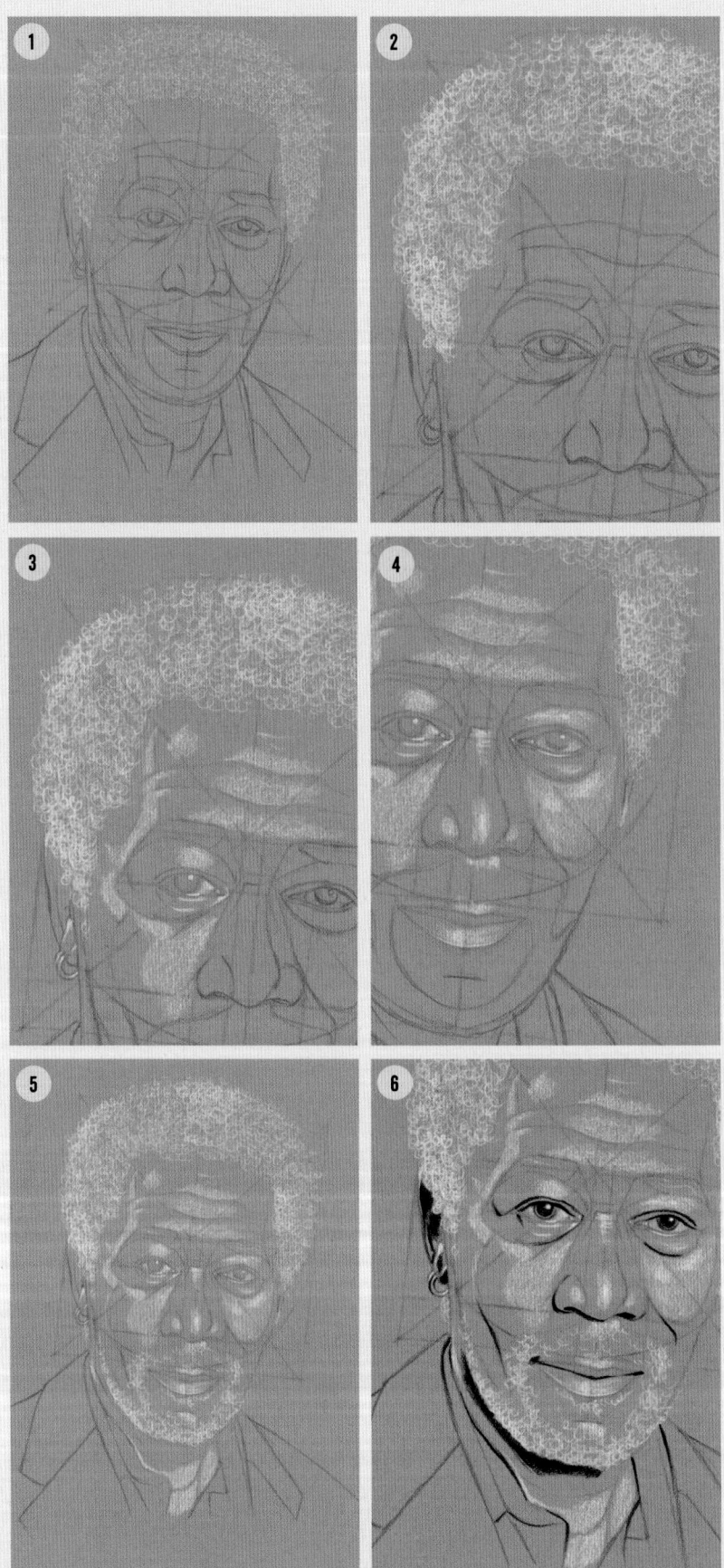

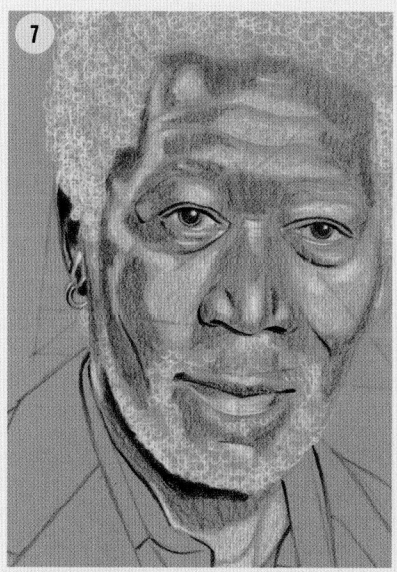

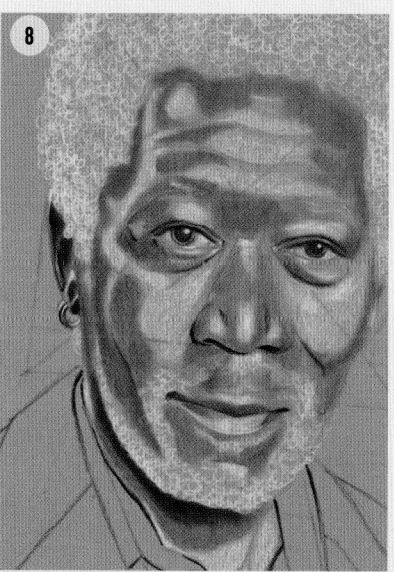

7 Shade the rest of the face with a 2B pencil and a light-to-medium grip. For this step, keep the shading uniform as you will build on this first layer with more details.

8 Blend only the darks at this stage, using a blending tool.

9 Using a clean blending tool, blend the dark and white charcoal pencils together. Make sure you keep cleaning the tip of the blending tool, using a sandpaper strip, before blending into the whites. This completes the first layer of shading.

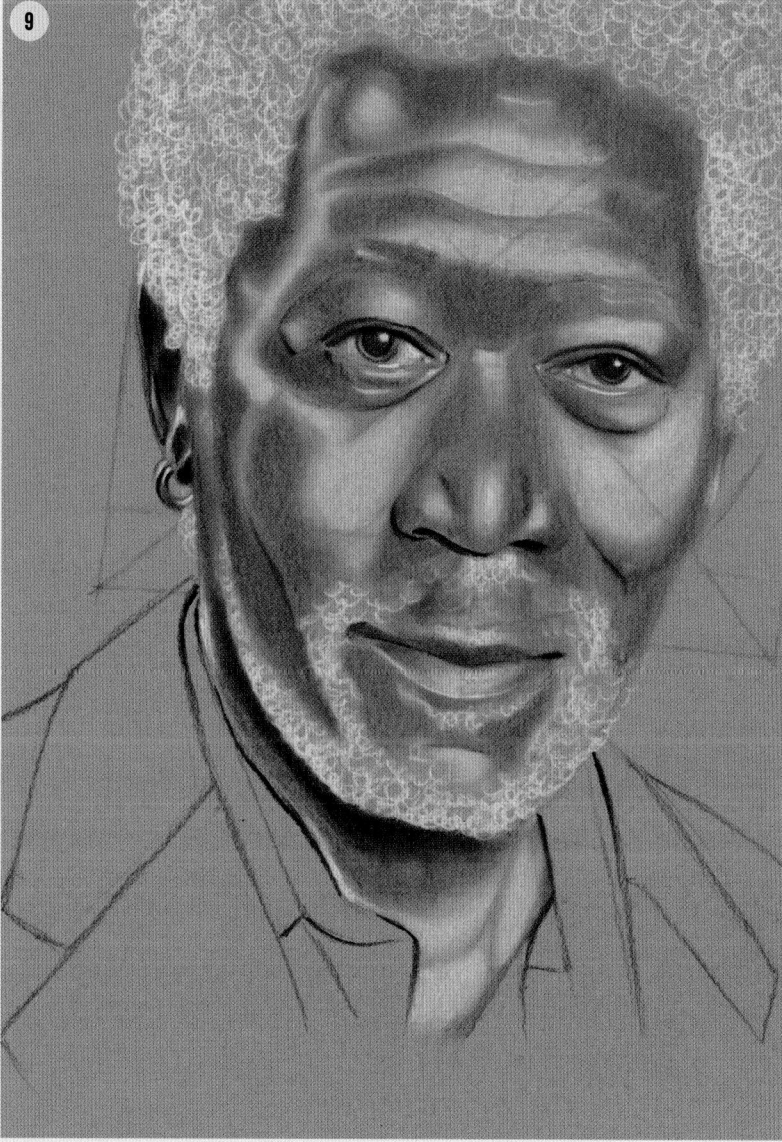

BE BRAVE!

Don't be afraid to shade boldly with graphite in these early stages. Experiment with varying pressures and blending tools to create a system you're comfortable with.

10 With the softer 4B charcoal pencil, shade the darker regions of the face starting with the right eye and right side of the forehead.

11 Shade the left side of the face in the same way.

12 Go on to shade the rest of the face, ear and neck.

13 Now, go back to blending again, using a paper stump. As you work, keep cleaning your blending tools after working on a darker value. That way, you can control the level of transition, and avoid the darks bleeding into the lighter tones more than required.

14 In this step, use the residual charcoal on the blending tool to add depth to the hair. Go over the hair with a squiggle motion to darken the shadowy parts of the hair. It is preferable to use a blending tool with a sharp point for this.

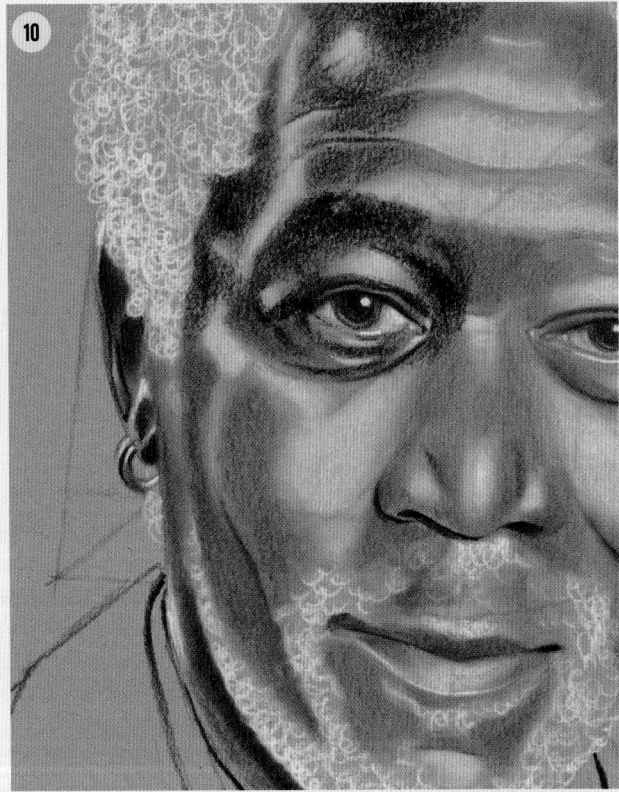

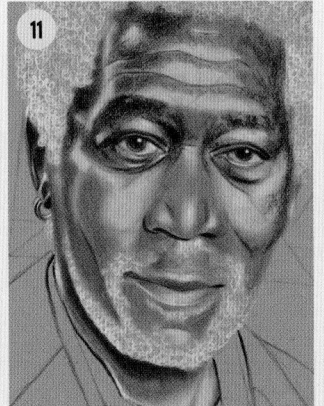

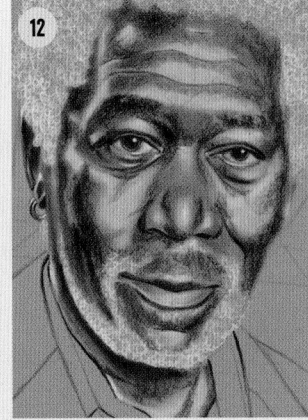

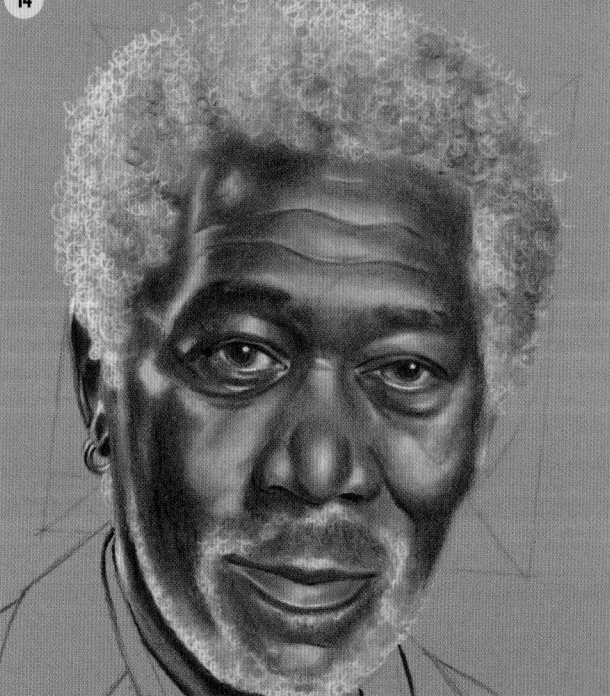

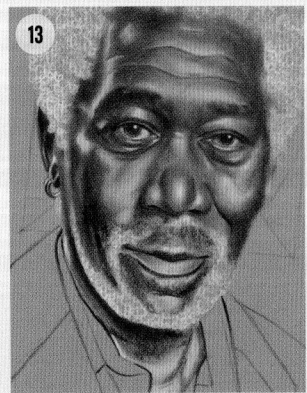

WORK IN LAYERS

Splitting the hair into layers captures its volume. Identifying and applying the different layers from a reference is key to achieving realism.

15 To create more depth, repeat Steps 10–13 with a 6B pencil.

16 As you did in Step 14, blend the shading using a paper stump.

17 Still using the 6B pencil, draw the freckles across the cheeks, eye area and forehead.

18 Go over the face with the white charcoal pencil to enhance the highlights. Go over the hair and eyes again, and any other areas that need to be made sharper to enhance the contrast of the portrait.

19 Complete the clothes, using charcoal powder and a blending tool (such as a sponge brush)

directly as a first layer. Use a pencil eraser to add pinstripes. Now refine your portrait. I have made adjustments, including the hairline and adding more shadows near the inner corner of the eyes. The bottom of the nose is made darker and there is a minor proportion adjustment to the lips.

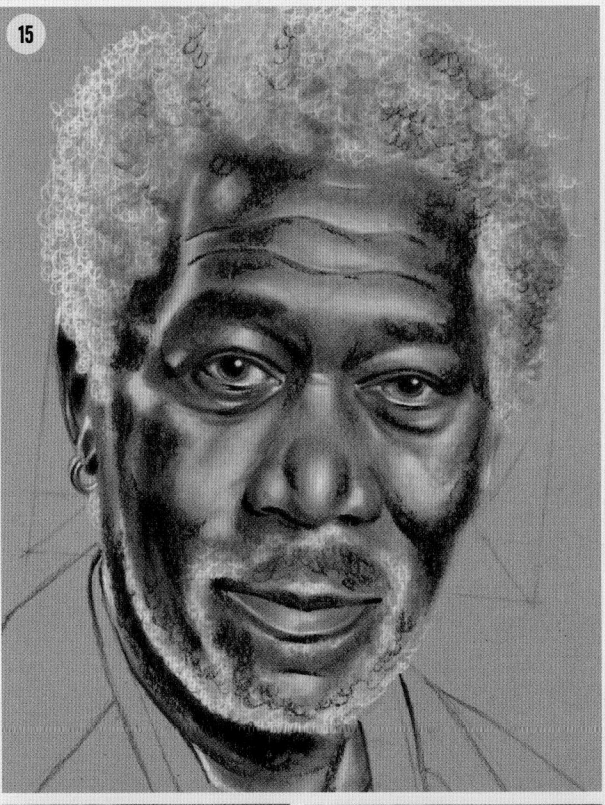

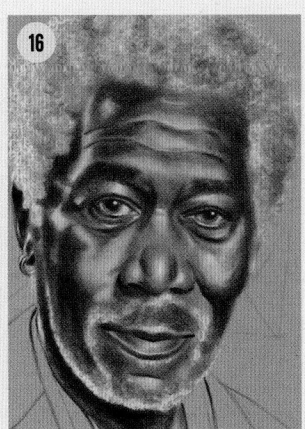

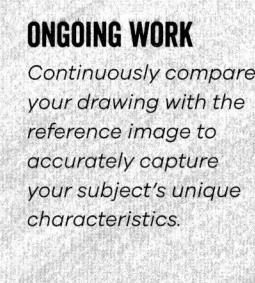

ONGOING WORK
Continuously compare your drawing with the reference image to accurately capture your subject's unique characteristics.

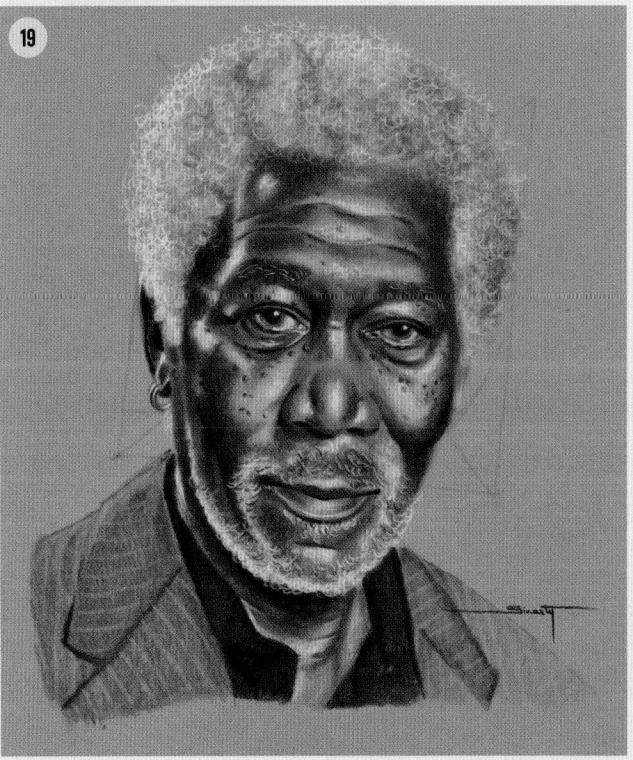

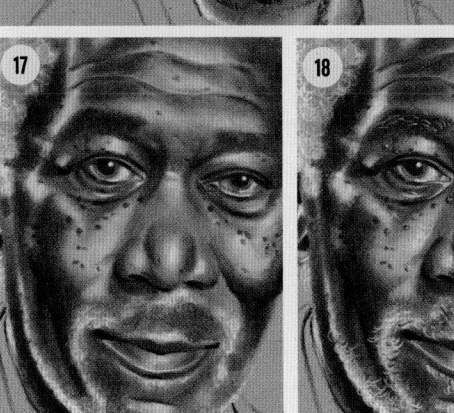

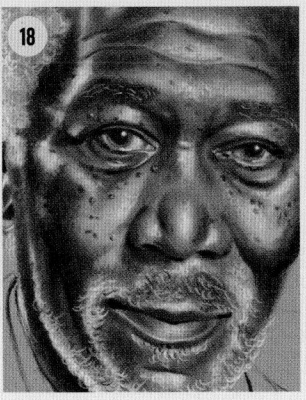

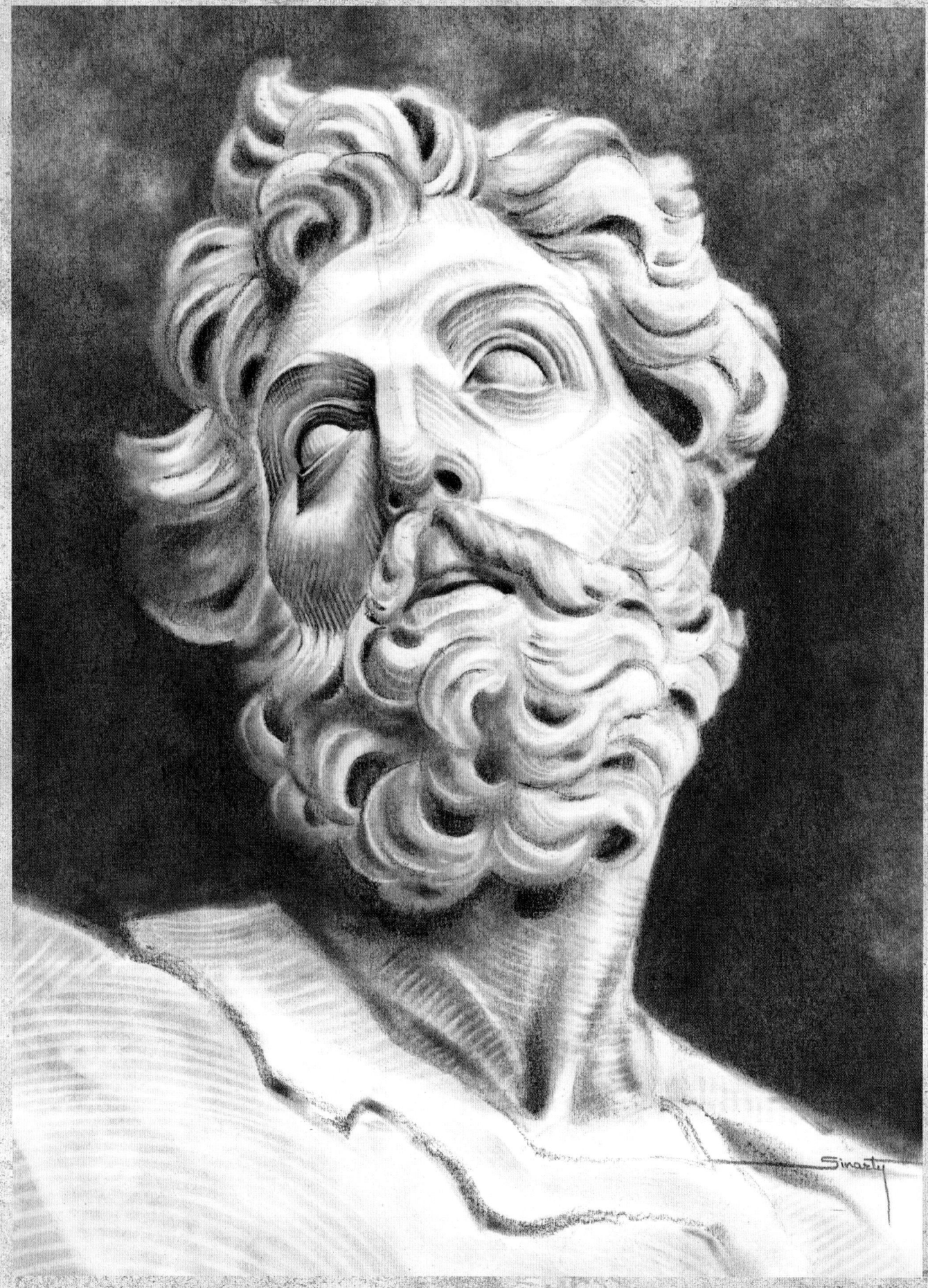

SAINT LONGINUS

This project is a study of the magnificent marble sculpture by Italian artist Gian Lorenzo Bernini. The sculpture was completed in 1638, and sits in St Peter's Basilica in the Vatican. Bernini captures the moment when Saint Longinus, a former Roman soldier, experiences spiritual awakening, looking up at the sky with a partially opened mouth as he regains his sight. We will try to replicate that emotion through this drawing. Let's begin!

Materials

- White sketching paper, 22.9 x 30.5cm (9 x 12in)
- Graphite pencils: 2B, 6B, 8B
- Graphite powder
- White charcoal pencil
- Paper stumps, sponge brush
- Kneaded eraser, pencil eraser
- Good-quality, long-tip pencil sharpener, one-sided sharpening blade as required

Techniques

- Proportion: Block-in
- Shading: Blending gradient with hatching and contour texture

BASIC OUTLINING

1 On white sketching paper, start by drawing a slightly tilted oval, slightly towards the top of the canvas, for the head (see the inset thumbnail for guidance). Add the vertical centreline and the browline, eyeline and nose line. Make these lines curved as if drawing on the surface of a balloon.

2 Draw the outline of the beard and the moustache.

3 Block in the outline of the locks of hair – start at the centre of the head and work outwards.

4 Outline the neck and shoulder to complete the basic structure.

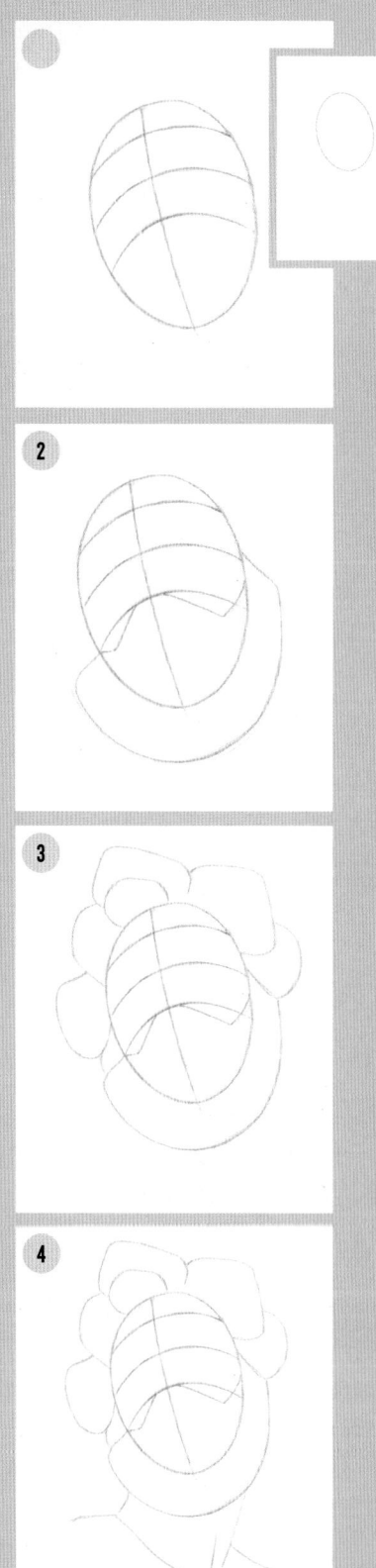

5 To begin creating the features, block in the planes of the nose, taking care to follow the horizontal and vertical guidelines.

6 Now draw the eye sockets and outline of the lips, again following the guidelines to position them.

7 Add basic details to these features. Begin by drawing two semi-circles for the eyes. Draw the tip of the nose and the outline of the nostrils. Also add details to draw the upper and lower lips. Then use curving lines to draw the locks of hair on the beard.

8 Develop the features by detailing more of their contours. Begin by drawing finer details around the eyes. Also refine the shape of the edge of the face near the forehead and the eyes

9 Draw details of the hair using curved lines. Follow the sculpted contours of the reference.

10 Finally, detail the beard. The curved sections you draw will be filled with different values of light and shade later on.

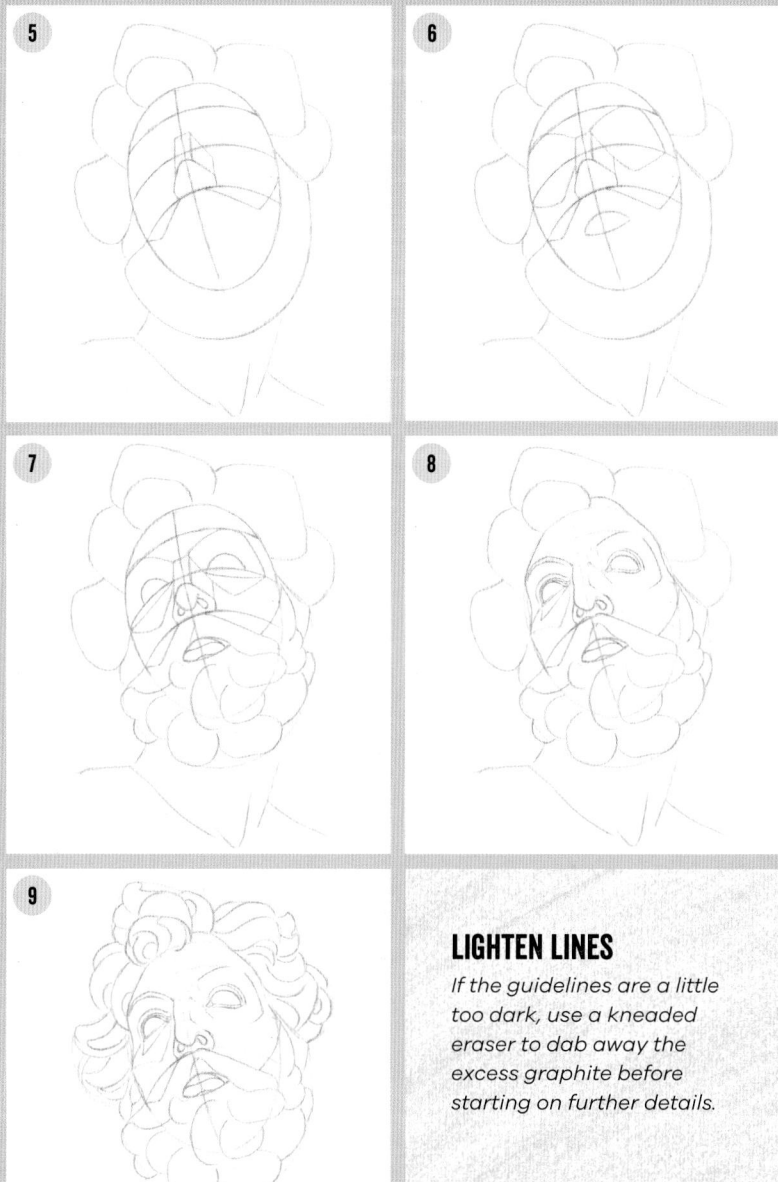

LIGHTEN LINES

If the guidelines are a little too dark, use a kneaded eraser to dab away the excess graphite before starting on further details.

GO STRAIGHT TO SHADING

Simply tracing the final outline drawing – Step 10 – provides an opportunity to jump ahead to practise shading (see Proportion Techniques: Freehand & Tracing).

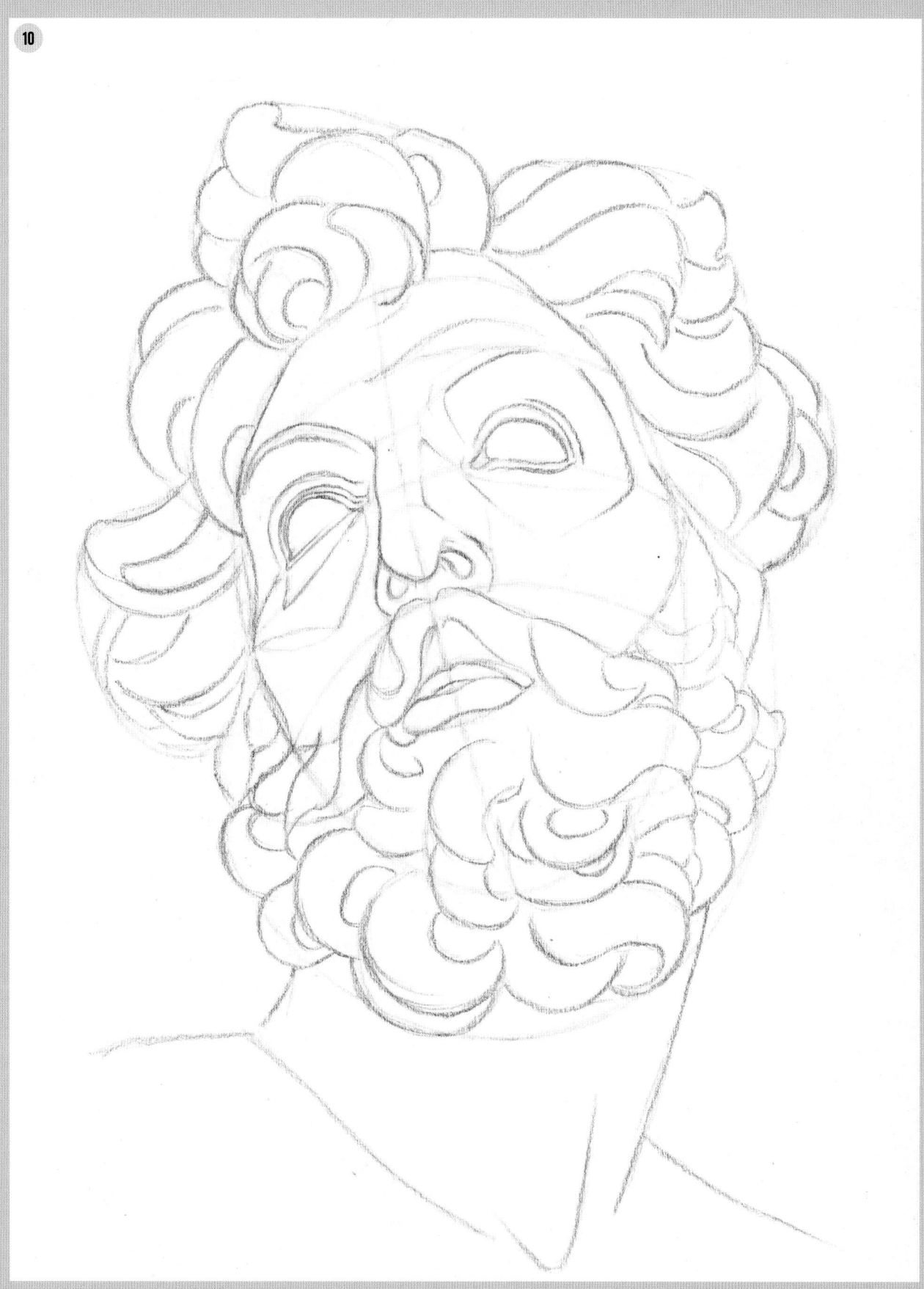

SHADING

At this point, you have completed the portrait construction and outline (either by following the previous Steps 1–10, or by simply tracing the image for Step 10).

1 Start with the first layer of shading. Using graphite powder on a sponge brush, shade the shadow region of the right side of the face.

2 With an 8B pencil (or the darkest pencil you have) hatch the details and extreme dark value near the right eye and cheek.

3 With the kneaded eraser, lighten some of the regions as shown using small dabs to lift a little of the graphite pencil and powder.

4 Now use the paper stump to smooth over the hard edges (*see* Sketching Fundamentals: Shading Basics). With the pencil eraser, draw some texture on this area of the face, ensuring the lines follow the contours of the sculpture. This is an optional step, but it creates movement in the drawing of a static piece of sculpture.

5 Use the paper stump covered in a small amount of graphite powder to shade the opposite side of the face.

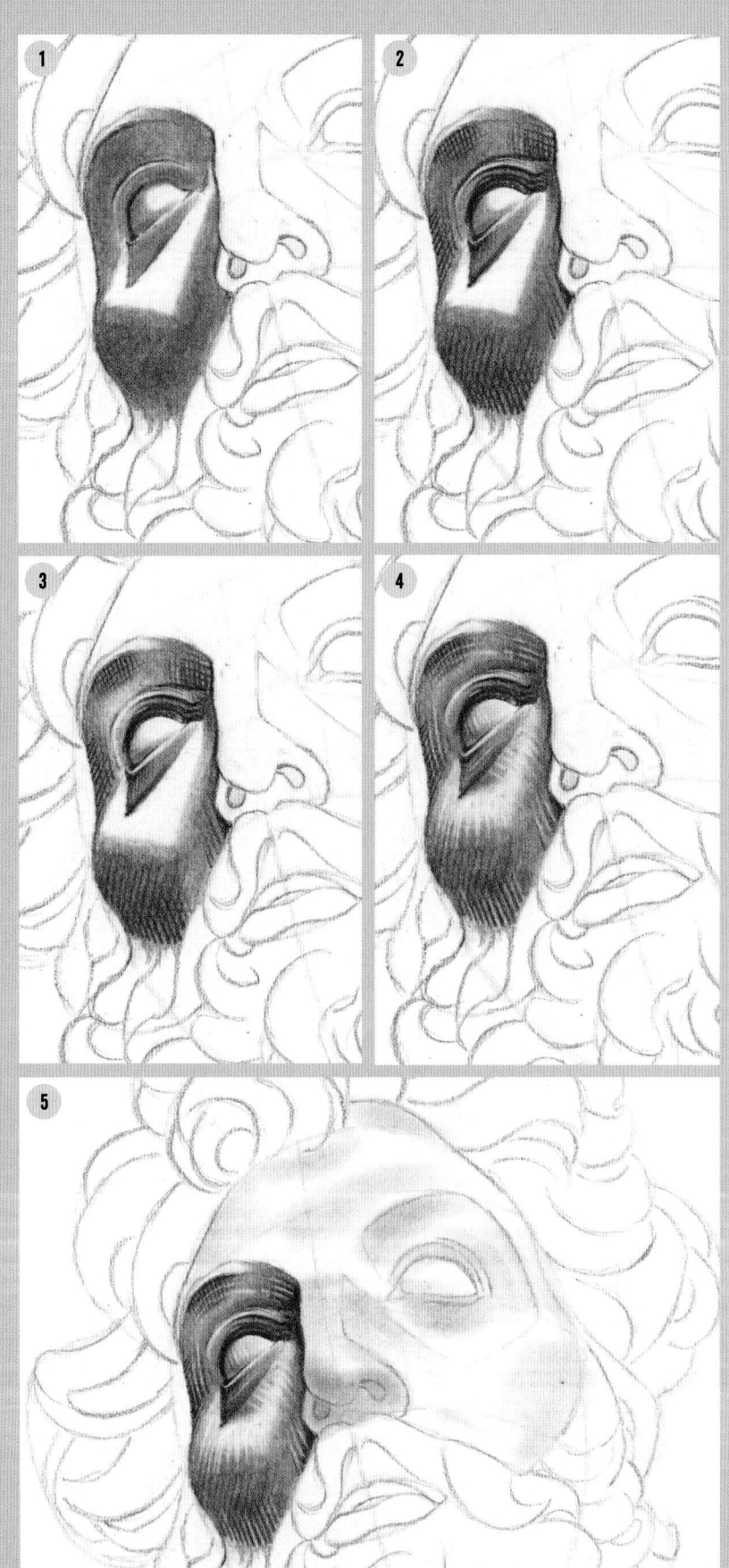

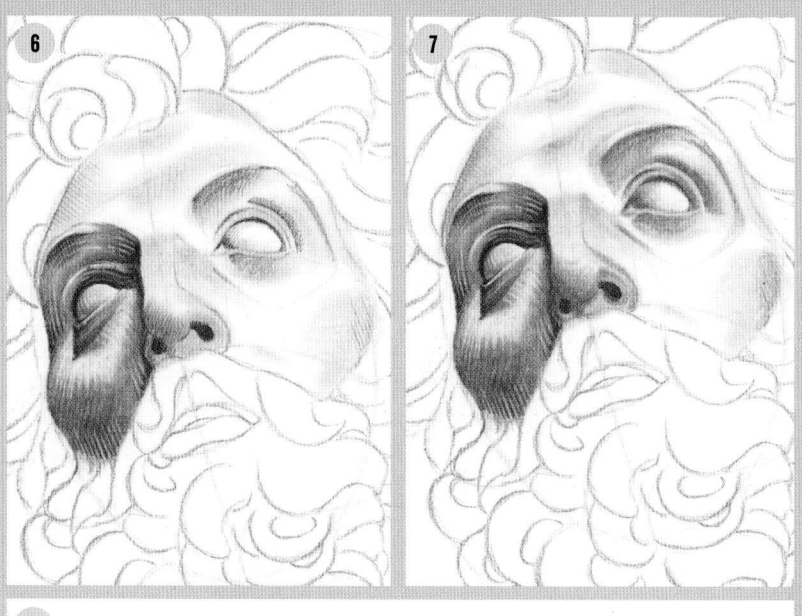

6 Use an 8B pencil to darken the nostrils and the details near the left eye. You can also begin to lightly hatch the contours around the forehead and right cheek using a 6B pencil.

7 Use a medium-sized paper stump to soften the edges near the eyes and darken the nose. Also slightly darken the contours on the forehead and the cheek to give a sense of form.

8 As you did in Step 4, use a pencil eraser to give texture to this side of the face as well. With some graphite powder on a sponge brush, shade the first layer of hair, including the facial hair. From here, you can work towards both value extremes over the next two steps (*see* Sketching Fundamentals: Shading Basics).

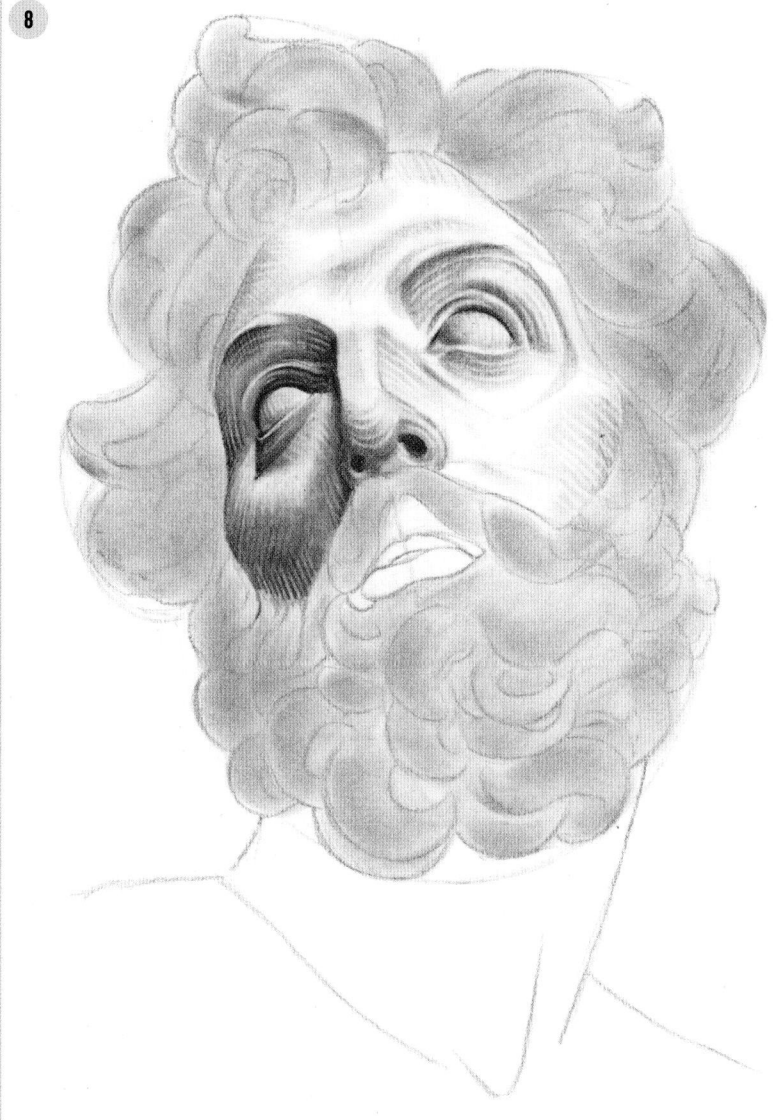

DRAWING HAIR

Take your time drawing the hair. It can be slightly tedious, but the good news is that you don't have to be too accurate with the proportion in terms of each lock of hair. Make sure the movement of the hair is correct.

9 Use a 6B pencil to shade the darker shadowy areas of the hair, following the reference and the outlines you created earlier.

10 Use a kneaded eraser to reverse shade highlights on the hair, keeping in mind the direction of the light source (top right).

11 Use a paper stump to soften the edges and merge values.

12 This step may seem very similar to the previous step, but you are in fact correcting the value of the overall drawing to give a better sense of where the light is falling on the sculpture. Using a kneaded eraser and paper stump, work over the areas to balance out the values. Notice the change in values on the right side of the hair (lighten) and the left side of the beard (darken).

13 Begin work on the lips and the neck with the first layer, shading the areas you previously outlined.

14 Now use a 6B pencil to mark details and shadows, including around the lips and to pick out the anatomy of the neck. Also outline the armour around the neck. (This is part of the armour St Longinus renounces as a symbol of the withdrawal of his job as a Roman soldier.)

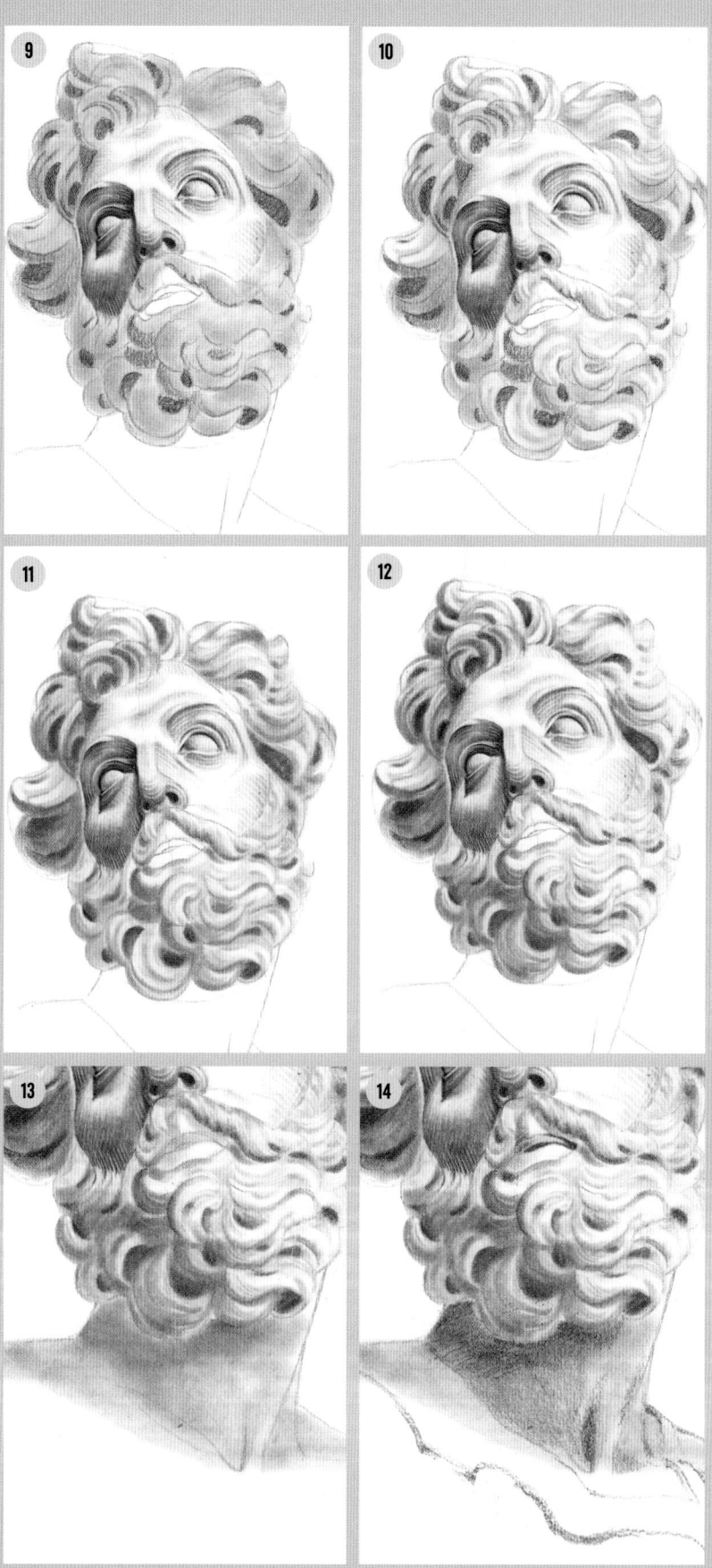

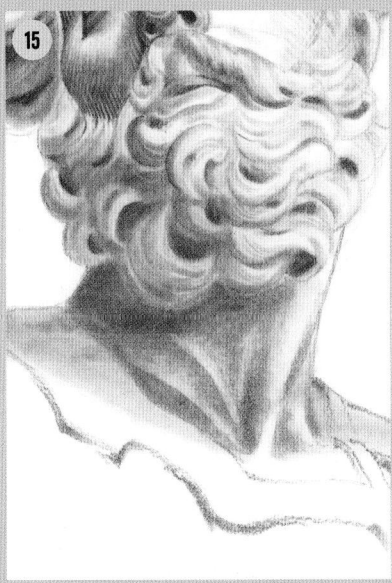

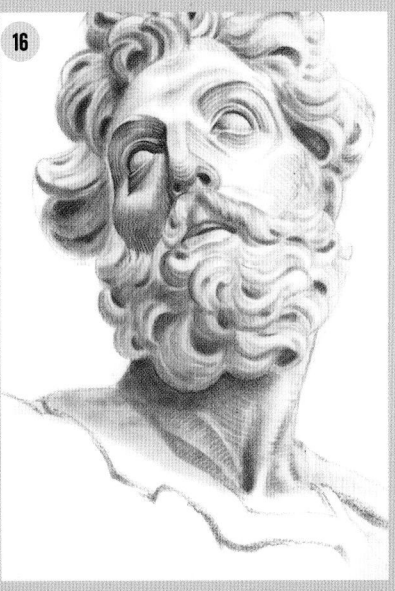

15 Use a paper stump and kneaded eraser to add further details around the lips and neck.

16 Use the pencil eraser to draw texture, following the planes and contours of the lips and neck. Then use an 8B pencil to sharpen some edges and enhance the contrast a bit further.

17 Finally, shade the background. To create a sense of the heavens at which St Longinus is gazing, use a mix of graphite powder, graphite pencils, blending tools and a kneaded eraser. Then add shadow details and texture to the armour and body. This completes our rendition of this masterpiece by Bernini.

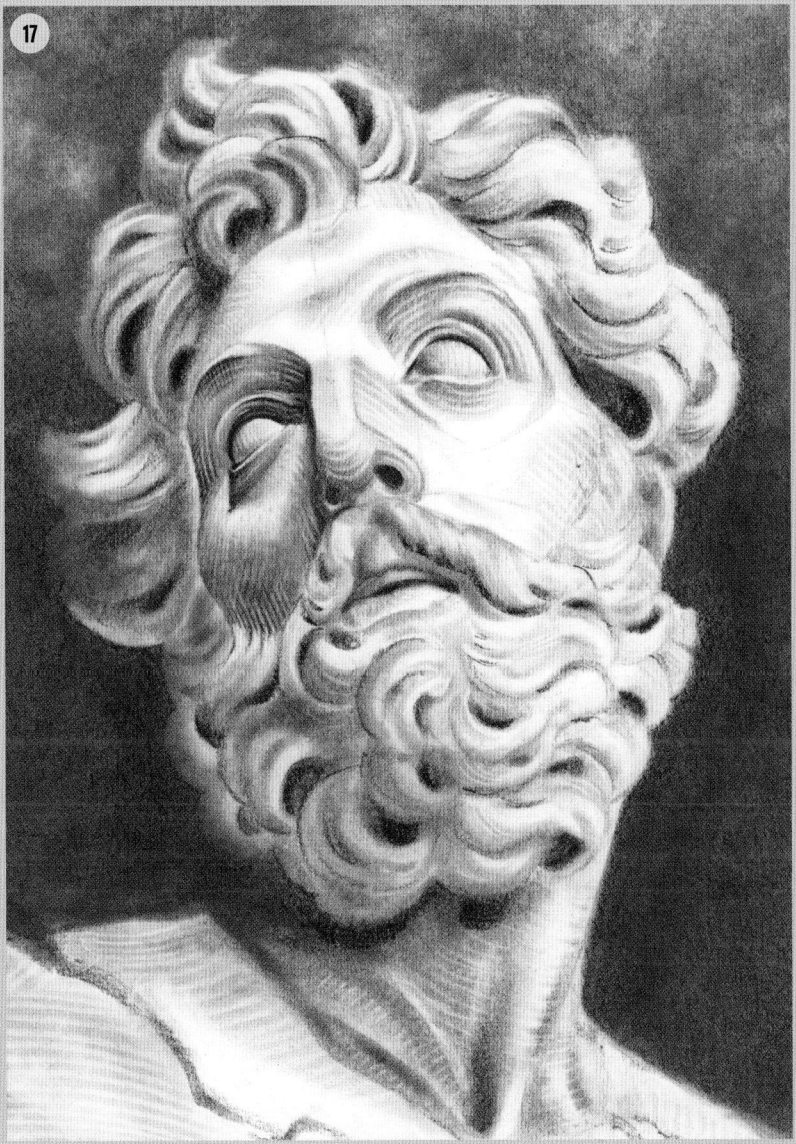

THE MACRO VIEW

It is important to look at your drawing from a distance to get an overall impression and compare it to your reference. The process I usually follow is moving from macro to micro, then back to macro (see Proportion Techniques: The Block-in Method). The final macro view allows you to step back to assess the finishing touches and value adjustments made in Step 12.

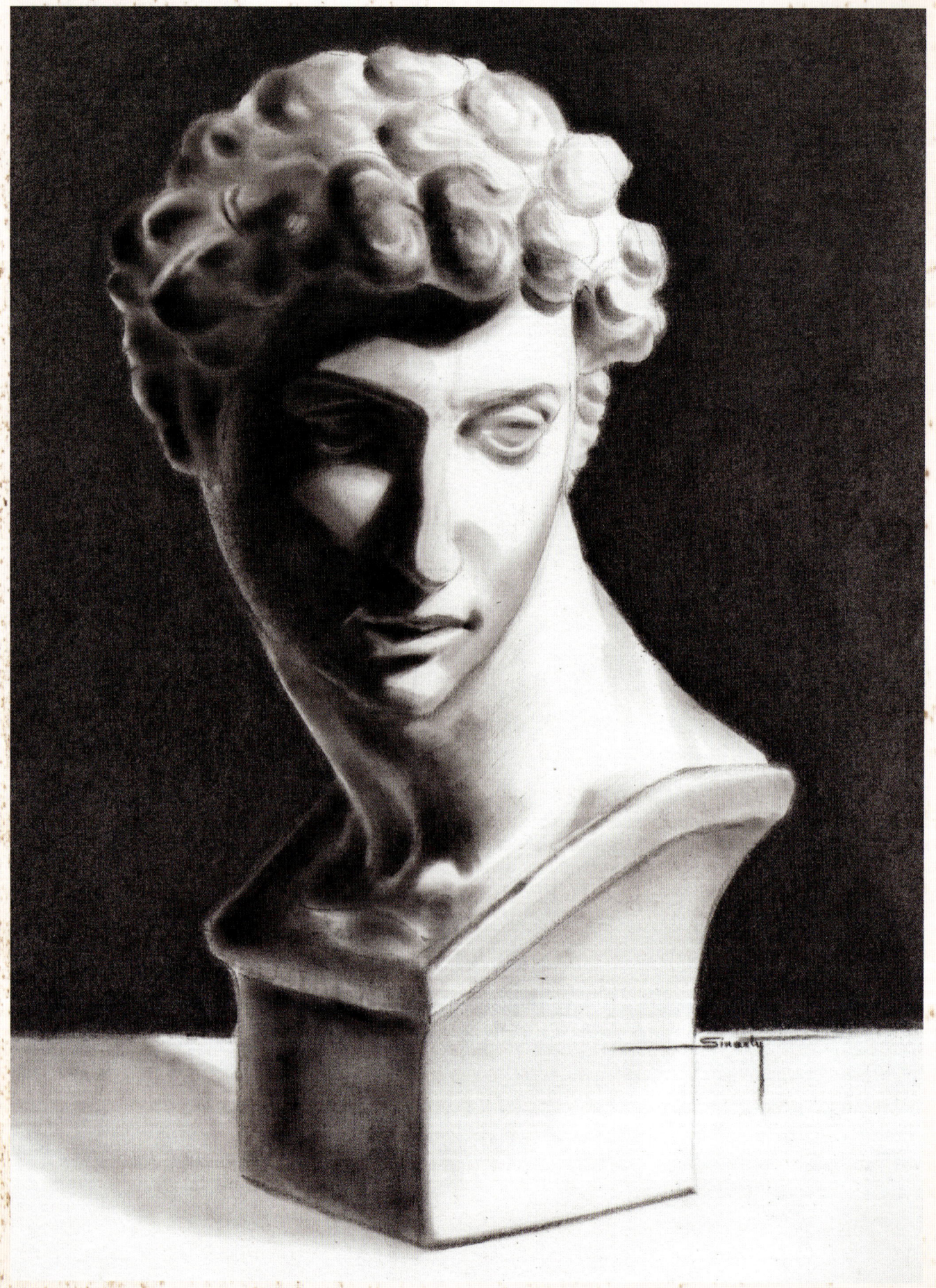

GUILIANO

Our subject is the bust of Giuliano de' Medici (1453–1478) who was the ruler of Florence, Italy. I particularly like this sculpture as it depicts vision and focus. From a drawing perspective, the light perfectly illuminates the left side of the face, a great exercise in values. We will explore a new technique – abstraction. Abstraction in this context is the process of depicting detail with only a few strokes, giving a "sense" or an illusion of detail, rather than drawing the detail itself. Using only blending tools for shading (no pencils at all) will result in soft edges that help to form the features.

Materials

- White sketching paper, 22.9 x 30.5cm (9 x 12in)
- Graphite pencils: 2B, 4B
- Graphite powder
- Paper stumps, sponge brush
- Kneaded eraser, pencil eraser
- Good-quality pencil sharpener or one-sided sharpening blade

Techniques

- Proportion: Block-in
- Shading: Gradient blending

BASIC OUTLINING

1 Draw an oval for the head, tilted slightly clockwise and towards the top left of the page (see the inset thumbnail for guidance). Then draw a vertical centreline for the face, slightly towards the right of the oval.

2 Add horizontal markings to depict the hairline, browline and nose line.

3 Draw a basic outline of the hair and the ears. On the left side, The hair and ear are blocked in together. On the right side you can see only the hair coming down in front of the ear, hiding it.

4 Add the outline of the neck, then the base of the sculpture.

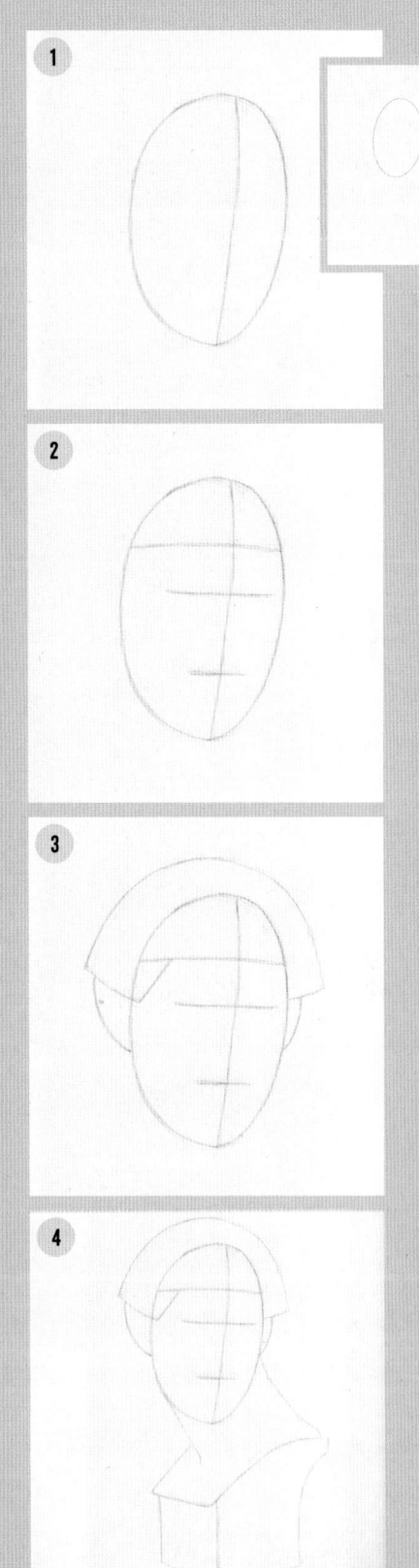

5 To add the details, start by blocking in the shadows on the face, beginning with the forehead and working down to the nose and lips. The light source is at the top right of the sculpture.

6 With a 4B pencil, further refine the line of these blocks to depict the contours of the nose and the lips. Block in the position of the left eye, and mark the jugular notch on the neck.

7 Following the outlines created in Step 3, refine the hair and define the outline of the face and neck.

8 Block in further rudimentary details of the shadows on the cheek, eyes and the lips. Notice the portion of highlight on the right cheek.

9 Solidify the line of the neck and the base of the sculpture, including the area where the neck becomes part of the base.

10 The hair is simplified (abstracted), so draw ovals of various sizes, mixing the shapes a little too. These ovals need not be pixel accurate to the reference – you can detail these as part of the shading process to get a sense of the shadows and highlights.

GO STRAIGHT TO SHADING

Simply tracing the final outline drawing – Step 10 – provides an opportunity to jump ahead to practise shading (see Proportion Techniques: Freehand & Tracing).

GUILIANO

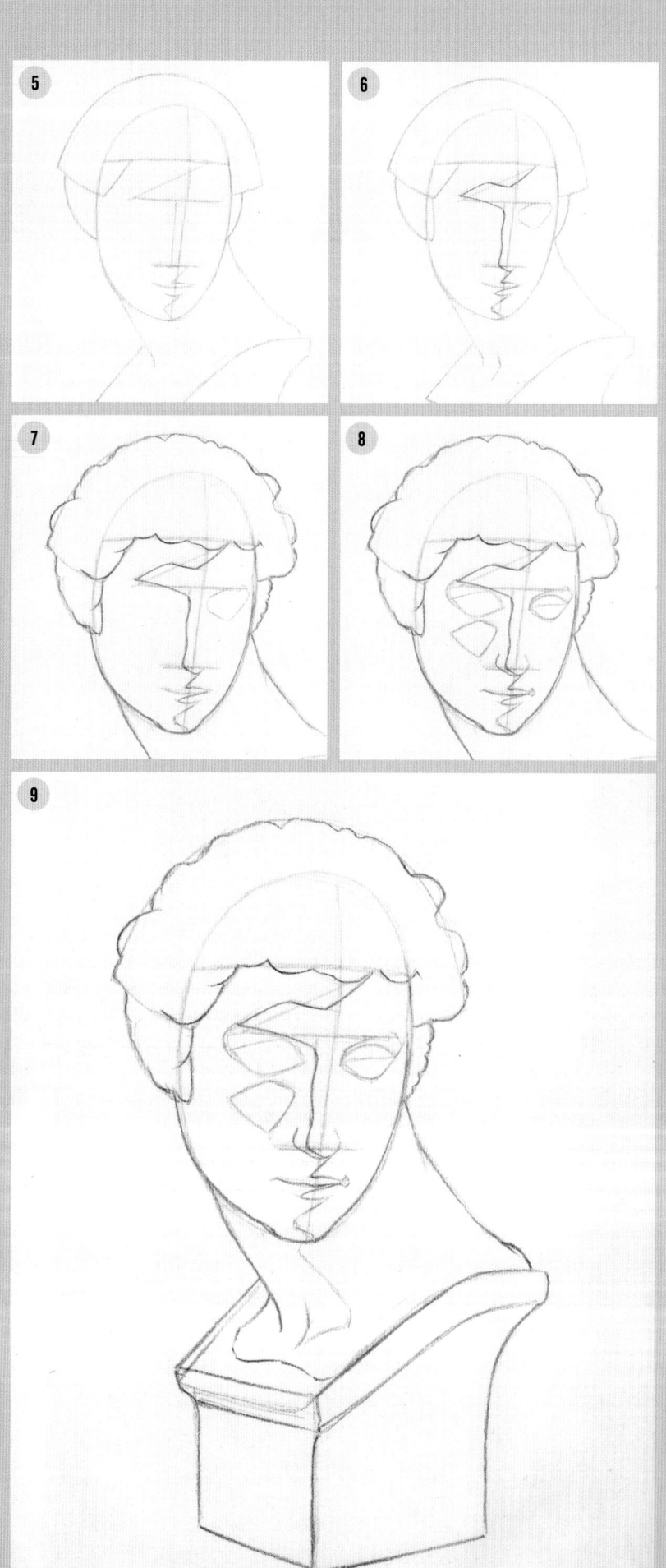

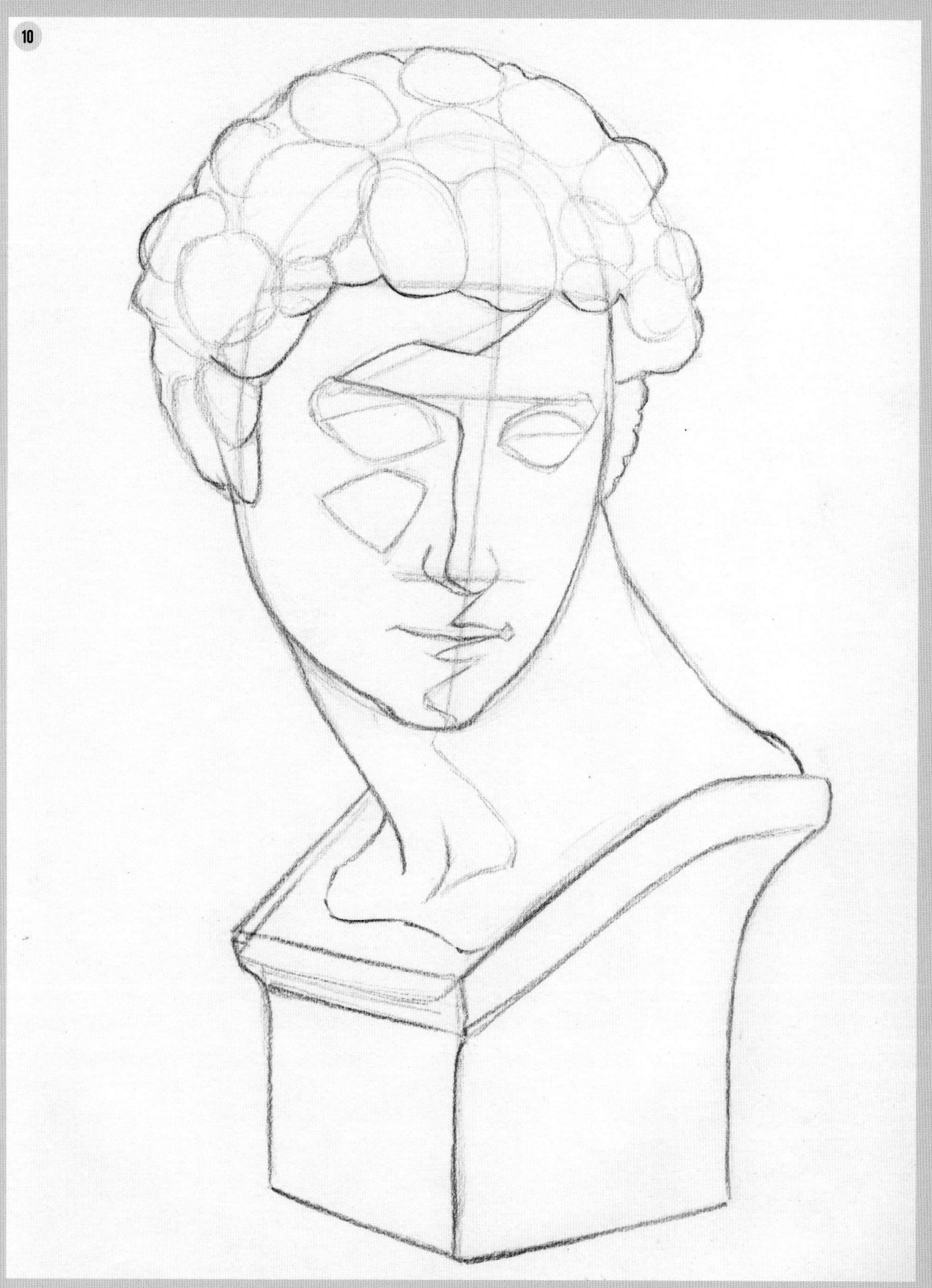

SHADING

At this point, you have completed the portrait construction and outline (either by following the previous Steps 1–10, or by simply tracing the image for Step 10).

1 Use charcoal powder and a sponge brush (or paper stump) to shade the previously blocked-in shadows on the right side of the face. Note the unshaded portion on the right cheek depicting the highlight.

2 Use a kneaded eraser to pick up some of the charcoal to "draw" the details of the eyes and lips. Think of this as reverse shading where we are essentially shading with the eraser instead of the pencil. Also remove some of the charcoal from the jaw to create a highlight.

3 Use the sponge brush and a very small amount of charcoal to smooth the transition of the cheek highlight. Also draw a few more details on the eye, nose and the lips.

4 With a small amount of charcoal powder on the tip of a medium-sized paper stump, shade the left eye and some shadows on the highlighted side of the face. Then using the sponge brush, shade the shadows on the neck and the base.

5 With the kneaded eraser and a small paper stump, sharpen some edges and adjust values on the eyes, eyebrows, neck and base.

6 Define the darker shadows on the neck using charcoal powder and a broad paper stump or medium sponge brush.

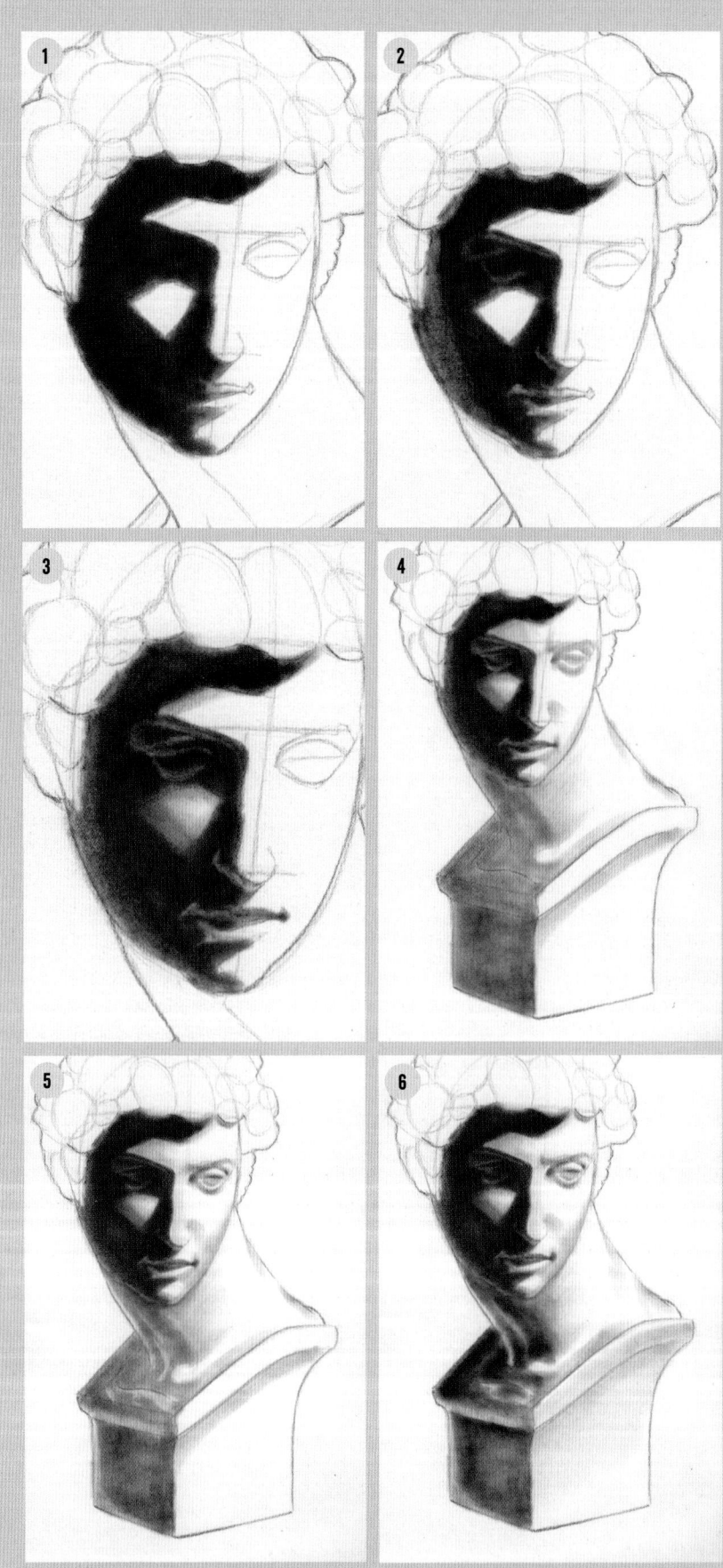

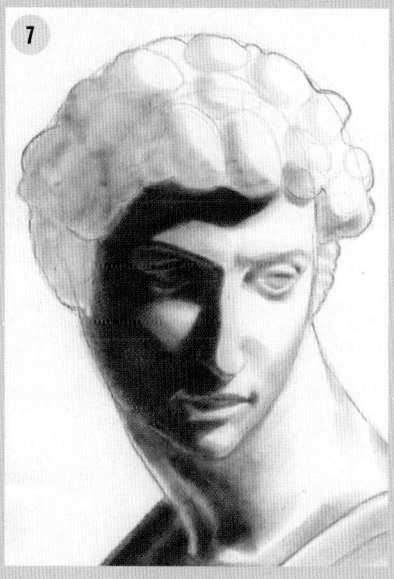

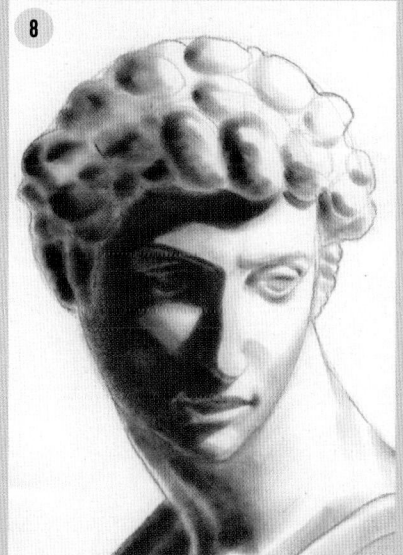

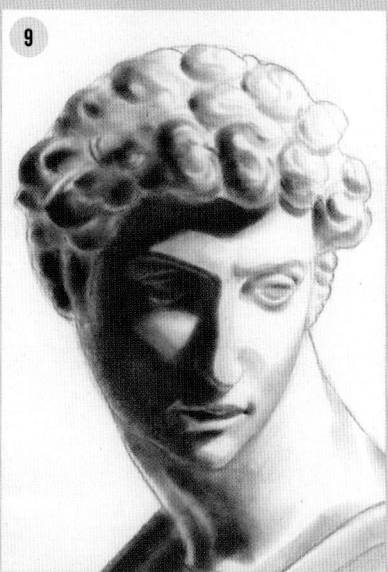

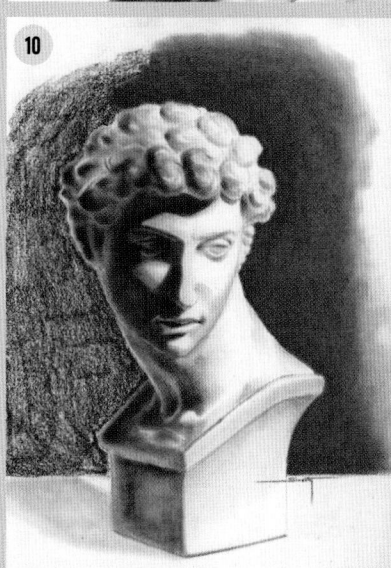

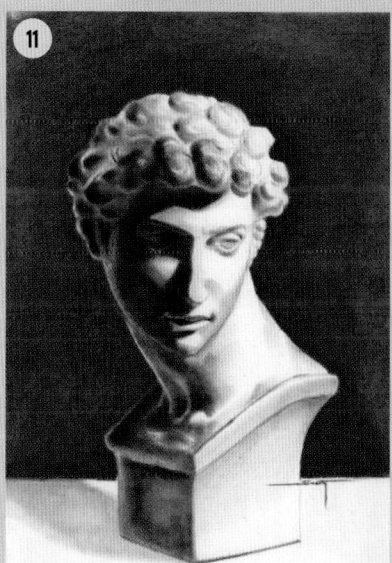

7 As you begin shading the hair, keep in mind the direction of the light source and the form of the sculpture. Using the sponge brush, shade the first layer of hair. Start with the left shadowy region, shading the left curve of the ovals to give depth to the locks. This is similar to the additive and subtractive method of freehand drawing (*see* Proportion Techniques: Freehand & Tracing).

8 Now shade the darker regions to the left and front of the locks, using charcoal powder on a sponge brush.

9 Add a few more details using the kneaded eraser or pencil eraser. Keep these details abstract and slightly soft.

10 Go over the whole sketch and sharpen any values and features that need to be corrected. On the left side, add the shadow of the bust with a light brush of charcoal. Now start shading the background using a neutral-value charcoal pencil and paper stump to create a smooth backdrop. This step shows both the blended and non-blended sections of the background.

11 Finish blending the background, extending it out to the edge of the paper if required (you can also fade it out). This is a style choice. Notice how much more the sculpture pops with the added background due to an enhanced contrast.

ABSTRACTION IN HISTORY

An example of this abstraction technique is the painting "Girl with a Pearl Earring" by Vermeer. He depicts the shine and the "idea" of an earring beautifully with just a few brush strokes.

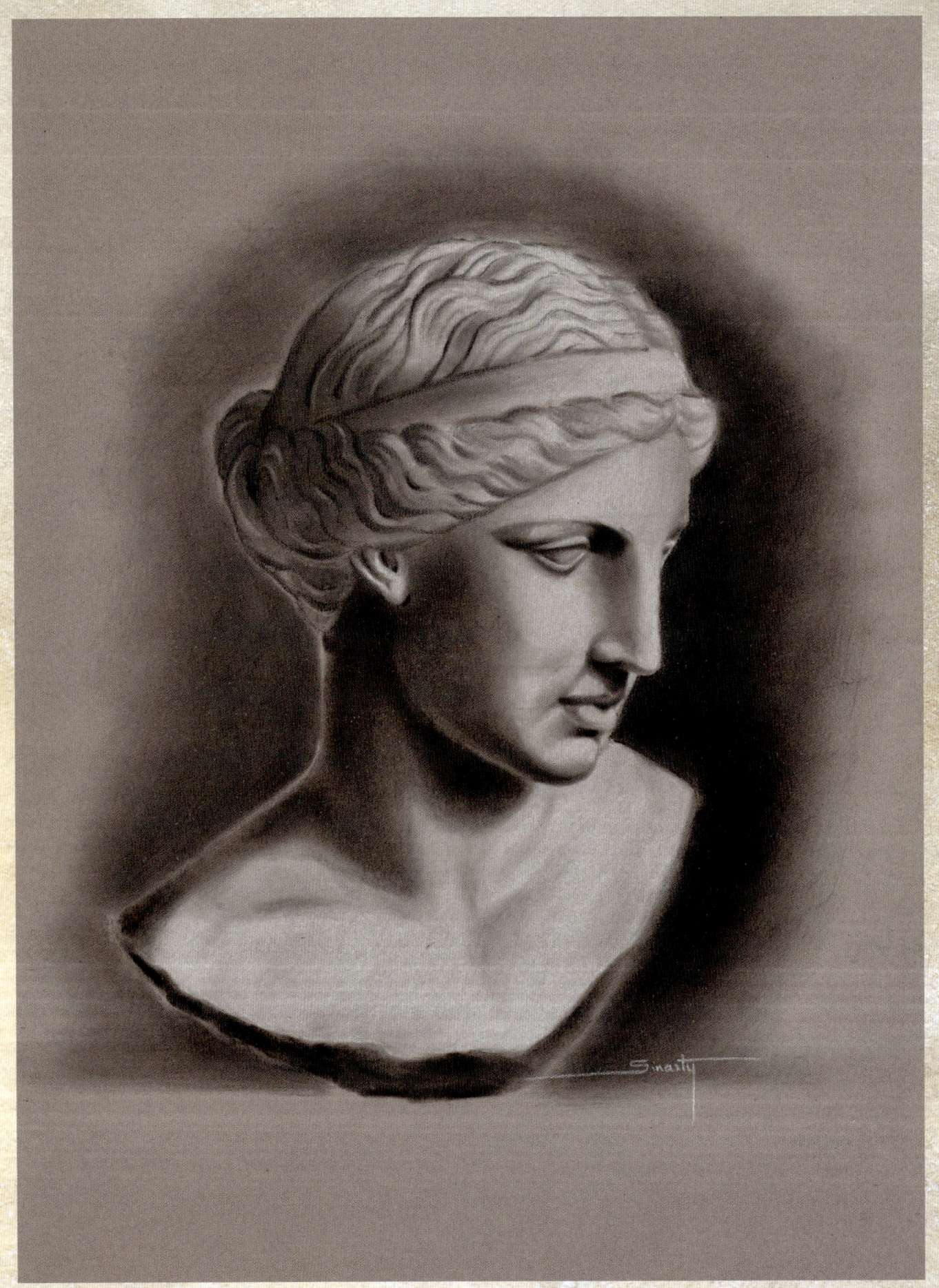

VENUS

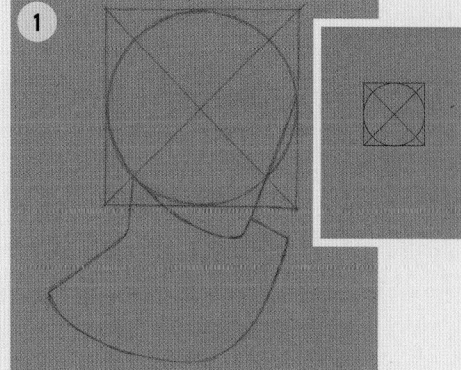

In this project, we will draw the bust that was modelled on the marble sculpture *Venus De Capua,* the Roman goddess of love and beauty. This rendition bust of the famous full figure of Venus is believed to be a copy of a lost sculpture of Aphrodite. This subject especially intrigues me due to its soft features and smooth contours.

Materials

- Toned grey sketching paper, 18.2 x 25.7cm (7¼ x 10in)
- Black charcoal pencils and charcoal powder
- White charcoal powder
- Paper stumps, cotton buds, sponge brush
- Kneaded eraser, pencil eraser
- One-sided sharpening blade

Techniques

- Proportion: Block-in
- Shading: Gradient blending

BASIC OUTLINING

1 Draw a square slightly above the middle of the page (see the inset thumbnail for guidance) and divide it into diagonal quadrants. Draw a circle within the square – this will contain the cranium. Draw a basic outline of the face and jawline, then draw the neck and extend it downward. This will be the base of the sculpture.

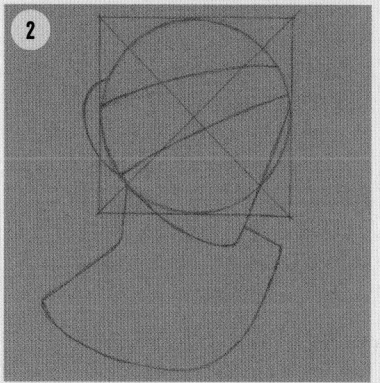

2 Draw a basic outline of the hair marking the hairline, the headband, and the visible part of the bun at the back of the head.

3 Mark the browline and nose line, using the reference and square diagonals as a placement grid. Draw a basic outline of the nose.

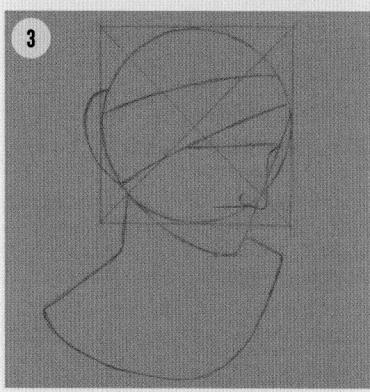

4 Draw a basic block-in outline of regions around the eye, nose and ear. The ear is partly hidden by hair, but draw the whole ear to judge the correct proportion and size. Mark the jawline, extending up to the ear. Draw further details, starting with the eye, lips and hair. Do not focus too much on the details, but on the proportions of the features. Correct any inconsistencies in proportion now, before adding more details. Add dimension to the base, noting the shape in the reference.

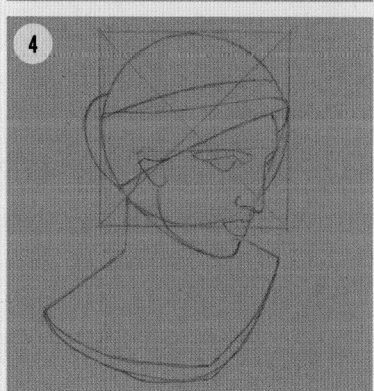

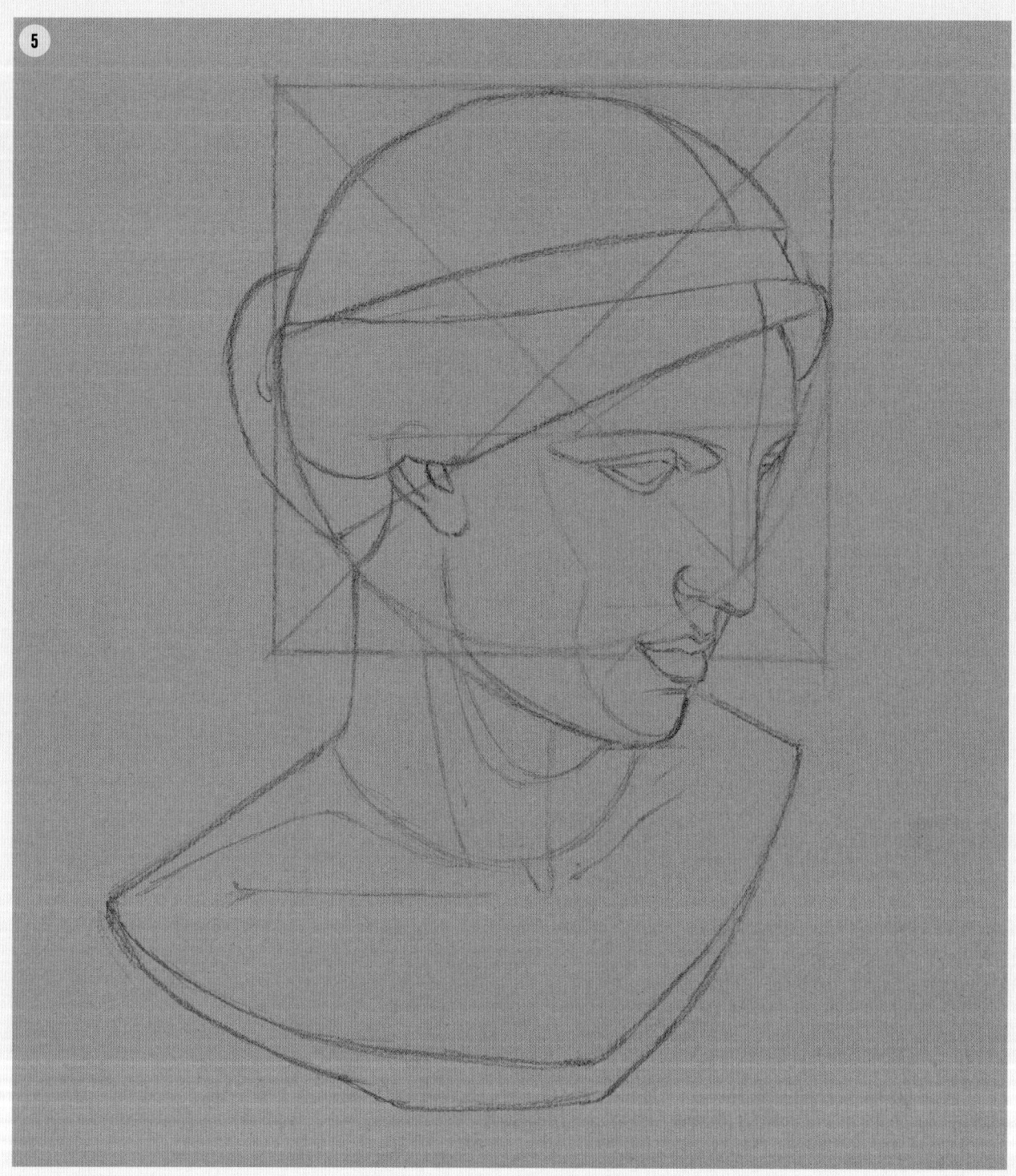

5 Now that the proportions are correct, prepare the sketch for shading. Add a few more details, including the shadows and highlights, to the face, hair and base.

GO STRAIGHT TO SHADING

Simply tracing the final outline drawing – Step 5 – provides an opportunity to jump ahead to practise shading (see Proportion Techniques: Freehand & Tracing).

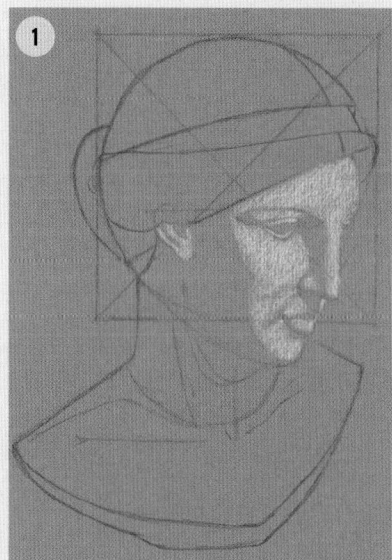

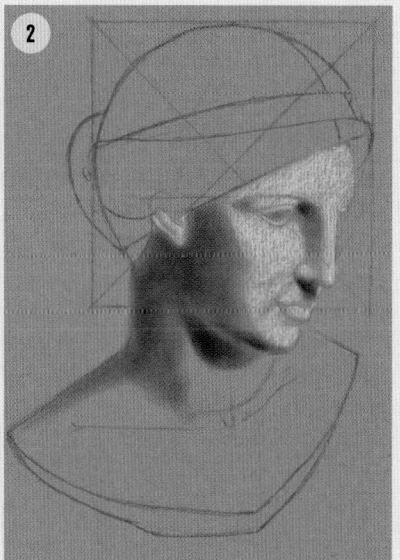

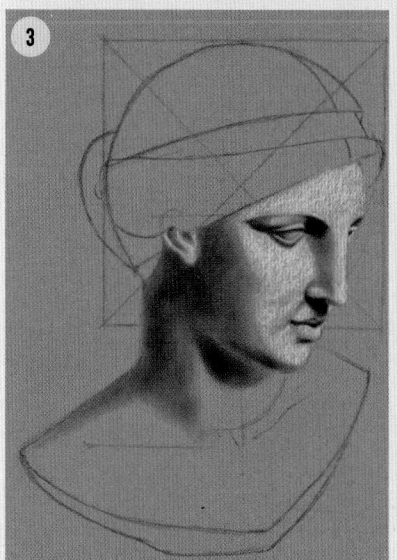

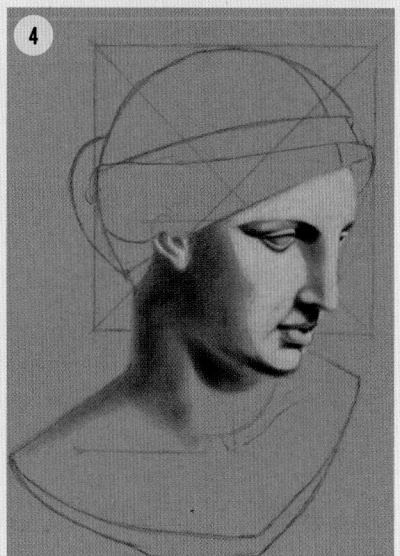

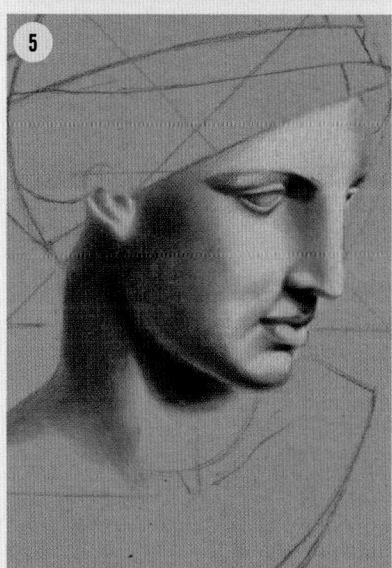

MACRO FEATURES

In the block-in technique, we focus on the macro shadows and highlights of the face, more than the individual features (see Proportion Techniques: The Block-in Method).

SHADING

At this point, you have completed the portrait construction and outline (either by following the previous Steps 1–5, or by simply tracing the image for Step 5).

1 Begin by shading the white value extreme (*see* Sketching Fundamentals: Shading Basics). Use the white charcoal pencil with a medium grip (*see* Sketching Fundamentals: Pencil Exercises) to shade the first layer of the front of the face and ear. These will be the highlights – the light source is top left of the sculpture (top right of the viewer's perspective).

2 Use charcoal powder and a paper stump or cotton bud to add a first-layer wash to depict the shadow regions. Don't blend the black charcoal with the white just yet.

3 Draw some details around the eyes and ear using a charcoal pencil. Blend with a small paper stump or a tortillon. Repeat to draw the details of the nose and lips.

4 In preparation for blending the darks into the lights, blend just the white charcoal using a clean paper stump. To ensure there is no trace of drawing medium on your paper stump, clean it using a sandpaper strip (*see* Tools & Materials: Blending Tools).

5 Blur the transition lines between the value extremes, merging the darks into the whites, use a broad paper stump or sponge brush.

6 Repeat Shading Steps 4 and 5 for the neck. Start by using white charcoal for the first layer, then switch to charcoal powder and pencil for the darker layers. Notice now the edge of the forehead – the transition between the light and dark values was not smooth enough in the previous step. We use a clean paper stump to smooth it out.

7 Without merging it into the darks, blend the white layer using a clean, broad paper stump or cotton bud. Also shade the broken edge of the bust using some charcoal powder and a blending tool such as a stump.

8 On the neck and ear, merge the white into the darks, and use the blending tip to draw details that show the collar bone anatomy. Notice that the collar bone shadows are very subtle. Make sure your blending tool has very little charcoal on it.

9 Split the surface of the hair into dark and light areas, using charcoal powder and white charcoal pencil respectively to shade. Don't worry about the individual strands at this point – since this is a marble sculpture, the hair will be drawn a little differently to the hair in regular portraits. This will use the additive/subtractive techniques we talked about in The Freehand Method (*see* Proportion Techniques: Freehand & Tracing).

10 Use the charcoal-smudged tip of a paper stump (scrape off any excess on a spare sheet of sketching paper) to mark the outlines of the hair and band.

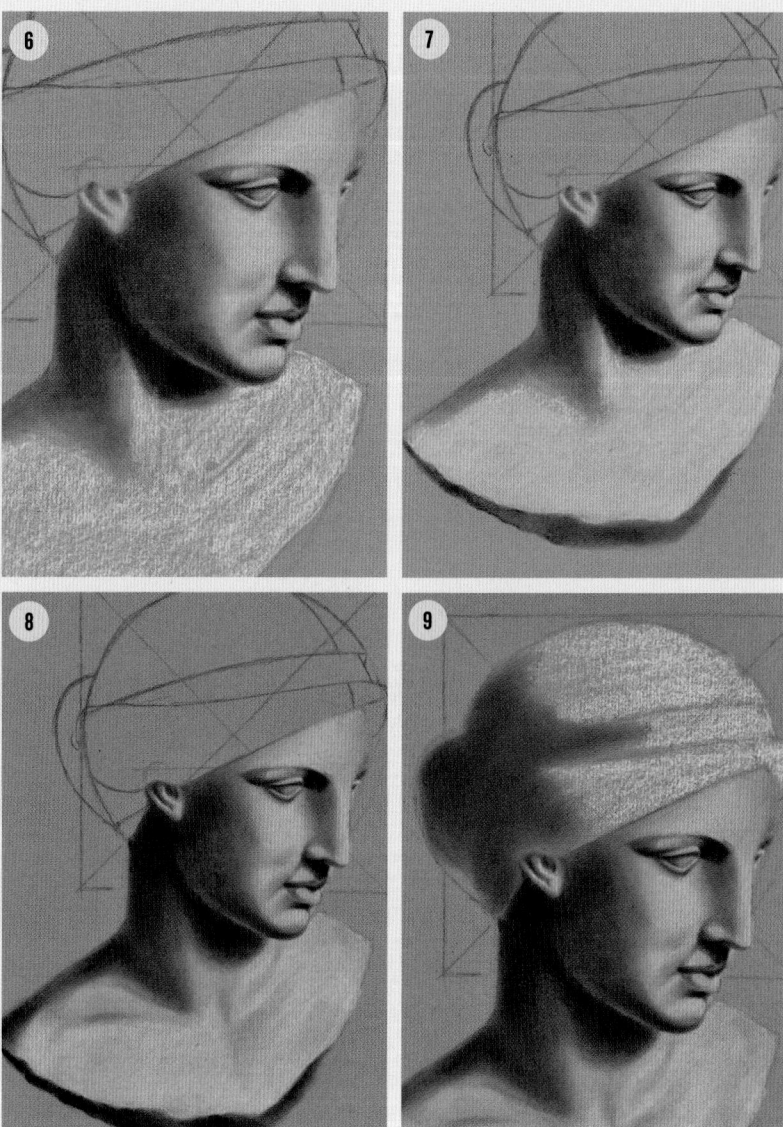

SOFT SHADOWS

Although the shadows on the neck are cast by a strong light source, they should be very subtle as the details do not have sharp edges or precise contours. Therefore, they would not cast dark shadows. Use an extremely small amount of black charcoal while blending. Before working on this area, remove excess charcoal from your paper stump or sponge brush using a rough sheet of paper. View your drawing from a distance to work on these subtle shadows.

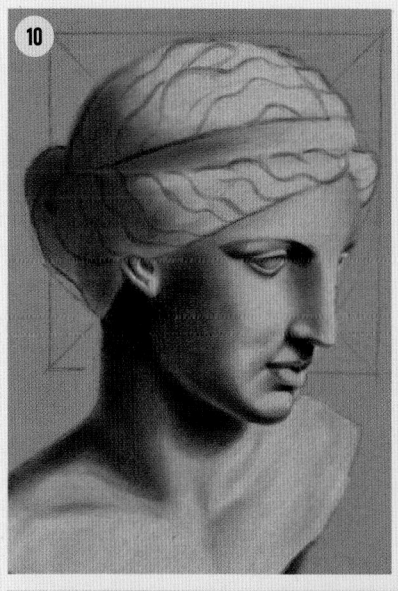

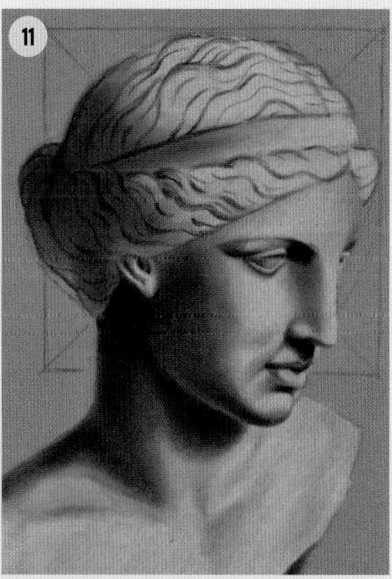

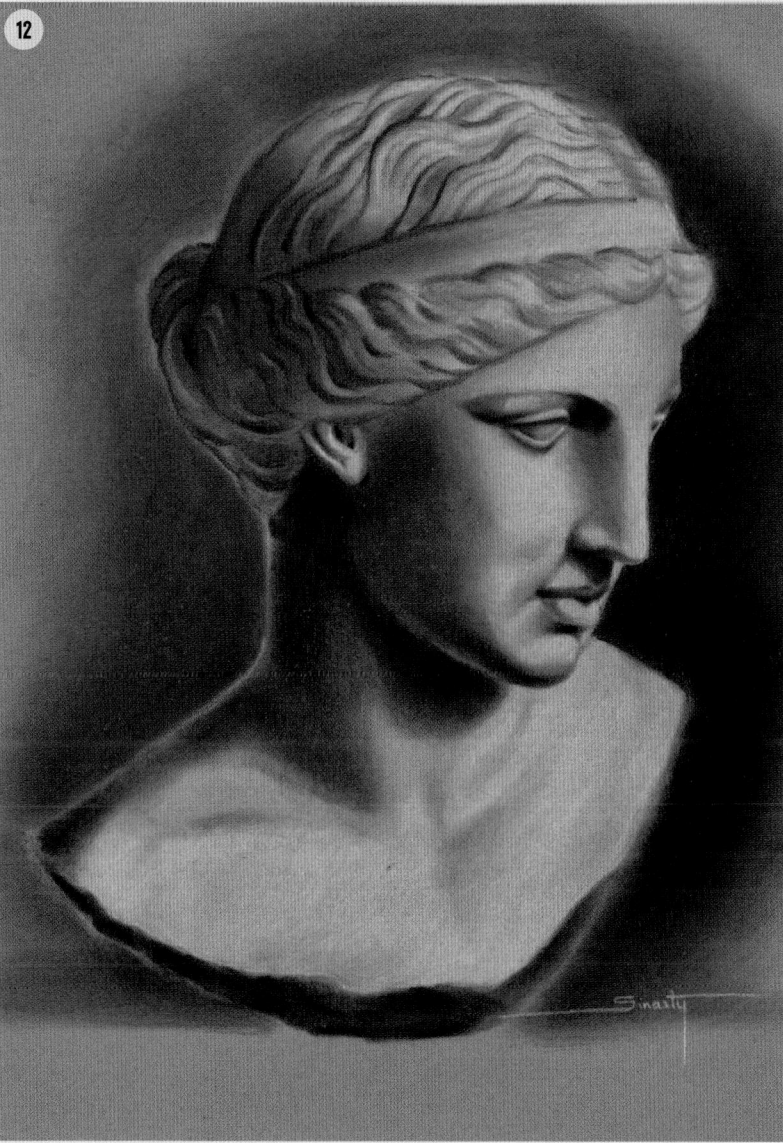

11 Now focus on individual locks of hair – this step requires a little more time and patience, but will be worth it. This is the "additive" part of the freehand method. Consider the shadows of the physical marble falling on other parts of the sculpture to give your portrait a truly sculptural feel. To create highlights in the darker regions of the hair, simply remove the excess charcoal using a pencil eraser. This is the "subtractive" part of the freehand method

12 Finally, a dark background is required to allow the sculpture to "pop out". The dark background behind a highlighted face also enhances the contrast, so shifts the viewer's focus to the subject.

BACKGROUNDS

The great masters played around with light and dark backgrounds and foregrounds to engage the observer. It is a whole different discussion and study when it comes to light and composition. I have shown a small example of this to give you an idea of how background affects our portraits (see Proportion Techniques: Reference Images).

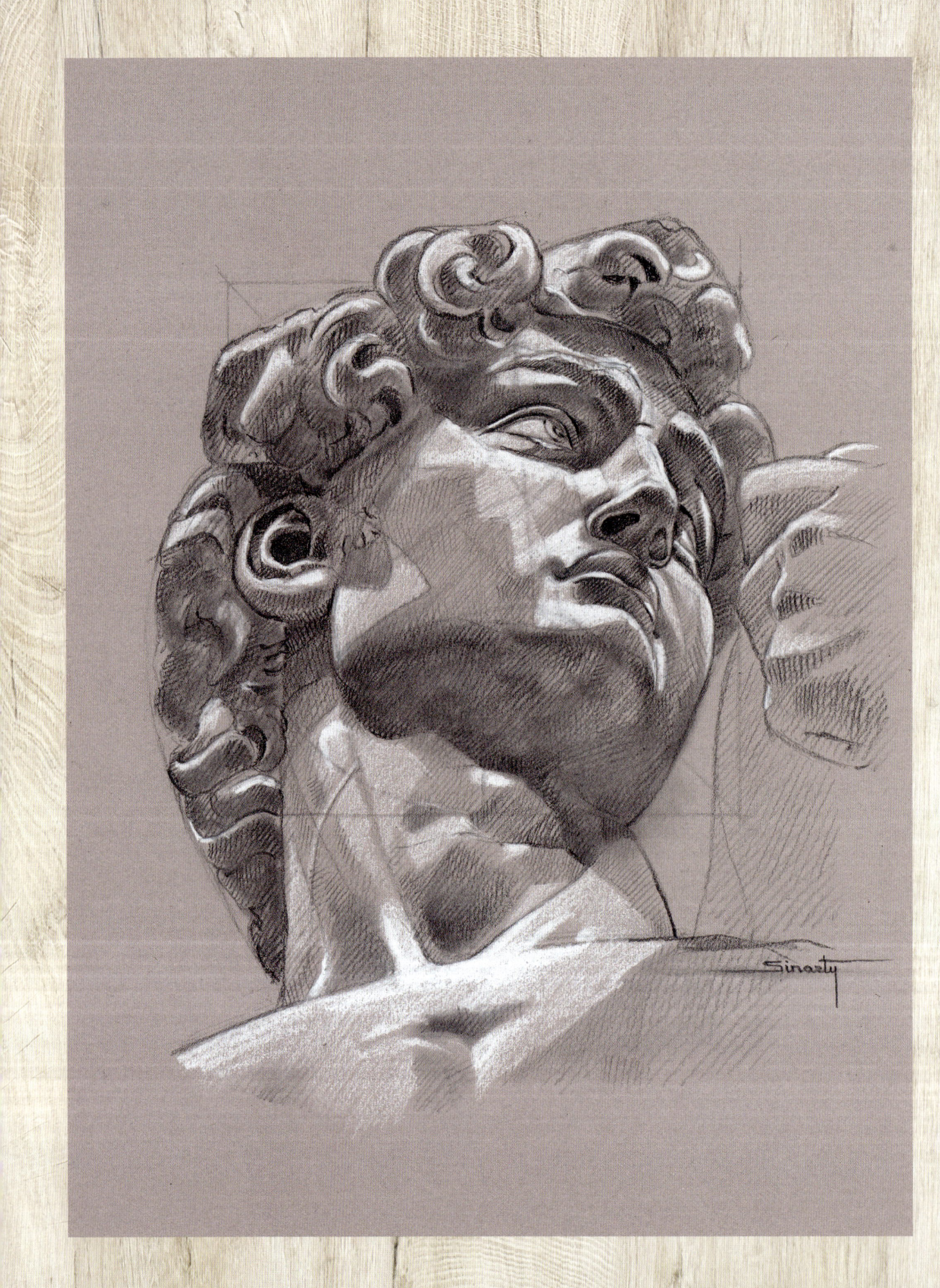

DAVID

Michelangelo's *David* is an iconic masterpiece of Renaissance art, renowned for its meticulous craftsmanship and extraordinary beauty. Drawing this portrait allows artists to interpret and recreate the powerful expression and gaze, intricate details, and timeless elegance.

Materials

- Toned grey sketching paper, 18.2 x 25.7cm (7¼ x 10in)
- Graphite pencils 2H, 2B, 4B, 6B, 8B
- White charcoal pencil
- Paper stumps
- Kneaded eraser, pencil eraser
- Good-quality, long-tip pencil sharpener, one-sided sharpening blade as required

Techniques

- Proportion: Loomis head
- Shading: Cross hatching and gradient blending

BASIC OUTLINING

1 Draw a square towards the top half of your page (see the inset thumbnail for guidance). Split this into four smaller squares of equal area. Use this square as a guide to draw a circle – the cranial sphere.

2 Draw the two diagonals of the square. Draw a tilted ellipse in the top left area of the circle to depict the side plane of the head (*see Proportion Techniques: The Loomis Method*). Draw a curve along the bottom to position the jawline and chin. The viewing angle is from beneath, looking up at David.

3 Draw the jawline extending upwards along the side of the head, splitting the side plane in half vertically. Draw a line on the side plane, perpendicular to this vertically extended jawline. Use the square guidelines to mark the positions of the browline and the bottom of the nose.

4 Draw curved guidelines along the cranial sphere to mark the brow and nose lines. Draw a facial centreline along the cranial mass at the top to complete the basic Loomis head.

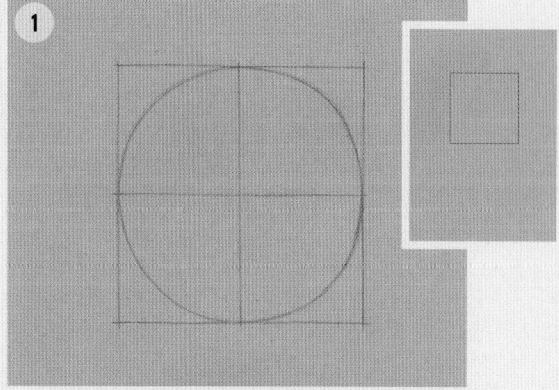

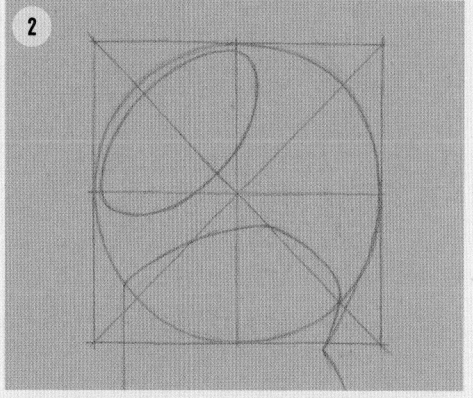

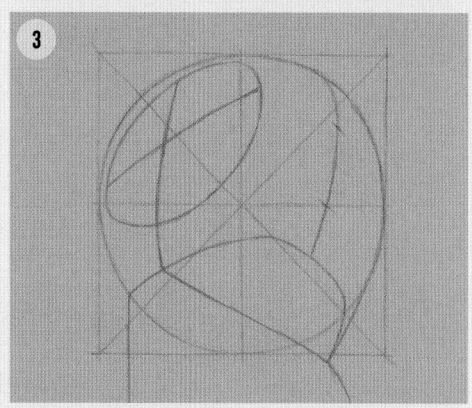

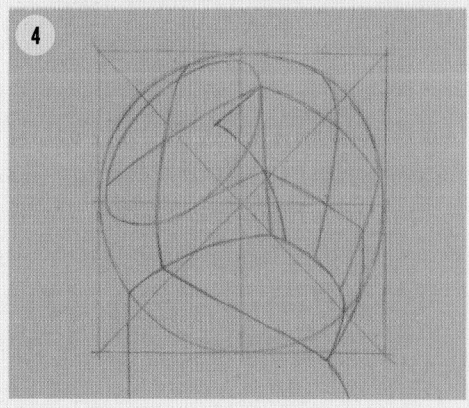

5 Use the facial centreline as reference to draw the basic planes of the nose (*see* Facial Features: Nose). Also draw the right eye socket plane.

6 Draw the left eye socket plane and draw a rough construction of both the eyes.

7 Draw curved lines to depict the lips and the chin. Notice that the upper lip touches the bottom reference line of the nose because of the viewing angle.

8 Draw a semi-circular arc to depict the ears and draw the outline of the hair. This is the finished construction sketch – now onto the details!

OUTLINE DETAILING

While drawing the following steps, use a 2B graphite pencil and a light-medium hand (*see* Sketching Fundamentals: Pencil Exercises).

9 Use the guidelines to draw details of the right eye and the eyebrow. Also depict the shadows and highlights as shown.

10 Complete the other eyebrow. Draw the nostrils on the bottom plane of the nose.

11 Detail the lips and ears keeping in mind that the reference is a low angle shot of David. Also depict shadows and highlights on the side of the face and the neck.

12 Draw the details of the hair. Capture the movement of the hair without the need to be pixel accurate. Draw part of the hand on the right side.

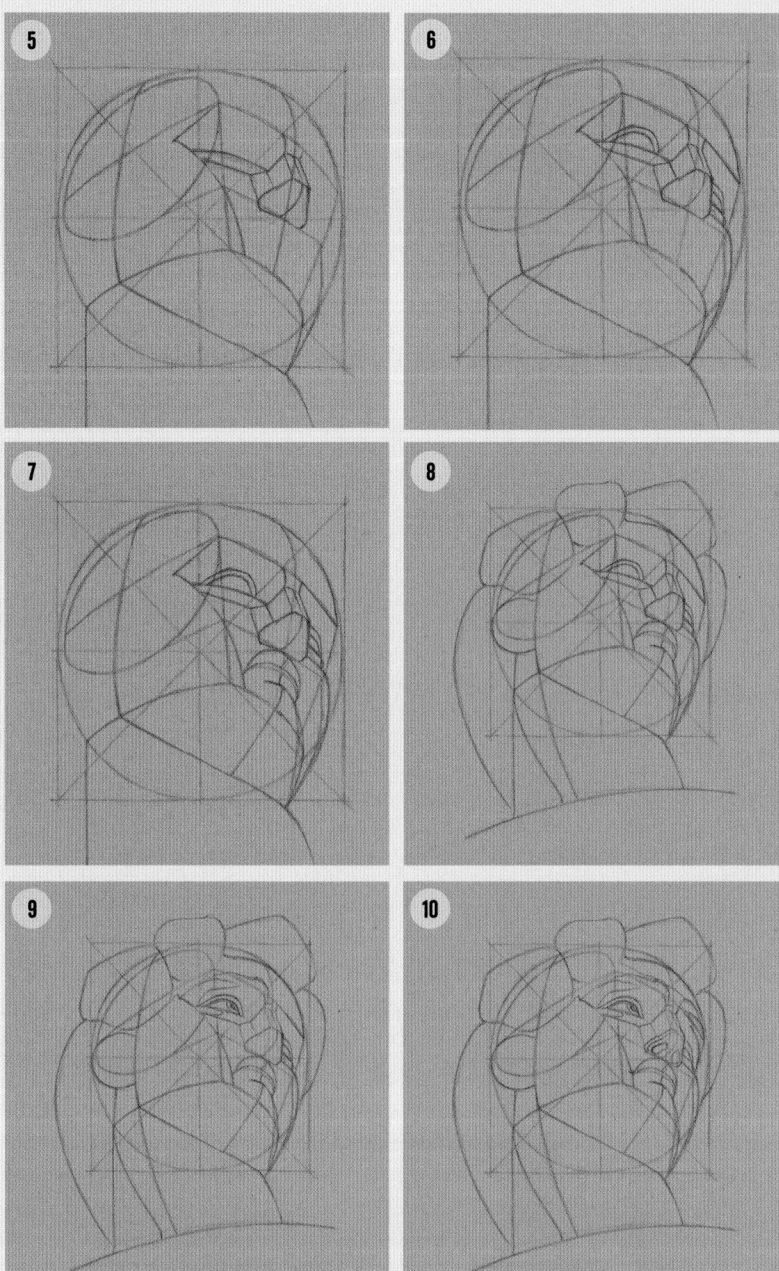

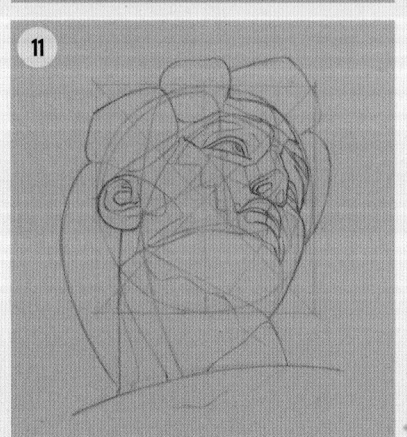

GO STRAIGHT TO SHADING

Simply tracing the final outline drawing – Step 12 – provides an opportunity to jump ahead to practise shading (see Proportion Techniques: Freehand & Tracing).

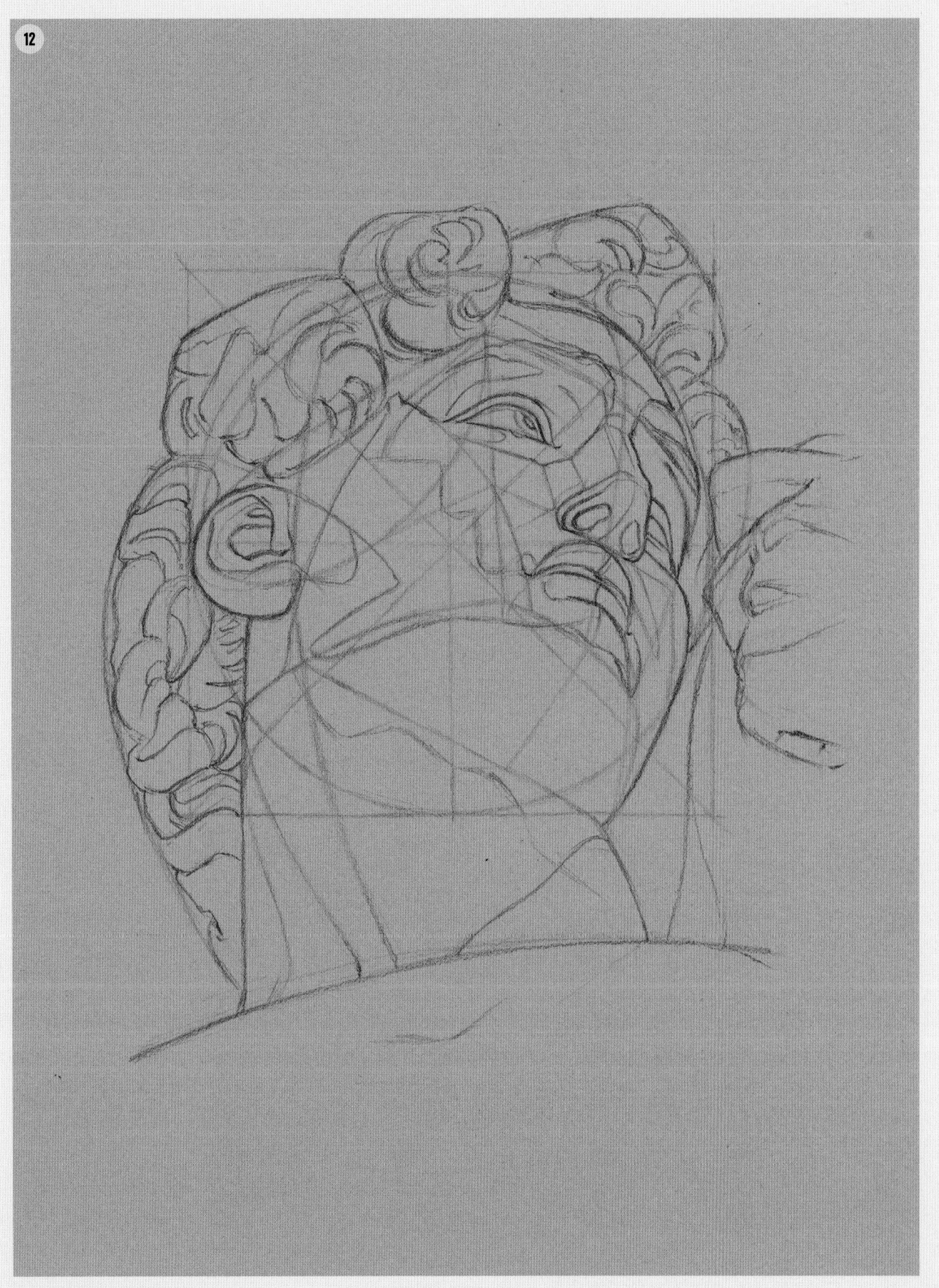

SHADING

At this point, you have completed the portrait construction and outline (either by following the previous Steps 1–12, or by simply tracing the image for Step 12).

1 Use a white charcoal pencil to sketch the highlights on the eyebrows, nose and the cheeks. Also depict highlights on the ear, neck and hand.

2 Draw highlights on the hair. Now define the other value extreme using your darkest, 8B pencil. Do this by shading the darkest parts of the ear, nostrils and the outlines of the eye.

3 Now that you have the value extremes defined (see Sketching Fundamentals: Shading Basics), move on to a mid-value using the 4B pencil. Use the hatching technique to build the first layer. Try to hatch more or less in a single direction on this first layer and keep the distance between the hatches as well as the pressure on the pencil constant (*see* Sketching Fundamentals: Pencil Exercises). Take your time.

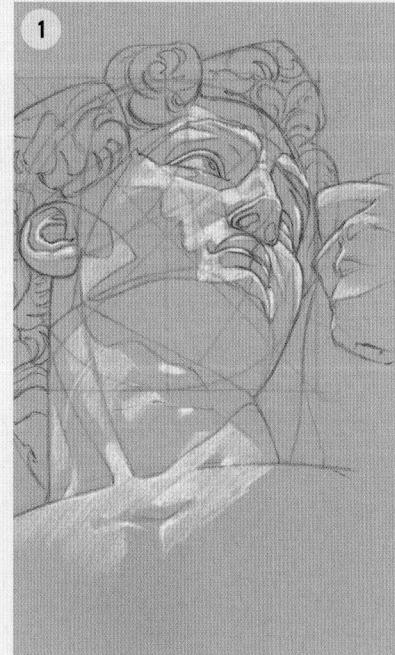
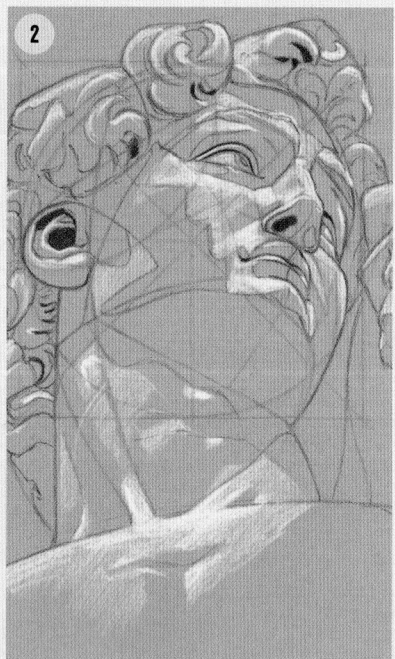
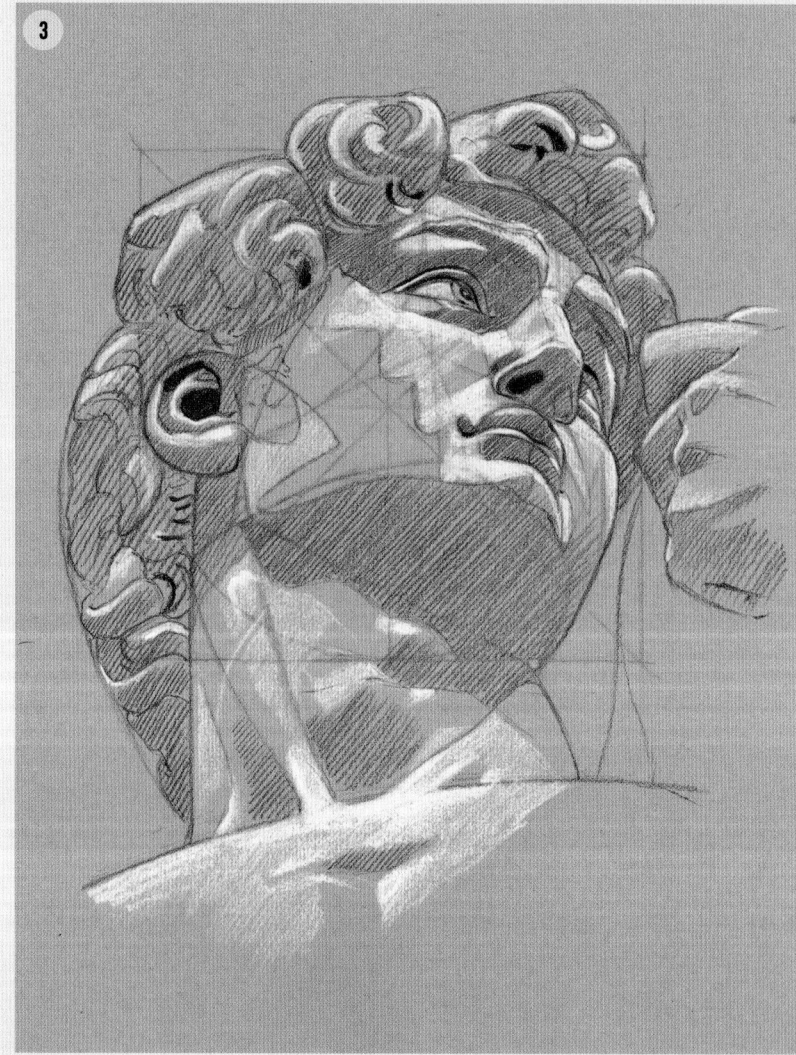

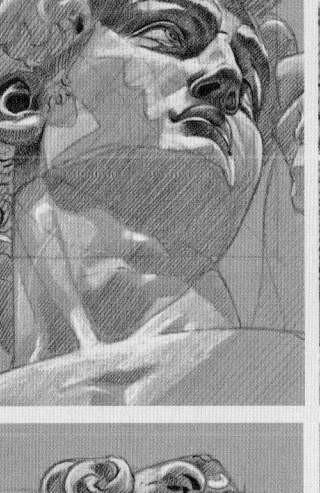
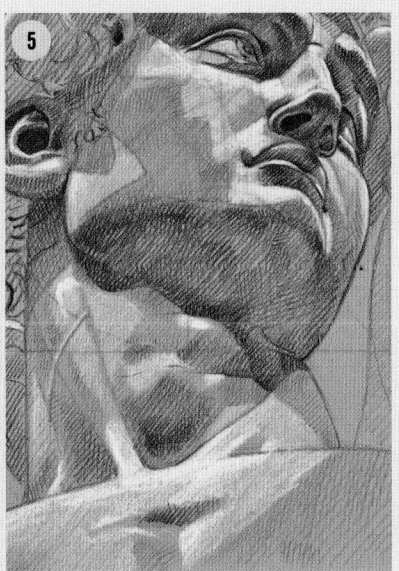
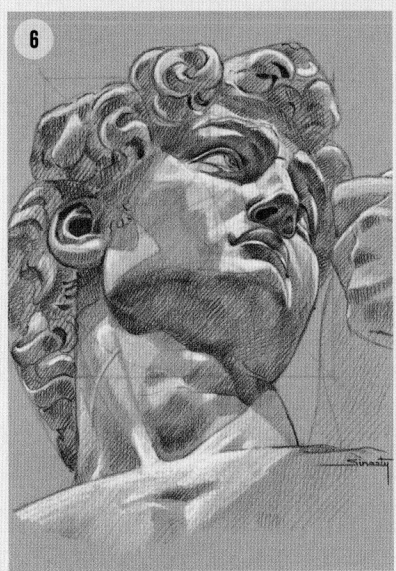
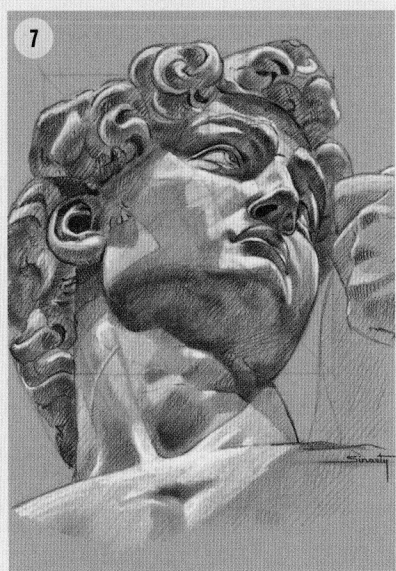

4 Let's focus on detailing the features. Use the cross hatching technique and a 6B pencil to shade the darker parts of the ear, eyes, forehead, nose and lips.

5 Use cross hatching to shade the darker regions under the chin and the neck.

6 Finish up the rest of the hair using the same technique. Again, you don't need to be that accurate for the hair, only being careful about the contours of the locks of hair. Use a 2H and 2B pencil in this step to cover up the lighter portions of the skin on the cheeks and the neck.

7 Use your paper stump to blend the darker shadows to give your sketch some depth. Be careful not to overdo your blending since the cross hatching needs to be visible. Hatch shadows in the hair with a 6B pencil. Finally, use your darker pencils to make your features crisp and you're done! It is preferable not to erase any of the guidelines – these give your drawing character.

SHADING ANATOMY

Shading the muscles on the neck can get tricky. Pay close attention to the anatomy of these muscles while building your layers. Observe your sketch from a distance to gauge any value adjustments needed.

TAKING IT FURTHER

A desire to be better at anything is all about passion. Being passionate as an artist means improving every day through practise, so here are some ideas for practical ways to elevate your drawing.

HOW TO IMPROVE

The quickest way to improve is to identify your weaknesses and work on them. The goal is to be a good critic of your own work. You can then research and design development exercises for yourself. Here are some of my personal exercises for improvement:

Study the face
For a portrait artist, it is important to study the facial structure, including the underlying bones and muscle groups. This knowledge will help you accurately capture the proportions and features of the face. Spend time observing different faces in various lighting conditions. Notice the unique characteristics, subtle nuances, and expressions that make each face distinct.

Seek inspiration
Diverse sources such as nature, photographs, and the work of other artists will energise and inspire you.

Make time to practise
To improve in drawing, consistency and practise are key. Set aside regular time for drawing and experiment with different subjects, styles, and techniques.

Learn to self-critique
Being a good self-critic is as important and necessary as seeking constructive feedback from peers or professionals to identify areas for improvement. Look at the work of other portrait artists to see how they approach the subject. Pay attention to their use of light and shadow, composition, and technique.

Keep a sketchbook
Have somewhere you can easily capture ideas, observations and daily sketches.

Remember, improvement comes with time and dedication, so stay motivated and enjoy the journey of continuous learning and growth.

If you struggle with proportions, try drawing small-scale freehand portraits. A small notepad, such as A7 size – 10.5 x 7.4cm (2⅞ x 4⅛in) – is great for this. At this scale, the margin of error reduces, so you can practise defining freehand proportions and become better at critiquing your own work.

> **"TALENT IS A PURSUED INTEREST."**
> BOB ROSS

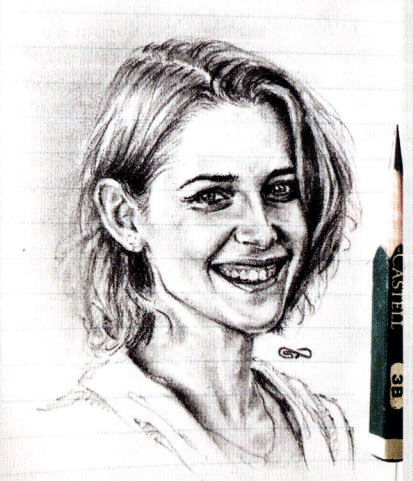
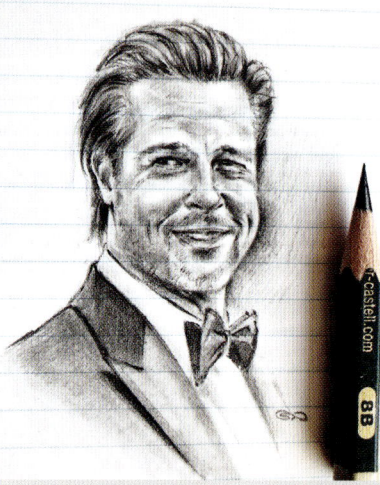
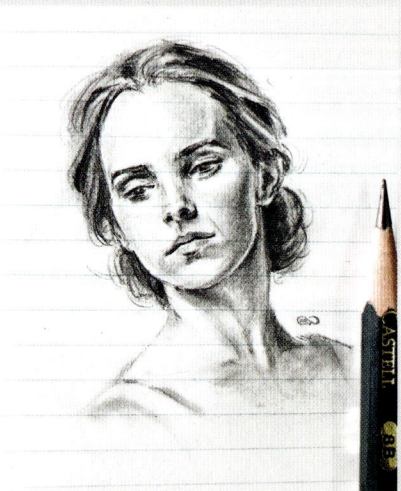

FINDING YOUR STYLE

This is a journey of self-discovery and artistic exploration – step out of your comfort zone and try new things. Experimentation offers the chance to identify what resonates with you and feels most authentic.

A "style" is basically a niche in any art form that is uniquely singular. Begin by studying the styles of the great artists, focusing on what separates them from the rest. Artists I admire include Johannes Vermeer, Rembrandt van Rijn and M.C. Escher. I am inspired by Vermeer's exceptional realism captured with just a few brush strokes, Rembrandt's manipulation of light, and Escher's breaking the barriers of visualization with his graphite drawings. It is fascinating how each of these great artists has something completely different to offer – each is identified by the style of their art.

Wherever this quest takes you, every artist walks the same path during the first half of their journey. In the meantime, mastering the fundamentals is necessary before you can deviate from the norm in search of that art form that defines you. Finding your style is a fluid and evolving process. Embrace experimentation, stay true to yourself, and allow your style to develop organically as you grow as an artist.

MAINTAIN A CALM MIND

Drawing is as much about the mind as it is about your hands. While drawing, there are ways to help keep your mind relaxed and calm.

- From the start, visualize your final portrait on the blank canvas.
- Take time to feel every line and slow down the pace of your drawings.
- Don't be afraid of failure – confidence and consistency come from failing several times in your quest to get it right.
- Find a quiet and comfortable space to work. Eliminate distractions and surround yourself with elements that promote tranquillity, such as soft lighting or soothing music.
- If your mind feels overwhelmed or restless, take short breaks to stretch, meditate, or engage in activities that help you rejuvenate.
- Patience is key – a drawing need not be completed in one sitting. Returning to it with a refreshed mind can bring a renewed sense of outlook and creativity to your work.

My recent drawings show the style I have arrived at after spending some years practising the basics of portraiture.

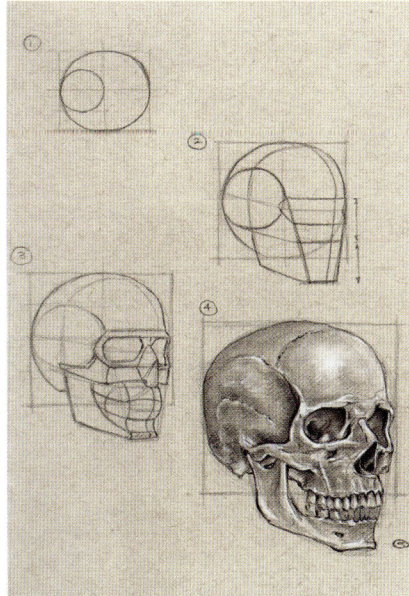
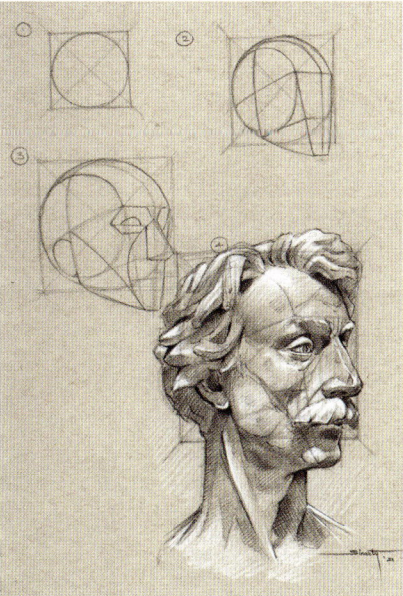
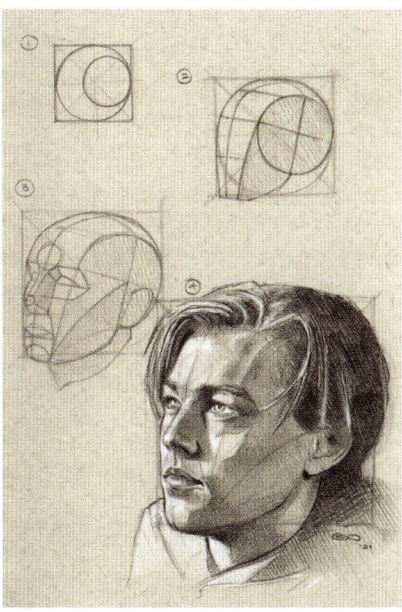

ABOUT THE AUTHOR

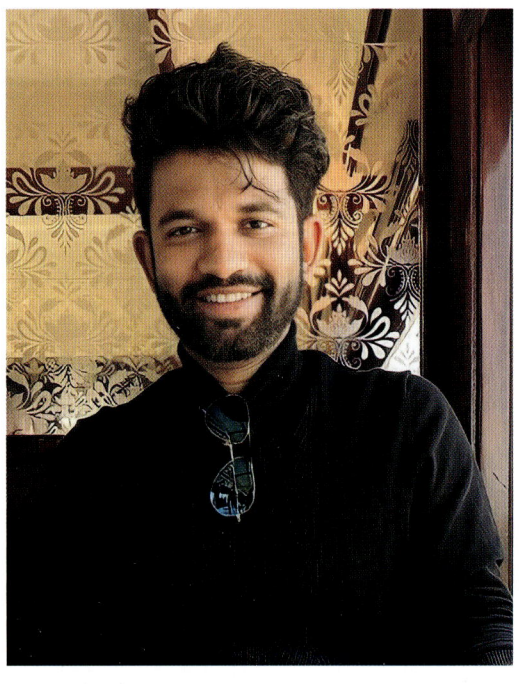

Satyajit Sinari aka SinArty is a graphite and charcoal sketch artist from India. He has been sketching since the age of five, and since starting to showcase his art in 2016, now has over 250,000 followers on Instagram. He has trained under a number of accomplished veteran artists in India and has also judged art competitions in India and the US. With over fifteen years of experience, he is skilled in different media including watercolour, acrylics, and oils. However, his favorite medium remains the graphite pencil.

Focussing mainly on portraits, human anatomy and sculpture studies, SinArty specializes in proportion techniques and simplifying drawing from complex references. To motivate novice art enthusiasts to embark upon their sketching journey, SinArty shares tutorials and process videos on platforms including Instagram, YouTube and DeviantArt.

He formally trained as an electrical engineer at the University of Michigan. In his spare time, along with sketching, he also likes to play football, travel and create music on the Tabla, an Indian percussion hand instrument he has been studying for the past twenty years.

INSTAGRAM: @SINARTY77

YOUTUBE: @SINARTY

ACKNOWLEDGMENTS

This book is a dream come true. A rudimentary vision turned into reality is what every artist craves. There are many people without whom this book would not be possible. I'm forever indebted to my parents and grandparents for the support and motivation behind following my passion. I'm forever thankful to my art teachers and the artists who motivated me to get to the next level in my personal art journey. I am grateful to all who have been following, appreciating my work and supporting me through all the social media platforms over the years.

I would also like to thank Ame and the entire team at David and Charles for seeing the potential in my methods and making this dream come true. I hope to work with you again on a new journey.

Finally, I want to express my gratitude to the readers who have chosen to embark on this artistic adventure with me. Your interest and enthusiasm for the world of drawing continue to motivate me to pursue excellence in my craft.

INDEX

RECOMMENDED BRANDS

These are the brands I'm currently using and recommend for tools and materials.

Paper
- Canson
- Stonehenge
- Strathmore
- Papelsino
- Arteza

Graphite
- Prismacolour
- Faber Castell 9000
- Caran d'Ache
- Staedtler Mars Lumograph

Charcoal
- General's
- Faber Castell

Other tools and materials
- Derwent (pencil extenders)
- Winsor & Newton (workable fixative)
- Caran d'Ache (sandpaper strips, paper stumps, sharpeners, pencil eraser)
- Faber Castell (kneaded eraser)
- Tombow (barrel eraser)

A DAVID AND CHARLES BOOK
© David and Charles, Ltd 2024

David and Charles is an imprint of David and Charles, Ltd, Suite A, Tourism House, Pynes Hill, Exeter, EX2 5WS

Text and Art © Satyajit Sinari 2024
Layout and Photography © David and Charles, Ltd 2024

First published in the UK and USA in 2024

Satyajit Sinari has asserted his right to be identified as author of this work in accordance with the Copyright, Designs and Patents Act, 1988.

The author and publisher have made every effort to ensure that all the instructions in the book are accurate and safe, and therefore cannot accept liability for any resulting injury, damage or loss to persons or property, however it may arise.

Names of manufacturers and product ranges are provided for the information of readers, with no intention to infringe copyright or trademarks.

A catalogue record for this book is available from the British Library.

ISBN-13: 9781446310007 paperback
ISBN-13: 9781446310014 EPUB
ISBN-13: 9781446310274 PDF

This book has been printed on paper from approved suppliers and made from pulp from sustainable sources.

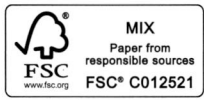

Printed in China through Asia Pacific Offset for: David and Charles, Ltd, Suite A, Tourism House, Pynes Hill, Exeter, EX2 5WS

10 9 8 7 6 5 4 3 2 1

Publishing Director: Ame Verso
Managing Editor: Jeni Chown
Project Editor: Jenny Fox-Proverbs
Head of Design: Anna Wade
Designers: Sam Staddon, Laura Woussen and Marieclare Mayne
Pre-press Designer: Susan Reansbury
Photography: Jason Jenkins
Production Manager: Beverley Richardson

David and Charles publishes high-quality books on a wide range of subjects. For more information visit www.davidandcharles.com.

Share your portraits with us on social media using #dandcbooks and follow us on Facebook and Instagram by searching for @dandcbooks.

Layout of the digital edition of this book may vary depending on reader hardware and display settings.